Preface

In the United States the legal system by and large is ill suited and fairly inhospitable to those who represent themselves. A myriad of laws and rules have been imposed that make navigating the legal system both challenging and treacherous for the novice. If that were not enough the legal profession, seeking to protect its absolute monopoly on the furnishing of legal information under the guise of "protecting the public" has made it extremely difficult for people to have meaningful access to legal information.

Recognizing the need for a resource for people in this proverbial Catch-22 trap, Be Your Own Lawyer (www.beyourownlawyer.org) was established in 2012. With virtually no marketing or commercial promotion, the results have been overwhelming. In the past few years Be Your Own Lawyer has helped people across the country represent themselves in civil court matters ranging from personal injury to domestic to business disputes in courts from California to New York.

Because of limited size and resources, Be Your Own Lawyer can only accommodate a fraction of the people that seek information and help. This book was written to help bridge that gap. To make relevant information available to anyone interested.

Contents

INTRODUCTION

If you are representing yourself in a civil legal matter, or thinking about it, this book was written for you. First and foremost, this book is about representing yourself in civil matters, which means everything EXCEPT criminal cases.

And no, after reading this book, you will not be able to go out and pass the bar exam in whatever state you find yourself in. Nor will you have the knowledge, skill or expertise of a practicing attorney. No one should be foolish enough to think that there is some magic potion that will, after reading a few hundred pages, put you on par with someone that's not only been to law school and studied in much greater depth the topics in this book, but has had years of experience in dealing with them.

The purpose of this book is to give you an understanding of the issues and challenges that will confront you as you gather the facts and law about you and head off to do battle.

Everyone has heard the old adage: "He who is his own lawyer has a fool for a client."

Fortunately, the relevance of it is questionable at best. While its origins are not completely clear, it is thought to have been derived in 1814. The problem is that in 1814 there was no internet, there was no online legal research and there was no resource such as Be Your Own Lawyer. Things have changed!

Not only is it both possible and realistic to represent yourself, in some cases there simply are no other options.

In terms of legal issues in America today, people increasingly find themselves in a difficult position which is the result of two arguably separate but actually intertwined forces.

On the one hand litigation has literally become a growth industry. One has but to read the headlines to see the multitude of lawsuits being brought. As a society we have been imbued with the mindset that no matter what misfortune befalls us, someone else should be accountable and responsible. In Florida there are billboards hawking a website: Who Can I Sue! The United States has more lawyers per capita than any other country in the world. If that doesn't convince you, wander down to your local courthouse and casually ask a clerk there what the average time is for a case, once filed, to go to trial. If it is anywhere near the national average the answer will be in the neighborhood of two years. Everybody it seems is suing everybody and "sue the bastards" has become the American mantra!

Along with that, in this environment of increasing litigation, the costs of being represented by an attorney are going through the roof. It's not just that attorney hourly rates border on the obscene (the average attorney hourly billing rates for 2012 were over $500/hr for large firm partners, and $342.95 for attorneys in smaller firms), but the increasing complexity of litigation requires more and more hours at these rates. A typical civil lawsuit taken to trial will cost in the neighborhood of $50,000. A complicated case can cost many times that amount.

These two trends have combined to place the average American in a potentially disastrous conundrum. The likelihood of being involved in litigation is steadily increasing while the cost of being represented by an attorney is getting further and further out of reach. The inevitable result is that more and more, people are resorting to representing themselves. Some do it after weighing all the factors. Others, being sued and without funds to hire an attorney, simply have no choice.

Of course the law and the procedures related to litigation of a case are not simple. Representing yourself, while definitely a viable option, requires a lot of work. In approaching the idea of representing themselves, people tend to orient themselves to varying degrees in one of two directions. This book will try to navigate you toward a reasonable midpoint between extremes.

Some people take a look at what has to be done and see it as an insurmountable obstacle. Something they can never hope to accomplish. Others naively see it as no obstacle at all. They incorrectly assume that because they do not have the benefit of an attorney, all the rules and procedural requirements will be magically waived for them, akin to the parting of the Red Sea, and all they have to do is show up and "state their case".

The extremes of both positions are simply wrong and glibly adhering to either one will be the precursor to proverbial train wreck. The purpose of this book is to keep you sanely in the middle. On the one hand, the obstacles are not insurmountable. The legal knowledge necessary to understand and handle your own case is readily available if you know where to look for it and how to filter and organize it. On the other hand, it will not materialize as from heaven at your feet, and you will not absorb it by osmosis. That won't turn out any better than when you attempted it the night before your high school chemistry exam. To represent yourself it is absolutely essential that you acquaint yourself not only with all the necessary law that pertains to you, but with the rules and procedures as well. In representing yourself you will find that you are fully expected to know and comply with the same requirements imposed on everyone else.

The purpose of this book is to give you a roadmap – a template if you will - for representing yourself.

It is not intended to give you the legal knowledge that you might need for each and every case since that would fill hundreds of volumes. Instead, it is intended to get you pointed in the right direction and to understand the steps that you need to take in order to effectively represent yourself.

The book is broken down into three sections. The first is an introduction and is devoted to logical steps that you should consider in undertaking the challenge of representing yourself. Think of it as a sort of decision tree. It makes little sense to study the legal issues or procedures until you have determined that you both can and should represent yourself.

For example, while in the United States, with a few narrow exceptions, you have the right to represent yourself, there are things that need to be considered in reaching that decision. Likewise, you should be aware of the limitations of the judicial system and to appreciate that going to court may not always be the most prudent course of action.

Once you have decided to proceed, or circumstances dictate that you must proceed; you have to consider some of the options and choices that may present themselves, and weigh the merits and drawbacks of the various choices.

The second section is intended to provide an actual guide to handling a case from start to finish. It includes such things as filing court papers, going through discovery and presenting evidence. That section focuses on two goals. The first is to familiarize you with the mechanics and structure of the American judicial system in general. The second is to give you as much insight as possible into the anatomy of a civil case so that you can put the various aspects of representing yourself into perspective and appreciate what is going on

The third section gives you information and hopefully some insight into various legal topics that are likely to be germane to cases in which you could find yourself being your own lawyer. Consider it general legal information. It is not necessary that you read every section. If you are involved in a contract case, there is not much reason, unless you're simply interested, to read the section on bankruptcy.

It should be stressed that in terms of law and procedures, this book is not a final solution, but a starting point. There is no way that everything that you need to know about representing yourself in every possible kind of case could ever be condensed in one volume. The purpose of this book is to give a feel for what is involved and a basic understanding of the trial process.

This book gets you started!

Representing Yourself

Because people often do not understand what it really means, or requires to represent themselves in court, it would not be fair to launch into a book about it, without first making sure that the reader understands the basic questions. So before getting into "how", let's look at the questions of why you would consider representing yourself, and whether or not you should embark on such an undertaking.

The decision to represent yourself is not one to be taken lightly. There are a lot of considerations. This section will try to explore some of those issues and give you some insight into how to tackle them.

WHY

That's the first question that is often asked. Why would you want to represent yourself in a court case, or some other legal matter when law schools are cranking out lawyers like the proverbial hotcakes and you can't turn on your TV without seeing some clown standing in front of law books telling you why you need their services?

Why would you represent yourself when these guys are ready willing and able to take care of it for you?

There are three basic reasons why people find themselves in court cases without the benefit of an attorney.

Cost.

Lawyers are expensive. Hourly attorney's fees on the low end run around $250 per hour and go upward from there. Any kind of experienced trial lawyer will charge between $350 and $500 per hour. They will require advance payment, or retainer fees ranging from $2,500 for the most simple, straightforward cases, up to as much as $50,000 for more complex cases. Let's face it. Most of us don't have that kind of cash sitting around. And it shows. Recent research has turned up a very frightening revelation. Fully 65% of the civil lawsuits settled in the United States in 2011 were settled because one of the parties no longer had sufficient resources to pursue the litigation. That's a fancy way of saying somebody ran out of money.

So what we have is a legal system where you either don't get to play at all because you don't have the money, or the guy with the most dollars wins. In that context, there are of course two scenarios: you can be the one suing, or you can be getting sued. If you are thinking of bringing a lawsuit, you of course always have the option, if you cannot afford to hire an attorney, of bringing the lawsuit, or not. Pursuing your claim, or just walking away.

While that may be well and good if you are the one doing the suing, where does it leave the guy that's being sued? If someone with resources decides to bring a lawsuit against you, you have three choices and three choices only:

- Do nothing and end up with a judgment against you.
- Hire an attorney to defend you; or,
- Represent Yourself

If you don't have the money, the second option disappears. If you have assets that you want to protect, such as a home or a business, the first option is not acceptable.

Your lawyer is not doing a good job.

The second reason people choose to represent themselves is because they are disgruntled, disgusted and dissatisfied with their attorneys. Many people assume that the only reason to represent yourself is cost. This has turned out not to be the case. A substantial number of people who represent themselves could hire an attorney, and in many cases had hired attorneys, but prefer to represent themselves. Many grew disgusted and dissatisfied with their lawyers, fired them, and decided they could do just as well or better on their own. Why would that be? After all, attorneys are supposed to work for you and be your advocate. They're supposed to be on your side.

It seldom works that way. People are sick and tired of being over-billed for work that is not complex. If by the way, you don't understand attorney's fees, be sure to look at the part about attorney's fees in the section on Attorneys. They are sick and tired of telephone calls not being returned. They are sick and tired of not being informed of developments in their case. They are sick and tired of being spectators in something that is extremely important to them.

What many people do not understand and grasp is the amount of control of your legal fate you give up when you retain an attorney. Consider:

-       All communication to and from the court and to and from the other side is with your attorney. You are not in the loop.

-       You are not permitted to be heard (except as a witness). It must come through your attorney. You are not allowed for example to say anything during a hearing unless it is to testify.

-       Your attorney has the absolute authority to bind you to anything in the case. If he settles a case, even without your authorization, you are bound.

-       If he is not paid, or grows disenchanted with your case, your attorney can usually withdraw, leaving you high and dry, often at the worst possible time.

Many people when they learn these hard cold facts decide that they are better off on their own. They like that they are in complete control of their case. Everything, whether from the court or the other side, comes to them. They get to make all the decisions.

And after all is said and done, remember: You are your own best advocate! Nobody cares as much or is as interested in your case as you!

Representing Yourself Levels the Playing Field

When you have armed yourself with the tools you need in order to properly represent yourself, you will have a distinct advantage in terms of the cost of litigation if your opponent is represented. As you delve into the intricacies and procedures of a lawsuit, you will quickly learn how time consuming so much of these things can be.

Depositions (an integral part of the discovery process) which require preparation as well as participation, can consume hours and hours of attorney time. Your opponent is paying thousands of dollars in attorney's fees for depositions while you are paying nothing. Many courts schedule groups of hearings at one time, working their way down a docket sheet case by case. If there are thirty motions for example scheduled to me heard at nine in the morning, it may literally take hours to reach yours. If the other side is represented, this means those hours, where nothing is being accomplished except sitting there waiting to be called, are costing your opponent money.

Don't underestimate the value of this. Any opponent is going to get tired of writing checks month after month, not knowing if it will ever pay off. It's about time you were able to turn things around a little!

11

CAN YOU?

People always ask whether they can in fact represent themselves.

The answer to this question is, with a few exceptions in extreme cases, YES! ABSOLUTELY!

All the courts in the United States are originally established under a constitution – either the United States Constitution or a constitution of a state. There are various additional courts that are set up by statute, but the underlying authority to have courts is always constitutional. Under all those constitutions EVERYONE is guaranteed equal access to the courts. They are for everyone – not a select few. And that right cannot be burdened or eroded by saying, "you are only entitled to avail yourself of this right if you can afford a lawyer."

So yes, you have the right to represent yourself.

Now understand this right is only for you. You cannot represent your spouse, or your children, or your mother-in-law! You cannot represent a corporation – even if you own it.

But you can definitely represent yourself!

BUT CAN YOU REALLY?

Ok now that we've established that you have the right to represent yourself, the next question is can you really pull it off?

After people understand that they have the right to represent themselves, the next question is often, "ok I understand. I have the right to represent myself. But can I really do it? Can I really put everything together and represent myself?"

Part of the problem is that the "system" is intimidating. In some respects it's meant to be. Or at least it's meant to inspire respect and awe. Courthouses are always imposing buildings. In early America they often dominated village and town squares. Even today they are huge, impressive structures. Then there is the hustle and bustle. When you go into one of these edifices, everyone is running around, looking important, looking busy, looking like they belong. While all of this is worthy of respect, it should never be intimidating.

Those buildings with all the trappings belong to everyone? They belong to you! All those clerks and official looking people – guess what? They work for you! You have no reason to be intimidated. You are doing nothing more than using a part of the government (paid for with your tax dollars) that is there for everyone.

Of course the next question is "How will I know what to do?" "What papers do I have to file?" "How do I find out what the law on my cases is?" Those questions give rise a completely different topic – the reason you're reading this book.

The truth is that the legal system can appear complicated and even insurmountable. While it may be complicated, and require a lot of studying and research, it is certainly not insurmountable. It is not easy for someone, without help, to research the law. That doesn't mean you can't. It is not easy to know where to look for the rules that tell you how and what to do, but they can be found. You might stumble a couple of times, and you might get disillusioned. But you can do it!

You can represent yourself

You can do it successfully.

And with help, you can do it without re-inventing the wheel!

AND IF YOU CAN, SHOULD YOU?

Yes you should, but.... While you can represent yourself, there are always exceptions. In life there is always that "BUT". In the case of representing yourself, the "BUT" encompasses two categories.

First, there are just some cases where it is probably never a good idea to try to represent yourself. Ever. There are likewise cases where you could represent yourself, but are better off with a lawyer.

Second, the reality is that the adventure of representing yourself is just not for everyone.

First consider when representing yourself is not a good idea! For Some Cases You Should Have an Attorney! Yes, there are some cases where you should not represent yourself. For those cases you need to go and hire the best attorney that you can afford. Here are some cases where it is usually a very bad idea to try to represent yourself:

Any serious criminal case.

What does that mean? Any criminal case where if you lose you could end up spending time in jail or end up with a criminal conviction for more than a minor misdemeanor on your record. Money is just money, and things to argue over, are just things. You can make more money and things can be replaced. Your personal freedom, or reputation and having a criminal record are different. Where your personal freedom is at stake, spend as much as you can afford to hire the best attorney that you can find. The consequence of losing is just too big of a dice roll.

Juvenile Cases.

Just as with criminal matters, if your child gets into trouble, or if you are accused of child neglect or abuse, an attorney familiar with these cases should be involved. Not only do these cases have potentially disastrous consequences, they are dangerous because they are deceptive. They begin with interviews, meetings and what appear to be informal hearings. The problem is that they

15

often gain a momentum of their own and the consequences on the lives of those involved, you and your children, can be devastating. Get a lawyer for these!

Complex Civil Litigation.

There are just some cases that may be too complicated to be handled without an attorney. While the decision is not as critical as in serious criminal or juvenile cases, there are cases where you are probably just not going to be successful at representing yourself. Matters that involve complicated or highly technical fact issues, or intricate legal issues, need the involvement of an attorney. While representing yourself can be advantageous, there are times when it is necessary to be pragmatic and realistic. It is not reasonable to expect that in representing yourself you can catalog and summarize the thousands of pages of documents that will emerge in some complex cases. It will be very difficult for you to work effectively with expert witnesses as would be required in a highly technical case. Taking the dozens of depositions that would be required in a complex case would present a substantial challenge. Even many attorneys shy away from these cases. These are cases that should be handled by an attorney, in particular an attorney competent and experienced in that particular area.

Outside of those kinds of cases, you, and only you, can decide if representing yourself is a good idea. For some people it's great. For others, not so much.

Representing yourself takes work. It's that simple. You have to research the law that pertains to your case. Court papers have to be prepared, organized and answered. Your own papers have to be filed and sent to the other side. You have to prepare and organize your case, keeping track of the issues, the facts and the evidence. It will take you at every step of the way longer than it would take an attorney because you have a learning curve to deal with. While an attorney might take twenty minutes to dictate a motion to compel discovery to his secretary, it will take you hours. Not only will you have to type it yourself, but it will probably take a lot of time to research to see how it's done.

It's not insurmountable, but it's not for everyone. So if you have the option of deciding whether or not to represent yourself, here are some of the questions you should ask yourself:

- Do you have the time? If you're working forty hours a week at a job and have other responsibilities, is it realistic for you to think that you can set aside the time to do research, prepare papers and go to hearings?

- If you are bringing the lawsuit (as opposed to being sued) what will the costs be? By representing yourself you save on attorney's fees, but there are other costs involved in litigation. Having a court reporter at a deposition for example can cost several hundred dollars. Filing fees in some states have increased to the point of being absurd.

-       Is your personality suited for the conflict that inevitably arises? Some people are naturally contentious. These are the people that are in the debating club in high school or college. These are the ones that want to argue all the political and other issues with anyone up for the challenge. Other people are far more benign. They don't like confrontation. They avoid arguments. They are more passive. Still others are easily upset and excitable. You have to objectively assess your own personality before going down this road. If the idea of getting into a courtroom and arguing to the judge seems like the greatest thing since sliced bread, that's great. On the other hand, if though the thought of doing that makes your palms sweat and you feel yourself getting dizzy, representing yourself might not be the best plan. Only you can decide, but this is the time to be objective.

These are some of the questions that will help you decide whether or not to undertake Being Your Own Lawyer. On the other hand, if you're the one being sued, or foreclosed on, or whatever, and you've been to half a dozen lawyers that are demanding a retainer of several thousand dollars, that you just don't have, then it is all academic. Your decision has been made for you.

Either way, before you embark on this adventure, be sure to carefully consider all the issues.

HANDLING A CIVIL CASE

The first section of the book dealt with the actual questions surrounding representing yourself. It addressed issues about what is involved, relevant questions and the logistics.

This section addresses the actual process. Here you will learn what it means to be in a civil case, from start to finish. What it takes to lay out a viable plan and to put it into action.

The last section, the one following this is oriented toward giving you more information about the law itself. It begins with an overview of American Law and outlines the different courts available in America to resolves disputes. Once you have been given an overall background, various legal topics, relevant to representing yourself in court are explored.

To get the most out of this book you should refer freely to the last section. Here there will be references to things like evidence, or court rules. Don't hesitate to stop and go to that part of the last section to get a better feel.

Also, understand that in terms of actually going to court, things differ a lot from state to state in terms of details, but generally, it's pretty much the same. The clerk of court in South Carolina does pretty much the same things as the prothonotary in Pennsylvania. Things have different names in different places, but with a little research and common sense, they will all fall into place.

Planning

Ok, you understand that not only are you allowed to represent yourself, but you actually can pull it off. You understand in general terms what it takes. You've been given things to consider in deciding whether to represent yourself.

You're saying to yourself, ok enough already! I get it! Tell me how to do this!

Ok – here we go. But no, it's not time to head off to the courthouse just yet. First comes a lot of detailed planning and decision making.

To understand how to represent yourself you have to have an understanding of the whole picture. How the legal system works. How a case gets from start to finish and what happens along the way. In the following sections you'll learn how to handle a case from start to finish.

Now let's get things going.

There are two points of view on this – plaintiff and defendant. To make it easy they're presented separately.

When You're the plaintiff

When it comes to beginning a lawsuit, obviously the plaintiff has more choices than the defendant. The plaintiff for example, has the option of bringing or not bringing the lawsuit at all. That's a pretty potent choice, and it, like other options to be considered should not be taken lightly.

The research and analysis of your civil case begins long before you trot down to the courthouse with papers in hand.

Get it Together and Decide

Something has taken place in your life that makes it obvious that you may be going to court. Either you've been injured, or cheated, or a business relationship has gone sour. You've paid for something and haven't gotten it. You've lost your job unfairly. The list goes on and on. Every day, all over America, people find themselves being pushed from watching Court TV to being in it.

Before you ever file the first paper, or respond to a paper in any way, it is absolutely critical that you get a good grasp of the entire picture. First, you can't make any meaningful decisions without understanding the whole thing – law, procedures and rules. If you don't grasp that, then your decision making has about the same level of accuracy as tossing darts and seeing where they hit. Beyond making decisions if you don't understand what's going on you'll spend the whole case reacting and dodging bullets. You will spend the rest of any lawsuit you are in stumbling around from tree to tree in the proverbial forest. In the end, you will lose.

You need to be able to understand the total and complete picture of civil lawsuit. The entire picture in a lawsuit consists of the facts surrounding the dispute, the law that pertains to the lawsuit (all of it) and the rules and procedure that must be followed. If you omit any one of those three you are doomed. If you understand those three elements you will be in a position to make rational and objective decisions. With knowledge of those three things, you will win!

In this section you will be taken through the steps that you need to follow in order to get this entire picture but first things first.

Perhaps a good way to see this "whole picture" concept is to compare a civil case to a football game. There are more similarities than you might think. After all in a football game there is an offense and a defense. In a court case there is a plaintiff and a defendant. In both the football game and the court case both sides want to win. In both a football game and a court case it is absolutely imperative that you have a detailed game plan and strategy. Just as a football coach has a detailed playbook, written and prepared long before the team takes the field, you must have your whole strategy mapped out and planned well before you ever get near a courthouse.

And there is a caveat to that. It means before you do anything else, you lay out the facts and the law. Then you ask yourself some critical and hard questions, starting with, "do I even want to play?"

That's right. Before you map out the grandiose plan for victory, the first hard question you have to ask is, do I really want to be in court at all.

The question may at first seem somewhat silly. After all if you think you've been wronged, that's what the court system is for. "Sue the bastards" is such a familiar refrain that it seems like everyone swears by it, because it sure looks at times like everyone is suing everyone.

Is this Lawsuit Really A Good Idea?

First, if you're the one bringing the lawsuit, or thinking about it, you've got an option that the other side doesn't have. After all, the defendant being sued has basically two options – fight or surrender. Contest the lawsuit or lose. The plaintiff on the other hand has the option of bringing the lawsuit or, deciding that doing so may not be the best possible option.

So what are we talking about here? What are the issues? What are the factors that go into that decision?

The process of deciding whether or not to go to court is really just the first step in laying out the whole playbook - the master plan of representing yourself. Of course should your analysis lead to the conclusion that going to court is not in your best interests, the "playbook" stays very short.

Look at the decision making process at this level. Here are some things to consider:

- What are you trying to accomplish with the lawsuit? What are your goals?

- Can you realistically achieve those goals?

24

- What will you really get in the end?

- What will it cost you to win?

Let's look at these issues in a little more detail.

What Are You Trying to Accomplish?

It may seem like a silly question at first, especially in most basic lawsuits where the plaintiff is seeking a money award. But it's often not nearly that simple.

The reality is that lawsuits are brought for a lot of different reasons. Seeking a money judgment is the reason that people are most familiar with. You've been injured, or your property has been damaged, or you've experienced losses when a contract was breached. You want to recover those losses.

You go to court to try to recover the money value of any of these things by have a judge or jury award you a judgment. In a perfect world you receive the amount of that judgment.

But while that kind of lawsuit is far and away the most common, there are plenty of other reasons to sue someone or something.

Lawsuits can be brought to order people to do or refrain from doing something. If you live in a subdivision restricted to single family residence and someone starts to construct a five story apartment building, you would go to court for an injunction. Here you couldn't care less (at least at this point) about a money judgment. You want the construction stopped.

Lawsuits can be brought so that a court can give a ruling on a legal question, such as the interpretation of a contract or deed or the legal effect of a statute.

And too, lawsuits can be brought for less noble, albeit practical purposes. They can be brought to harass or cause the other party to incur expense. Large companies or wealthy individuals routinely bring lawsuits that they know they cannot ultimately win, or collect on, with the sole objective of requiring their opponent to either pay huge sums in litigation or make concessions that they otherwise would not.

So the very first thing that you need to lay out is what it is you want. The preparation for a lawsuit seeking money damages will be substantially different than a lawsuit you file just to cost the other side expense and trouble. Likewise, a lawsuit filed to stop some activity, will require completely different planning and organization that a lawsuit to enforce a contract.

Can you realistically achieve those goals?

The next issue that you need to subject to cold, objective scrutiny is whether the goals are achievable.

26

There are two separate areas to explore here, and both of them require that you put emotions aside and be objective and realistic.

The first area is the legal side. The second is the reality side.

On the legal side you have to do enough research and studying to make sure that your goals are attainable at all as a matter of law.

First, can a court even give you what you are seeking?

The question at first glance may appear silly in light of the obvious response of "that's what courts are for."

The problem with this as with many simplistic answers is the power of courts is not unlimited. For example, while they issue injunctions and restraining orders, and may require things like support payments to be made, no court has the power to require someone to keep working at a specific job, complete a contracted task, or engage in a specific activity. Slavery was abolished a hundred and fifty years ago.

If someone has contracted to construct your house and after payment refuses to do so, while a court can award you a judgment for the money paid or other damages, it cannot issue an order requiring the builder to go on the job-site and swing a hammer.

You also have to take into account the jurisdiction – the reach of a court. Can it help you? The answers to some situations are crystal clear. Others are considerably murkier.

If you go on a road trip to Mexico, and purchase a "genuine native" souvenir, only to find upon your return the "made in China" label, it is clear that you have grievance against the seller. But… is there anything a court in say, Milwaukee Wisconsin can do for you about something you bought in Mexico? Of course not.

Less clear are situations involving more complex issues. You are in New York and a car with diplomatic plates backs into your car causing damage. All sorts of issues need to be resolved, none of them simple.

These issues need to be carefully researched before you head to the courthouse. Why would you want to spend hundreds of dollars in filing fees, hours of time drafting, filing and serving a complaint, and the time to go to court only to have the judge say "case dismissed" at the first hearing.

The second aspect of this issue is in a nutshell, can you win? Do you have the facts? What is the law? Are the damages you have suffered related closely enough to the misdeeds of the defendant?

Doing this analysis is fairly complex. This is where you have to do your homework. It requires applying the facts of your claim to the applicable law.

If for example you are alleging that you had a contract with the proposed defendant that he breached, all the aspects of contract law that pertain need to be examined. Was there a contract? Was it in writing? If it was oral is it barred by requirements that some contracts be in writing? Was there consideration? Was the contract actually breached? Was there justification for the breach? Were you actually damaged by the breach? Were the damages that you are claiming foreseeable? Some of these are what is referred to as indispensable elements of a cause of action. If any of them are missing you cannot prevail on that cause of action. Think of it as a checklist. You have to go down the list and be able to check ALL the boxes.

Every potential lawsuit presents these kinds of questions that have to be addressed. This is what is referred to as an objective case assessment. Stated another way, in possibly overly simplistic terms, the question becomes: "Will it fly"?

Fortunately, while it appears outright intimidating and overwhelming it is far from insurmountable. Applying a systematic approach based on research of the law and an objective assessment of the facts will give you the answers you need.

What will you really get in the end?

Put another way, what will you receive, where will you be if you win?

This may not be such a difficult question to answer where your goals are something other than money, such as in interpretation of a contract, or getting a restraining order. But it becomes a huge factor in deciding whether to proceed with a lawsuit where you are trying to collect money damages. In the realm of money judgments, lawyers refer to it as pursuing a defendant with deep pockets. Among attorneys it is a major determining factor in whether a lawyer will take or pursue a case, and it should be for you, representing yourself as well.

Being awarded a judgment is not the same as being handed actual money. A judgment is nothing more than an order from the court that declares that you are entitled to receive that amount from the defendant, and authorizing certain legal mechanisms to be employed against the defendant's assets to pay the judgment. It does NOT require the defendant to pay the judgment.

It is so important that you understand this principle that we will repeat it.

A judgment does NOT require a defendant to pay anything!

A judgment creditor (you, if you win your lawsuit and get a judgment) can have the defendant's property seized (subject to exemptions), his bank accounts (that are subject to the jurisdiction of the court) can be attached, and in some states, his wages can be garnished. But understand that there is no mechanism to require the defendant himself to pay the judgment. No one can haul the defendant into court and tell him to pay up or go to jail!

So the reality is a judgment in your favor for a million dollars is absolutely worthless if you can't collect it.

It is important that you determine to as great extent as possible, well before a lawsuit is filed, whether the defendant has assets from which a judgment can be paid. If there is no likelihood of collecting on a judgment, is it worth going through the time and expense of a lawsuit?

It actually may be for one reason or another. Judgments are valid for years and in some states can be renewed indefinitely. That means years later, if the defendant acquires assets, perhaps unintentionally through inheritance or by virtue of receiving marital property through divorce or death, you can proceed to collect.

A judgment against a defendant may help you in other ways, such as constituting an impediment to a competitor. It will be difficult for example for a judgment debtor to obtain business financing in the face of a judgment. In today's internet environment a prospective customer or client can easily determine the existence of a judgment. A judgment will seriously affect an individual debtor's credit rating making obtaining credit either impossible or at least difficult and significantly more expensive.

So there actually may be reasons to pursue a judgment even when there is no immediate prospect of collecting it.

The key is that you understand what you can and cannot accomplish with any given lawsuit and on the basis of that understanding make a rational and objective decision. If you are fine with a judgment that you can't collect immediately, that's perfectly reasonable. Just be sure that you understand that going in.

What will it cost you to win?

The next issue, assuming that you've defined what you're after and objectively believe you can get there, is to make a judgment call as to value. Will whatever you get by winning outweigh the cost and effort?

This is nothing more than doing an objective and realistic cost/reward/risk evaluation and analysis.

Let's face it, filing a lawsuit is going to cost you money. Even though you won't be looking at huge attorney's fees when you represent yourself, there are still costs.

With budget cutbacks court filing fees have become more than just a nominal fee. A recent case filed in Pennsylvania cost the plaintiff over eight hundred dollars to file. Even after the initial filing of the case, subsequent filings require fees. Many courts charge a fee every time you file a motion. In the course of any case it is likely that you will have to take a deposition. Court reporters charge by the page so depending on how long, people ramble on, you could easily end up spending hundreds of dollars for a transcript. There are witness fees, costs to make copies, possibly fees for reports from third parties.

Hopefully you get the picture. Even though you can save substantial amounts by representing yourself, a lawsuit is going to cost you money.

It is also going to cost you time. The mechanism that allows you to save thousands of dollars in attorney's fees does not dispense with the work that has to be done. It just shifts it from an attorney and their staff to you.

You have to make an honest assessment on two levels: do you have the time at all and are you willing to devote the necessary time to the pursuit of your goals?

It is important that this assessment be made honestly and objectively. Consider where the suit is filed. Consider the kind of case. Consider how many witnesses will have to be contacted and interviewed. Consider what kind of evidence will have to be gathered. Do not let wishful thinking and initial exuberance deceive you into believing that you can or will devote the time necessary to attaining your goals when in fact it is not true.

Along these same lines also consider the intangible costs and the burdens you will experience other than your time. Not everyone is suited to representing themselves. Appearing in court, especially for those easily intimidated can be a daunting experience. It can be stressful. A lot of us thrive on this sort of thing. Others avoid it like the plague. It is for you to decide whether or not you are willing to put yourself in those situations.

Against these you have to balance the reward and the probability that you will realize the award.

We come back to how much you stand to recover if it is a money judgment you're after. How likely are you to win the case, and how likely you are to collect the judgment if you win it. If it is something other than money that you're seeking, the same kind of analysis applies, though the factors may be a bit more subjective. If someone in your neighborhood, restricted to single family homes, wants to build that five story apartment building mentioned earlier, you may be ready to do whatever it takes to get an injunction. On the other hand, if someone is building a nice house, but it turns out that it will be only 1800 square feet when the restrictions specify a minimum size of 2000 square feet, are you still willing to go to the mat to stop them? Is the cost worth the reward? Is it a big enough deal to go through litigation over?

The bottom line is that you need to take a long hard look at any lawsuit that you are thinking of brining. You have to look at all the factors outlined. You have put emotions aside and be objective. You have to do it long before you get near a courthouse.

If it won't fly, leave it alone. If it will fly but there is no pay-off, leave it alone.

If it will fly and you can get what you want - go for it!

You've Decided – Now More Decisions

You've decided to sue someone. You've been to talk to a couple of lawyers. They want huge fees upfront and then want to charge you $300 an hour – OUCH!

You've decided that you can do this on your own. You've done your careful assessment. You've weighed the cost and the risk and the reward and decided that going to court is the hot setup.

So it's time to get started.

Rule number one in handling a lawsuit is to do absolutely nothing!

That's right, don't do a thing. Handling a lawsuit begins with a deep breath and a lot of thought and reflection. Very rarely do you have to do anything immediately, so why rush headlong into a potential disaster?

Of course you're thinking as you read this. "I paid good money for advice like that? It's so obvious it's silly!"

Actually though it is far from silly.

Lawsuits in the wrong court. Lawsuits against the wrong party. Lawsuits for the wrong thing. Defendants waiving perfectly good defenses and losing their cases. All these and more have occurred in real cases filed by, or responded to by people that for one reason or another didn't stop and take a deep breath.

The best way to win in a civil lawsuit is to approach it systematically and methodically. There is no need to rush. Here are some steps and guidelines for getting started. They're not etched in concrete, but generally, you should have a good handle on step one before you go to step two and so forth.

And for those who don't like instructions, give it a shot. You'll find that it is a lot like putting your kids' swing set together. After you first toss the instructions off to the side, after your project looks like the obvious disaster that it is, you'll find yourself coming back to them...

Here are the initial steps you need to go through in order to represent yourself as a plaintiff in a lawsuit.

1. Research jurisdiction and venue.
2. Define your causes of action or defenses and the parties.
3. Research your causes of action or defenses.

So here we go!

STEP ONE: Research and Decide on Jurisdiction and Venue

Before you even begin to look at causes of action, and the details of the court papers, you should look at jurisdiction and venue. Those are technical terms for what court and where. Most people fail to appreciate how important these issues are and how they can be used. They are so important that I have devoted an entire chapter to jurisdiction. For now, here are some things you should be aware of and factor into your analysis:

From the plaintiff's perspective there are a lot of options presented and a lot of different considerations go into picking the right court to file your lawsuit in.

First is the issue of what is called subject matter jurisdiction. You have to research the court system where you are to see what court fits. Many states have courts with different dollar levels of jurisdiction. There may be small claims courts that handle any dispute involving less than $10,000 or some other figure. Obviously there are courts that handle only specific kinds of cases, such as family or domestic relations courts. You have to make sure you pick the right court.

Second there is the issue of jurisdiction over the parties. If both you and the defendant live in the same state, there is no issue. But if you live in different states, the question of whether a state will be able to exercise jurisdiction over a non-resident becomes important.

Venue refers to the geographical area within a state. All states have different counties or the equivalent, and courts of the same kind in those counties. It is important that you file in the right county based on the rules and statutes of your state.

The most important thing is to understand that both jurisdiction and venue can be changed and manipulated by careful planning and some creative thinking. You need to be aware of the ways that that can be done and the advantages and disadvantages. Here are a couple of examples:

Pick a court that suits you. If your state has different levels of court based on amount in dispute, depending on what you are trying to accomplish, the court you pick may make it easier for you and more difficult for your opponent. Let's take a typical sample case. You needed a new roof and found ABC Roofing in the phone book. They gave you an estimate, you signed a contract, and they got started. But they never finished. You're out money that you've paid them and your roof is a mess. Assume that the initial payment was $8,000, and because they didn't finish, you didn't pay anything else. You want your money back. Let's say that you are in a state where in small claims or magistrate's court the owner of a corporation is allowed to represent it[1]. And let's say that the amount you are trying to recover is $8,000 in a state where the jurisdictional level of small claims court is $10,000.

Most people, without doing their homework and taking the proverbial deep breath, would simply file in small claims court. They would see that the amount they are

---

[1] Normally you can only represent yourself and no other person. A corporation is regarded for litigation as a "person" so you cannot represent one, even if it is your own corporation.

trying to recover is less than the upper limit of the subject matter jurisdiction of the court and would fail to look at any other options. They would have missed a great opportunity to cause their opponent a tremendous amount of additional expense. Why?

By increasing the amount in dispute you can force this case out of small claims court into a higher court.

How? By including in the claim (you were just initially asking for your money back) additional elements such as damage to your house or building resulting from the failure to install the roof, and any other expenses or costs that with a little imagination you can come up with.

Remember, you don't have to ultimately be able to prove these. You just be able to have some basis for alleging them to begin with.

What is the point? Mr. Jones, the owner of all the stock of ABC Roofing is now no longer able to represent ABC Roofing, Inc. as he could in small claims court. He has to go hire a lawyer. Suddenly after being asked for a $5,000 retainer to defend the lawsuit, with no guarantee that he'll win, paying you the $8,000 back looks a lot more attractive.

What? That sounds unethical! It's an abuse of the court system!

The first thing you need to understand is that you are in litigation to win. There are no extra points for being Mr.

Nice Guy. Your job is to get your money back from a guy that should have finished the roof or refunded your money without a lawsuit. If holding his feet to the fire a little gets you where you what you want, so be it.

STEP TWO: Define your causes of action and parties.

The next step is to define your causes of action. In the United States the combination of common and statutory law provides an impressive collection of things you can sue for. Use logic and an organized approach to pick the ones that will work for you.

Begin by identifying your beef. Why are you suing? What happened? How did it happen? Who did it? Did someone breach a contract? Did they kill your dog? Did they cheat you out of money?

This is an important first step, and it is not as easy as it sounds. We all have an inherent sense of right and wrong. We know that when we pay for something and don't get what we paid for it is wrong. We know that when we break someone's window with a baseball that it is our fault and we have an obligation to make it right.

But not everything is that simple and very seldom are things black or white. There are always some gray streaks. Now is the time to get the lawsuit right. If you chase the wrong cause of action, or the wrong defendant, or leave out a claim or a defendant, it may be hard, if not impossible to fix it later.

To get a better picture, continue the ABC Roofing example. You signed a contract with ABC Roofing owned by John Jones to install a roof on your house. You paid part of the price for the roof. It never materialized. You want your roof or you want your money back.

At first glance the obvious lawsuit is for breach of contract against ABC Roofing. You have a signed agreement from ABC Roofing that for a certain amount of money they would install a roof. You paid the money. They didn't install a roof. All the legal elements of a contract are present (offer, consideration, meeting of the minds) and the breach is as plain as day. Let's go!!

Not so fast.

Yes, everything, as far it goes 100% correct. You have a clear breach of contract case. But is this the way you want to go? Are there other options? Are there better options?

Take a long hard look at ABC Roofing, Inc.

A major reason for people to set up corporations and limited liability companies is to safeguard their own assets. The business world is a risky place and people naturally want to protect what they've worked long and hard for. That is why if you go to the online database of the secretary of state of any state, you will find thousands of small, one or two person corporations or limited liability companies. People set these companies up to insulate themselves from personal liability. If it is done correctly, the corporation itself which is the entity that does business with you and the rest of the world, will have nothing. If it does business from a building, it will not own that building. Instead will lease the building and everything in it from its principals (in this case Mr. Jones) or if he is smart, from someone (his mother, wife, or cousin) who has nothing to do with the business.

Trying to follow the sage advice of researching and planning, you do your homework on ABC Roofing and realize to your dismay that the company itself is effectively worthless. It appears that Mr. Jones has indeed gotten some good advice. The building from which ABC Roofing operates, according to the county property records by some person who, as near as you can discern, has no connection with ABC Roofing whatsoever. You may for an online service to perform an asset check on ABC Roofing and find that the company owns nothing. No real estate, no vehicles, no manufacturing equipment- nothing! So here you are. You've figured out that you have the perfect lawsuit for breach of contract. But you have a defendant from which when you win, you will never collect a dime.

What Not to Do

Most people faced with this situation would have glanced at the internet, gleaned enough to know about breach of contract and run off to the courthouse. Someone there (if they were in a kind and generous mood) would have handed them some forms and told them to write (where is says nature of action) breach of contract. They would have taken their filing fee and then it would be off to the races suing ABC Roofing, Inc.

ABC Roofing, Inc. may or may not even bother to answer. It might be that Mr. Jones, the owner couldn't care less. After all, it only costs a few dollars to start a new corporation. But assume that ABC responds and the process of the lawsuit gets under way.

As the lawsuit progress our intrepid litigator finally realizes that something is dreadfully wrong. This is too easy. He does some more homework; maybe poses some questions to some legal advice websites, and realizes that he is wasting his time suing the corporation. No matter how large a judgment he gets in the end, it will be worthless. He realizes at this point that it is Mr. Jones he should be after. He tries to amend his complaint to add Mr. Jones. Because he has not read the rules carefully, he overlooks the fact that a complaint cannot be amended at this point except by leave of court. That is, he is required to file a motion and obtain and order from the court allowing him to amend. Belatedly, he files a motion to amend the complaint and goes to the hearing that has been scheduled.

The judge listens to our hero, and then denies the motion. Again, he has not read the rules. That should have been done three months ago. It's too late to add parties or causes of action. On top of everything else, other factors may come into play. While our hero was busy waiting for the ABC Roofing case to work its way up the trial docket, the statute of limitations for a new lawsuit against Mr. Jones may have run. Depending on how he worded his complaint, he may have put himself in a position where he is unable to properly raise other causes of action that may be inconsistent with his breach of contract claim.

What to do instead

Stop and lay it all out. Research the different options. At first this may appear overwhelming. How to figure out what to put in the complaint can seem intimidating. But it need not be. Not if you approach it logically.

Here's a trick that seasoned trial lawyers use in laying out cases.

Start at the end and work backwards.

That's right. Go back to the question of what do you really want out of the lawsuit. Then, with that as your goal, work backwards through the steps of how to get there.

We're a long way from being through with ABC Roofing and Mr. Jones, so let's apply our theory to them.

You now know that ABC Roofing is in and of itself not worth suing. You also know that Mr. Jones is the driving force behind ABC Roofing, and that Mr. Jones is loaded. You know that in the end, while a judgment against ABC Roofing will be worthless, a judgment against Mr. Jones would be easy to collect.

You have effectively answered your own question. You need a judgment against Mr. Jones.

Now with a clear goal in mind as compared to the original somewhat foggy "I want my money back", you can focus your research efforts.

If you research breach of contract cases you will notice some very important things. In virtually every case that you find, there are other causes of action asserted in addition to the breach of contract claim. There are causes of action for fraud, for violation of various unfair or deceptive business practices statutes, violation of licensing requirements, unjust enrichment, and the list goes on. The bonus is that unlike the breach of contract claim, which can only be brought against ABC Roofing, Inc., the party to the contract, many of these other claims can be brought against anyone involved.

What have you accomplished by taking a deep breath and doing some research before filing that lawsuit?

You've literally changed the whole ballgame!

When you started you had in mind, and were ready to file, a lawsuit against a worthless corporation for breach of contract. Now things have changed. If you've paid any attention at all to your research results, you now are ready to draft and file a lawsuit against ABC Roofing, Inc. AND Mr. Jones personally for not just breach of contract but possibly also for:

- fraud
- fraudulent inducement
- money had and received
- unjust enrichment
- conversion
- violation of your state's unfair and deceptive trade or business statute
- breach of fiduciary duty
- defective products (roofing materials)

Everything has changed. You've not only dramatically increased the prospects of prevailing, but you've added players to the mix from which you may actually recover something!

STEP THREE: Research your causes of action or defenses

This sounds a lot like what you've already done, but there's more. Once you have defined a cause of action or a defense, you have to research it to understand it completely. What you have to educate yourself on is what the elements of a cause of action are. That is what must be established (proven) in order for you to be entitled to recover. Every cause of action that you will plead in a complaint, without exception, has specific elements and parts.

Let's look at our example and one of the causes of action – breach of contract. To recover on a breach of contract claim, a plaintiff must plead (put in his complaint) and prove at trial (1) the existence of a contract, including its essential terms; (2) a breach of a duty imposed by the contract; and (3) resultant damages. The plaintiff in a civil case has the burden of proof. He must establish his cause of action. Therefore the failure to plead (put in the complaint) and prove any one of these will result in the case being dismissed. A defendant need only disprove or show the absence of any one of these in order to prevail. If fraud is included as a cause of action you should know that common law fraud has nine separate elements which must be alleged and proven. Leave one out and your cause of action is dismissed.

Be aware that properly identifying the elements of any cause of action which you elect to pursue accomplishes two things. First, the elements must be set forth (pled) in the complaint. Knowing these elements will allow you to properly prepare a complaint. Second, in the trial of a case the elements of a cause of action are what you have to prove, by evidence, in order to win. So from the plaintiff's perspective these elements provide a roadmap of the evidence you will need to present. Likewise, for the defendant, they provide a perfect blueprint of what the plaintiff will have to prove. This allows the defendant to develop its own evidence to counter, long before the trial begins.

So, since you have to have this information at your fingertips, both now and later, it's time to research it.

The problem with this is that as with so many things in life, it sounds much simpler than it is. Causes of action can be defined by statute, by case law, or both. You have to do a lot of digging.

In our example what you must understand is that there is no specific statute in any law book that will list these necessary elements for you. These elements came from an appellate court decision, which came from prior decisions, which came from early decisions and so forth. Common Law!

This research involves reading not only statutes and laws, but reading cases that have decided these issues. Even where a cause of action may appear in a statute, such as an unfair trade practices statute, it is critical to research the cases that have decided that statute. Often you will find that a court has interpreted a statute somewhat differently than would appear from reading just the statute.

Nor is it an area where you want to take shortcuts. There is no point in going through the effort and incurring the costs of filing a lawsuit just to have it dismissed because you have failed to allege the necessary of elements of a cause of action in your complaint. Likewise, there is no reason to lose a lawsuit as a defendant because you were not aware of the issues.

When You're the Defendant.

You thought you were minding your own business. Life is going along well but for the expected minor issues. All in all things are pretty good. Until...

This shady looking guy walks up to you and hands you a stack of papers and says: "You've been served!"

A quick glance at the papers tells you immediately that you're being sued.

You skim over the papers and while a lot of it doesn't make much sense, it's clear to you the plaintiff is seeking a judgment against you. Suddenly you have visions of losing everything. Your house, your car, the dog... You are overcome with a feeling of dread.

What do you do?

NOTHING!

That's right. You take a deep breath and do nothing at first. You don't get on the phone to the plaintiff or its attorney trying to "work things out". The best thing you can do is nothing.

Now in the context of court papers that will be addressed later that doesn't mean do nothing forever. It means you need to relax and look at it rationally. The first thing to do (after the calming down part) is to read the papers carefully.

First read the summons. How much time do you have to answer? Mark it down on your calendar.

Next read the complaint from beginning to end, then read it again. You should be able to discern who is suing you, why they are suing you, and what they want.

Even then you don't start typing your answer. You research, you analyze and you plan!

Does the Lawsuit Even Need to be Defended?

In many cases, this could be the end of your problems. Not all lawsuits are attacks on you. Not all lawsuits are over money. Not all lawsuits need to be defended at all.

Here are some examples of lawsuits that you really couldn't care less about, even though you are named as a defendant.

- a mortgage foreclosure against someone else that owes you money. When lenders foreclose a mortgage they want to make sure that they eliminate anyone that could have a claim in the property being foreclosed. Say for example that five years ago you had sued the property owner in small claims court and gotten a judgment. When the lender forecloses the mortgage they will include you as a defendant because of the judgment. They don't want anything from you. They just want the property they are foreclosing free of your judgment. This is a lawsuit that you can probably just forget about.

-    a quiet title action. Many times there are issues with real estate titles and deeds. Sometimes it is necessary to have a court issue a ruling. Often, especially if there is a questionable deed, everyone that might conceivably have an interest in the property is named as a defendant. If you were a former owner, or had some interest in the property that you no longer care about, this is another lawsuit that you can safely toss.

Some lawsuits seek something and name you as a defendant, but you are not the real party in interest. A good example would be in a lawsuit over an auto accident. Even though you are the proper defendant, this is really something for your insurance company. The only immediate obligation you have is to get a copy of the lawsuit to them and they will handle it.

Unfortunately though, most lawsuits will affect you and must be addressed.

You are not helpless and at the mercy of the plaintiff. You have a lot of options and the principles of planning and analysis apply to you just as to the plaintiff.

You need to go through the same kind of analysis that was laid out for the plaintiff as you ponder what to do with the lawsuit and layout your game plan for dealing with it.

Do I Even Want to Defend this Suit?

The plaintiff of course elected to bring the lawsuit, and they had an option not available to you. That does not mean you're without options and that there are no decisions that need to be made at this juncture.

Some lawsuits just make no difference in the long run and are not worth spending any time, effort or money on. The ones that don't matter or affect you directly have already been discussed. Others though might be less obvious, or take some consideration.

Remember that not all lawsuits are about money. An example might be a boundary line dispute between you and your neighbor. "Where exactly is the property line" has been food for lawsuits in America since shortly after the Pilgrims arrived. Sometimes it's an important issue to you, but sometimes it just really makes no difference. If the lawsuit is over the latter, this is a time when you can just call up the plaintiff or their attorney and say "Hey where is it you want this property line to be?" Chances are pretty good that it can settle it with a quitclaim deed to the "disputed" property.

Another example might be where a seller is trying to rescind a contract with you over the sale of some real estate. Do a careful and objective analysis and decide whether you really care enough about the transaction to get into litigation. If not, call them up and say "Hey we don't need to go to court. Let's tear up the contract"

Logic would dictate that the kinds of things that were just mentioned could have been resolved before suit was filed, however there is not much logic when emotions are involved.

Finally, you need to do the reverse analysis of the plaintiff in deciding what the downside is for you if the plaintiff wins a judgment. Obviously if you are affluent, own real estate, have lots of personal property and have bank accounts that can be taken to satisfy a judgment, there is no real choice. You defend that lawsuit. But what if you're retired? You have years ago deeded your house to your children, retaining a life estate. You own no other real estate and all of your money is in IRA or other retirement accounts exempt from judgment. Your income comes from social security and pension payments which likewise can't be touched.

How much time, effort and anxiety do you really want to put forth defending a lawsuit when in the end, the plaintiff will have a judgment against you on which they will never collect a dime?

Right out of the gate you see you have choices. There are other things to consider and decide!

Jurisdiction and Venue Issues

Just as the plaintiff has some options and choices regarding jurisdiction and venue, so too do you as defendant. You might not have as many, but you there are certainly things you should be looking at. Remember that given options, a plaintiff will always try to select a jurisdiction and venue that is convenient to them and as inconvenient as possible to you.

Do not just accept that when papers are served that the venue and court selected are correct or carved in stone. You can object to venue. You can file a motion to dismiss if the jurisdiction is not correct.

The jurisdiction issue will usually rear its head when the parties reside in different states. As is discussed in more detail in the jurisdiction section, there are circumstances in which a court in one state can exercise jurisdiction over a resident of another. But just because you are served with papers that say so does not in and of itself mean it is anything more than wishful thinking on the part of the plaintiff.

When you are being sued in a different state, examine the complaint carefully to see that the basis of the jurisdiction is. Many times attorneys will make unsupportable assertions as the basis for jurisdiction hoping that they will be overlooked. They hope the jurisdiction issue will be inadvertently waived, or not objected to, and they can handle the lawsuit in their own backyard. Others attempt to assert jurisdiction in the hope that a defendant in a different state will ignore the suit and they will be able to obtain default judgment.

Examine what the plaintiff is saying confers jurisdiction over you and determine whether the allegations are true. Research the long arm statutes of the state in which the suit is pending to see how jurisdiction over a non-resident (you) can be had.

This will put you in a position to decide whether or not to challenge jurisdiction.

The goal here is to make the lawsuit as convenient for you and as inconvenient for your opponent as possible. Jurisdiction, when citizens of different states are involved is one of the major areas in which to pursue that goal. If a plaintiff has sued you in his state, and you can force them into your own, you will have such an advantage that often the lawsuit will go away. Why? The plaintiff has to start over and potentially, with different attorneys. Unless they are licensed in both states, the attorney that filed the lawsuit in plaintiff's state will not be able to file it in your state.

Remember that if you have an issue with jurisdiction, it must be raised immediately. The best way is to file a Motion to Dismiss for lack of jurisdiction. If you file an answer first, you run the risk of waiving the jurisdiction issue completely.

You may also have some jurisdiction options with respect to the amount in controversy. Look at the ABC Roofing case discussed earlier. ABC Roofing sues you for the balance due on the contract which is $8,000. This amount allows them to file in small claims court where Mr. Johnson can represent his corporation.

The same tactic pointed out for you as the plaintiff applies to you as the defendant. Instead of just demurely answering the complaint and defending the lawsuit on grounds of poor workmanship, you counterclaim and you make your counterclaim not just for the amount you paid, but for the damages to your roof, etc., etc. Just as was suggested for you as the plaintiff, you will have accomplished a lot. You have forced Mr. Jones to spend money – possibly more money that the whole thing is worth.

The case is kicked out of small claims court into "big" court where Mr. Jones has to retain an attorney to represent ABC Roofing, Inc. His costs have jumped substantially. Once again, standing on some moral soapbox in these cases is pointless. You have been sued, unjustly from your point of view. You need to win the lawsuit and if jerking Mr. Jones around by running up his costs is a way to accomplish that, so be it.

Finally, look at venue. Usually you have the right as a defendant to be sued in your county of residence. Some states have venue provisions that allow for suit where the events giving rise to the lawsuit occurred, or where either the plaintiff or the defendant reside. If there are choices, you can still file for a change of venue based on the location of the witnesses, the evidence and the interests of justice. Again, if you can make things convenient for yourself, and inconvenient and more expensive for the other side, you're making progress.

Jurisdiction and venue need to be carefully examined and researched as a very first step!

Review and Consider Causes of Action and Parties

Never lose sight of what you are trying to accomplish. In this case you were the defendant, but only because ABC Roofing sued you first. You were after all pretty unhappy about paying part of the price for a roof that was shoddy and never completed. Chances are pretty good that you would eventually have brought the lawsuit if they hadn't. This makes your goal entirely different than if you had just been sued without a potential counterclaim. There your goal is simply to make the lawsuit go away or to get out of it as cheaply as you can. Obviously the goals shape the planning!

You must make the same analysis as was outlined for the plaintiff. The difference is that you don't have the option of deciding whether to commence a lawsuit. So in analyzing your goals the objective is to lay them out and dispense with the "is it worth it?" question and go right to the "how do I accomplish my goals" phase.

Finding all the right causes of action, and including as many parties as you can, are ways to work toward those goals.

One goal in defending a lawsuit is always to make it as painful, difficult and expensive as possible for the plaintiff to press their claim against you.

If this book accomplishes nothing else it will be considered a success if it makes you understand that a lawsuit is not an honorable encounter. Peel away the pomp and ritual and you see what it really is – a brawl. Your job is to win it, or at least minimize your losses. If that means doing whatever you can to make it as expensive as possible for the other side, then you need to accept that. If you try to engage in this encounter by adhering to some artificial ethical constraints, you will lose because be assured, your opponent won't!

You can inflict a lot of damage through creative and judicious use of causes of action and additional parties.

Revisiting the ABC Roofing case, let's add some facts to show you that you really are not powerless as it might first appear.

First consider adding parties to the lawsuit.

Let's say ABC Roofing installed the roof, but it leaks and is coming up. You have gotten into a dispute. ABC Roofing and its owner, John Jones want you to pay the balance for the roof. You want the roof properly installed or a refund of the money you have paid. You receive suit papers. ABC Roofing is suing you for the unpaid balance.

Without doing research and becoming aware of the options, most people just answer the allegations in the complaint or if the situation warrants it, as in the ABC Roofing case, file a counterclaim. Hopelessly unimaginative and boring!

Time to get the blinders off and have fun! You would be amazed at the havoc you can cause in the plaintiff's camp with a little creativity in this area.

You may not be able to decide the initial parties since that is at the option of the plaintiff. But you can certainly decide who else you might like to invite to the party.

In every jurisdiction when you are sued you can broaden the circle of frolicking participants not only by filing a counterclaim but also by adding parties by way of a third party complaint.

Adding people not named in the original lawsuit can open all sorts of possibilities. Under the right circumstances it can put enough pressure on the plaintiff to make the pursuit of the lawsuit considerably less interesting.

In this hypothetical case the first person you would add to the lawsuit is of course Mr. Jones. He's the driving force behind ABC Roofing. The posture he's put this lawsuit in is a win/no lose situation for him. Even if you file a counterclaim for what you've paid (his assumption going into the suit) the worst that can happen is that he gets nothing. Even if you win on the counterclaim ABC Roofing is judgment proof. So from his perspective he can win but not lose. When the plaintiff is in that posture, it is very difficult to resolve a dispute, so an important consideration is to burst that bubble of complacency.

By adding Mr. Jones as a third party defendant in addition to the counterclaim that dynamic changes drastically. Now he has just as much exposure as you do. He can still win, but now, he can also lose.

But you can make it even more interesting by doing your homework and becoming creative!

The shingles or the roofing material may be defective. They are coming up and curling. They might have been improperly manufactured, or perhaps they were not properly stored at the wholesaler. You need to add those as third party defendants, alleging in your third party complaint that you have been damaged by their defective products.

What will this accomplish? A lot!

When these people receive the lawsuit, it will not be styled you versus them. That comes much later on the caption. What will be glaringly obvious when the manufacturer and wholesaler get these papers is that it is ABC Roofing, their customer that started this mess.

The phone will be ringing off the hook at ABC Roofing. These companies will let Mr. Jones know in no uncertain terms that he needs to get this resolved before they incur any expense. They will remind him that they will be asserting claims for any attorney's fees and costs that they are required to pay because of the lawsuit that HE filed.

If the dynamic of the lawsuit was changed when you added Mr. Jones personally as a defendant, this has really changed it! Poor Mr. Jones has gone from a win/no lose scenario, to a win/lose scenario to a lose/lose scenario. The best he can do is to collect from you the balance due. In the meantime he is looking at possibly paying the attorney's fees of the manufacturer and the wholesaler whether they win or lose. Worse, he is looking at possibly having his contract with his supplier cancelled.

Wow!!! Has this ballgame ever changed!

With just a small amount of creativity, you've changed the entire tenor of the lawsuit, and made it far more likely that Mr. Jones will want to reach a mutually acceptable resolution very quickly.

OK, you've seen what can be done with parties, now take a look at what a little creativity can do with causes of action.

First, the answer itself.

Of course you will deny the allegations of the complaint. But as you will learn in pleadings and court papers, there are a lot of other things that you not only can allege, but must allege or lose them as defenses.

Things in this group include what are referred to as affirmative defenses, and things like motions to dismiss for various reasons. What is the point of throwing away a perfectly good defense just because you were in a rush and didn't stop to take a deep breath?

Then there are all the potential causes of action that you can raise in the counterclaim. In addition to the breach of contract which is the obvious counterclaim, things like unfair and deceptive trade practices, maybe violation of licensing laws, negligence, just to name a few. Remember again, if your state has compulsory counterclaim rules, any of these that you don't include are effectively gone.

Finally, you have all the third party claims against the manufacturer and wholesaler. Defective products, breach of warranty claims, perhaps negligence on the part of the wholesaler if it turns out the roofing materials were not stored properly.

Are you getting the point here about taking a long hard look before you do anything?

Yes, you could have taken a look at the suit papers you received and fired off an answer. You could have even thought to include a counterclaim alleging that the roof was not properly installed. In the process you might have missed a lot of opportunities. By laying everything out and doing some basic research you've opened the door to a whole new array of options and opportunities.

Look at what you were able to accomplish instead!

Research Causes of Action and Defenses

Just as it's important to research each cause of action as the plaintiff, it's important for the defendant to research the causes of action in the complaint being defended, the elements of any affirmative defenses2 and any counterclaims or third party claims. The defendant has a lot more work to do, and it should be done before the first page of a response is typed.

Of course you have to research the elements of the causes of action that the plaintiff is alleging against you. How else can you defend? You can't just deny everything and be done with it. You need to know what the elements of the causes of action are so that you can determine if they've been properly pled.

Here is another approach. If you do your homework and find that the plaintiff has failed to plead an essential element of a cause of action consider not raising it by a motion to dismiss. Everybody for some reason does that, and it seldom serves any purpose.

Why?

---

[2] An *affirmative defense* to a civil lawsuit or criminal charge is a fact or set of facts other than those alleged by the plaintiff or prosecutor which, if proven by the defendant, defeats or mitigates the legal consequences of the defendant's otherwise unlawful conduct.

Because if you file a motion to dismiss, all you do is draw the plaintiff's attention to the problem. When a judge grants a motion to dismiss for failing to state a cause of action it will almost always be with permission to the plaintiff to amend. In some states this is even automatic. For example, in Pennsylvania a motion to dismiss is referred to as preliminary objections. The rule there specifically states that if the plaintiff in response to preliminary objections amends the complaint, the preliminary objections are disposed of automatically.

You've done nothing but show the plaintiff the error of his ways and prompted him to fix it.

The rules in almost every jurisdiction (Federal Rule 12(b)(6) require the defense of failure to state a cause of action to be raised in the first responsive pleading, which can be the answer. So instead of a motion to dismiss, just slip it into the answer as an affirmative defense.

Then do nothing. Chances are very good that if the plaintiff, having missed the issue when the complaint was drafted, will not pay much attention to it in the answer, where it appears among numerous other "boilerplate" affirmative defenses. Then later, when the time to amend the pleadings has expired, shortly before trial, you can file a motion for judgment on the pleadings. Technically it will be too late to amend the pleadings close before trial and there is a good chance you can get the case tossed. A sympathetic judge may allow the plaintiff to amend, but it is far from a sure thing and the plaintiff will in any event be in a far greater bind.

Once you've researched the complaint and defenses to be raised in an answer, the same kind of research must be done with respect to the counterclaim and third party complaint. With these pleadings you are effectively in the same position as the plaintiff. You must research the available claims and causes of action, establish the essential elements of each claim, and use that as a checklist as you draft your pleadings. If you have properly researched the required elements of a cause of action or claim, and make sure that every element is alleged in your counterclaim or third party complaint, you will be in good shape.

Now, you're ready to draft your lawsuit or your responsive pleadings and get things moving. You're ready to handle the lawsuit!

In the following sections you will find an explanation of the court papers you will be dealing with, and how to handle them. Later you will learn about discovery and the trial of the case. Along the way there will be sections about motions and related issues. By the time you get to the end, you should be ready to handle your case!

Pleadings and Court Papers

Now that you've done your risk reward analysis and researched the issues, you're finally ready to prepare that pleading and go to the courthouse.

In any court action certain things must be brought to the attention of the court. These include things like the matters in dispute, what the plaintiff is seeking, why the defendant disagrees and what issues are to be decided are. They must be presented to the court in an organized and understandable way. This is accomplished with court papers and pleadings.

The lawsuit that you're involved in will be started by the filing and service of a complaint. You will be doing that if you're the plaintiff. The plaintiff will have done that if you are the defendant. In some jurisdictions this initial paper will be called something else, such as a petition but for the sake of simplicity, here it will be the complaint.

It is responded to by the party being sued, normally referred to as the defendant, with papers that can come in different forms and flavors. Collectively referred to as responsive pleadings, these can include an answer, a counterclaim, a cross complaint, a third party complaint, or one or more motions or other papers.

This initial filing and exchange of pleadings is extremely important. What occurs at this stage, and how it occurs will have profound impact on the entire case.

It is a pleading, more specifically the complaint, which creates the case. The filing of this paper is what puts a controversy before the courts. It is the answer or other response that sets forth the position the defendant will be taking in the case. Effectively these first papers define the structure for the rest of the case, and unless amended, will form the framework of the case for its duration.

Because they are so important, a more detailed look at these first papers is appropriate.

The Summons.

The summons is not really a pleading at all. It is referred to as process. It is addressed here because it is a "court paper" and more importantly, it and the complaint3 are usually handled and delivered to the defendant (served) together. You will in fact commonly hear the initial pleadings referred to as the summons and complaint.

The party bringing the lawsuit or case is the plaintiff. The party or parties against whom the lawsuit is brought is, or are the defendant(s). The summons is directed to the defendant.

---

[3] The term complaint is used here, but it includes other terminology used in different jurisdictions, such as petition, bill of particulars, etc.

It does two important things.

The first and most important is to confer jurisdiction over the defendant. The second is to give the defendant notice of the lawsuit. More specifically, that he is now before the court and that he must respond to the complaint.

In the section on jurisdiction the issue of personal jurisdiction is discussed at length. The concept of personal jurisdiction defines over whom a court may exercise jurisdiction, but it does not exist spontaneously. Something must bring a party before the court. In the case of the civil lawsuit it is the service (more about that later) of the summons upon the defendant that actually brings the defendant before the court.

Until there has been service; until the defendant has received the summons in the manner prescribed by the statutes and rules addressing service, there is no personal jurisdiction. That means the court has no power or authority over the defendant.

The second purpose of the summons is of course to put the defendant on notice that a lawsuit has been commenced and that he must respond. This is a basic requirement mandated by the U.S. and most state constitutions. There must be due process and in any court action both sides must have the opportunity to be heard. "Opportunity to be heard" means not only must a defendant know that there is some action pending against him, but he must have notice of what he must do in order to respond, where it must be done, and within what period of time.

Because the summons is such a critical document, every aspect of it, from its creation and filing to service upon the defendant must be accomplished correctly. Often even failure to use the exact wording prescribed in a jurisdiction may result in failure of process. Failure of process means that effectively the lawsuit, and whatever occurred in it, as a matter of law, never happened.

Fortunately it is not a particularly complicated document and getting everything right is not overly difficult. It does require careful compliance with the rules and requirements in any specific jurisdiction.

First, the summons must be correctly worded and in the proper form. Some jurisdictions use summons forms, created by the court itself, so it's hard to get that part wrong. Other jurisdictions merely specify the format and the content of the summons, leaving it to the plaintiff to create the summons correctly. In such a jurisdiction it is important to create the summons EXACTLY as specified, down to using any language specified, word for word.

How a summons must be worded will almost always be found in either the Court Rules, or in a specific statute governing court procedures. If you are creating the summons it is very important to research these in your particular jurisdiction. If you get lucky there will be an appendix to the rules or the statute that will give you a sample of how the summons should look and how it must be worded.

The next issue is the issuance of the summons. This again varies from jurisdiction to jurisdiction. In some states the summons is issued by the clerk of court upon request. Either they use a pre-printed form, or you bring to them a summons that you have created, and they clerk will sign it. In other jurisdictions a form called a praecipe for summons is filed, which requests the clerk to issue the summons issued. In still others, the plaintiff merely types the summons in accordance with the requirements of that jurisdiction. Regardless of the procedure that applies it is important to follow the rules and requirements exactly. A failure to properly issue the summons means that process may be defective which means that the court may not have jurisdiction over the defendant.

There are a lot of areas in terms of compliance with procedures that getting close may be enough. The courts refer to this as substantial compliance. For example, if you missed a rule the requires a three inch margin at the top of the first page, it is highly unlikely that the judge is going to through your lawsuit out when you file the paper with a two inch margin. Issuance of the summons does not fall in that category. The issues are so critical in terms of conferring jurisdiction and giving notice that degree to which compliance is required cannot be overstated.

An example of this can be found in a South Carolina Supreme Court decision some years back. The required language in the summons included the words, in the context of failing to answer; "judgment will be taken against you". A summons was challenged as ineffective process because it stated instead "judgment may be taken against you". The court in that case held that the defendant had never been properly served with a proper summons and that the court had never acquired jurisdiction over him.

Of course by the time that this got to the Supreme Court the statute of limitations on the original lawsuit had long expired, leaving the plaintiff with no possibility of recovery. Because of one word in the summons!

The final step is the service of the summons. Once you have a proper summons in hand, whether issued by the court, or which you typed, it has to get into the hands of the defendant.

The person being sued has to receive the summons.

This is basic one of the most basic principles of due process. It underscores the concept that bad things under the legal system are not allowed to happen to you without notice and an opportunity to be heard. The principle is rooted in our common law, and in turn English common law which is the source of a lot of our law. It is also rooted in basic fairness. You cannot have action taken against you without notice and a chance to have the court hear your side.

Service of the summons, usually along with the complaint, is critical, and must be done correctly. The court rules for each jurisdiction specify the manner in which service can be had upon the defendant. If the rules are followed, the court has jurisdiction over the defendant and the lawsuit can proceed. If they are not followed then anything that happens afterward is subject to challenge.

Remember, it is the act of service that actually confers jurisdiction of the defendant on the court. Before that happens, the court in which the action is brought has no power whatsoever over the defendant. It cannot make him do anything. It cannot issue an order that binds him. It cannot issue a judgment against him. That is why this step in the lawsuit is so important. The importance of researching and understanding the rules concerning service of the summons cannot be over emphasized. Many lawsuits have been commenced and proceeded to judgment against defendants that did not appear only to be set aside, sometimes years later, when the defendant was able to show that they were never properly served with the summons.

Unfortunately, the rules on service of process can be lengthy and sometimes confusing. When the concept of service first presented itself it was easy. There was only one way to effect service upon a defendant and that was personal service. Someone had to physically hand the summons to the defendant.

Service requirements and options have evolved over time and have become rather complex. The rules and procedures for service upon a natural person are different than for corporations or partnerships. There are alternatives to the basic personal service where a person is handed a copy of the papers. Service can under the right circumstances be accomplished by various alternate means ranging from mail, to publishing in a newspaper, to leaving at one's office or residence.

All the acceptable methods and procedures of serving the summons can always be found in either the rules of court for a jurisdiction or in related statutes, or both. They must be followed exactly. Close will not be good enough.

Usually, if there is any proceeding to challenge the sufficiency of service it will be after the fact, usually when a judgment has been entered. Rarely will a defendant who has not been served learn of the lawsuit and jump in. Instead, the first time a defendant who has not received notice of the lawsuit by service of a summons does anything will often be when he learns a judgment against him exists and someone is taking steps to enforce it. It is not uncommon for the first inkling an un-served defendant has of a lawsuit is when the sheriff knocks on his door trying to enforce a judgment.

The problem potential confronting the plaintiff if this happens is time. If following entry of judgment, no immediate effort has been made to enforce it, it may just sit there. If the defendant has not been properly served it is as if no suit had even been commenced. Everything that happened in the lawsuit has no effect whatsoever on a defendant that was not properly served. It may as well have never happened. And the clock is ticking on the statute of limitations. This by the way is part of the research you should have done early on, knowing how long you have to bring a lawsuit. Every jurisdiction has statutes which provide that if a lawsuit is not commenced within a certain time, it is barred. Some of these statutes are very short. Some malpractice limitations are as short as one year. It is easy to see how a plaintiff, thinking he has a valid judgment against a defendant could be blindsided when the defendant two years down the road files a motion to set aside the judgment for lack of jurisdiction.

The redeeming factor in all of this is that if a defendant appears in a court proceeding for any reason other than to challenge jurisdiction, then the issue is waived, as are any irregularities or objections to the manner in which service was affected. The gist here is that the whole point of the rules regarding the summons and service of the summons is to give the defendant notice and allow him to appear and address the allegations against him. Once it is clear that the defendant has received the summons and is appearing to defend himself, those objectives have been accomplished. The rules and procedures in that regard are no longer of great concern. So while you should be concerned and double check to make sure all the "I's" have been dotted and the "t's" crossed where a defendant does not appear, once an answer or motion to dismiss is filed that does not allege defective service, that issue is moot and need not be addressed again.

As a practical matter a defendant that appears will never bother challenging the manner in which he was served with papers. What's the point? As he's standing there arguing to the judge that the summons was not properly delivered to him, the plaintiff's attorney hands the court bailiff another copy, who in turn hands it to the defendant. He is served.

It is also important to research and understand the alternative ways that a defendant can be served. Personal service may not be possible or practical. It may not be possible to locate defendants. Defendants may be unavailable, either coincidentally or intentionally. Defendants in many cases believe that they can forestall a lawsuit indefinitely simply by not letting themselves be located for service. In other cases the absence is legitimate, such as someone travelling or living abroad for a period of time. To address these situations there are alternate ways of service that come into play. These range from leaving the papers with a responsible person residing with the defendant (delivering the papers to a defendant's spouse residing with them for example), to publishing a copy of the summons (and sometimes the complaint depending on the jurisdiction) in a newspaper.

Recognizing that in most cases defendants do not attempt to avoid process, realizing that it is nothing but an exercise in futility, many jurisdictions in an attempt to simplify the process, allow for service by certified or even simple first class mail.

Most jurisdictions require the mailing to be in a form where delivery to the intended recipient can be verified. Thus the rules in these jurisdictions require certified or registered mail, or some form of delivery where the defendant's signature indicates receipt. More progressive jurisdictions have gone further, allowing delivery by courier services, with the record of delivery establishing that the intended recipient in fact received it. There are even jurisdictions that provide for imposition of costs on a defendant that refuses to accept certified service.

Service of the summons on other entities varies depending on the kind of entity, whether the entity is actually present in the state, and whether statutory requirements regarding doing business in the state have been complied with. The specifics of service upon entities vary significantly among different jurisdictions, but generally:

A corporation is served by delivering the papers to its registered agent or to an officer of the corporation. Whenever a corporation is formed in or does business in a state, it is required to designate a registered agent. This can be a person, or another corporation, but it must be at a physical address. The registered agent does not have to be an officer, shareholder or even an employee of a corporation. It can be any person or entity that the corporation designates.

As an aside, if you have or are involved in the operation of a corporation it is very important to select an appropriate registered agent. Under the laws of every state service upon the registered agent is legal and effective service upon the corporation. And this is true whether the corporation ever actually receives the papers or not. The time in which to answer or otherwise respond to a lawsuit begins as of the moment the registered agent receives the papers. When the corporation receives them is of no consequence. So if you've appointed your estranged third cousin as registered agent, you are going to have a problem when they receive suit papers and just chuck them in the trash.

Moreover, the laws of most states provide that if a registered agent or officer cannot be found within the state, the secretary of state or some other designated official becomes the agent for service of process.

This is particularly dangerous for a corporation doing business in a different state because service is deemed complete upon delivery to the secretary of state (the clock is running) and there is no guarantee that the corporation itself will ever actually receive the papers. It could end up with a default judgment and never realize that it had been sued. These statutes have survived constitutional challenge with the courts generally holding that any failure of the corporation to receive notice is a result of the corporation failing to abide by or comply with the requirements for it to do business.

Service upon a registered agent or officer of the corporation can be accomplished by personal service and usually by way of certified mail.

Limited Liability Companies and Limited Partnerships are generally bound by the same rules as a corporation regarding a registered agent. It is always acceptable with respect to a Limited Partnership to serve the general partner, and with respect to a Limited Liability Company to serve any of its members. The general partner of a Limited Partnership, and the members of a Limited Liability Company can be served in all of the same ways that the rules or statute in a jurisdiction provide for service upon individuals.

A General Partnership is served by serving any partner.

Regardless of the kind of defendant, or the manner in which it is actually delivered, service upon the defendant is the second critical point in a lawsuit, after of course, the filing of it.

One thing to be very careful of in receiving any of these papers is to determine who the defendants are. Many lawsuits involving businesses will include as defendants not only the business itself, but the principals of the business as well. The manner of service can be critical in determining which party or parties the court has jurisdiction of.

Take for example a lawsuit naming ABC corporation and John Doe, it's president as defendants. The papers served on John Doe would likely be effective service on both John Doe as an individual defendant as well as on the corporation that he is president of. On the other hand, while delivering the papers to the registered agent of the corporation would be good service on the corporation, it would do nothing to bring John Doe before the court.

Service of the summons and the complaint triggers the start of the time to answer. This is always set forth somewhere on the summons itself. It will inform the defendant that if they do not respond within that time the plaintiff may take a default judgment. Typically this is either twenty or thirty days, depending on the jurisdiction. What the defendant must do within that time period is also spelled out.

The foregoing language is important. Make sure you know what your jurisdiction requires. In some places the response must be both filed and served within the allowed time. In others it is sufficient if the response is served on the plaintiff or its attorney, with it being permissible to file with the court later. In still others, it is sufficient if the response is timely filed, with service upon the defendant allowed within a reasonable time after that.

Just as the filing and service of the summons and complaint is critical, so too is a timely response. What that response is, depends on where you are and in what kind of court you are in. Typically the response to a summons and complaint is a written answer or motion. But this is not always the case.

Usually the defendant failing to respond within the time specified will result in default and open the door to the plaintiff being able to secure a default judgment. This is typically commenced with the plaintiff filing an affidavit of default, indicating that service has been had on the defendant and that the allowed time for responding has passed. There are separate procedures for obtaining a default judgment. They typically begin with a plaintiff filing a motion, with an affidavit setting forth the details of service upon the defendant and that no answer or response has been filed or received. These procedures also include protection for members of the armed forces4.

While there are always provisions for a court to set aside a default and allow a late response, this is normally only done for good cause, and is far from guaranteed. Consequently, if you are the defendant and have been served with papers, you absolutely do not want to default. It's akin to failing to show up at a ball game. The other side wins.

If a defendant is served with a summons and complaint and requires additional time to respond, court rules usually provide that the plaintiff can agree to an extension of time. Be cautious about using this provision because even of the plaintiff, or their attorney agrees, there are conditions. First the agreement must be in writing. Second the rules will specify how long of an extension can be granted. Very few rules allow for indefinite extensions and

---

4 Soldiers and Sailors Civil Relief Act of 1940 as amended.

even though the plaintiff might agree, a court may order the entry of a default judgment if the allowed time has expired. Third, the act of requesting an extension can constitute a waiver of any jurisdictional defenses.

The Complaint

Where the summons serves to put the defendant on notice that there is a lawsuit and that he must respond, it says nothing about what the lawsuit is about. The complaint is the paper that sets forth and spells out the allegations that the plaintiff is making, the legal theory of the lawsuit and what is being sought.

How the complaint is handled varies from jurisdiction to jurisdiction, but usually it is served upon the defendant along with the summons. In fact, the documents are usually stapled or fastened together, often with other forms related to local rules and procedures. Many jurisdictions require these papers to be in other languages, notably Spanish as well as English. Some jurisdictions require that information on lawyer referral services or legal aid be included. Still others require that alternative dispute resolution options be included. Regardless of what other forms and attachments might be included, the key documents are the summons and complaint, which frame the lawsuit and must be addressed.

The complaint is the document in which the plaintiff, the party commencing the lawsuit sets forth all the allegations required to set out a claim for relief, and proceed with a lawsuit. It is where the plaintiff sets forth why the court has jurisdiction to hear the case, what he thinks the defendant did or didn't do that creates a cause of action, why the plaintiff should be entitled to any award or relief from the court, and what kind of relief the plaintiff is asking for. The complaint should be organized in a logical order. Sometimes this is prescribed by the rules of the jurisdiction in which the lawsuit is pending, but if not, generally along the following lines:

- The caption identifies the parties and the court in which the proceeding is brought. It will include the case number which is important for all future papers.

- Allegations that refer to the jurisdiction of the court over the subject matter and the parties.

- If the court has different locations, why the location in which it was brought is proper (referred to as venue).

- A statement of the facts upon which the lawsuit is based.

- A listing of each cause of action, that is, each legal theory that the plaintiff contends entitles him to relief against the defendant. Here is where the plaintiff should set forth the essential elements of each cause of action.

- A statement of how the plaintiff has been damaged, or what harm will result if the court does not grant relief

- A statement of the relief sought – what is it that the plaintiff is asking the court to do.

While it is sometimes not necessary that the complaint follow this format or order, it is necessary that it include these items. The failure to include these elements in the complaint or to properly set them forth can result in problems with the lawsuit early on, including possibly having it dismissed. It is therefore necessary to understand what the complaint must state and how it must be worded. To make matters worse, the requirements vary from jurisdiction to jurisdiction.

Let's look at the elements of a complaint in a little more detail.

Why? First, you will have a better feel for how to put one together, and just as important, if you are a defendant, you will know what to look for in order to possibly challenge one that is served upon you.

All of the elements that we've listed are generally essential, at least to some extent. If a complaint does not contain all of these elements in some shape or form, it is defective. So let's look at the elements.

The purpose of the complaint is to set forth the allegations of the plaintiff's case. Part of those allegations are that the parties are entitled to be in that particular court and that that particular court is the proper place to resolve the dispute.

The caption is where the court and the parties are identified. Whether it contains the right "squiggles" or colons as you will often see is far less important than that it properly lists the parties, identifies the court, contains the case number, and identifies the pleading or motion which it precedes. You can easily find the proper form for a caption in your jurisdiction. Usually they are set forth as sample forms in the local rules. As various jurisdictions attempt to advance with technology, you can often find these forms on a local court website. If all else fails, just find another case filed in that court (anything filed is for the most part public record) and use that as a template.

The complaint, below the caption is often divided into logical sections. Some courts require these to be labeled, others do not. Some attorneys will divide the complaint into titled sections even when not required, others will not. So you may see a complaint with titles above the different logical sections, or you may just see a long series of numbered paragraphs. Whether a jurisdiction requires sections to be titled or not, almost all courts require the statements to be set out in separate numbered paragraphs. The complaint must contain in these paragraphs allegations that address the items we've laid out, whether they're separated into sections and titled or not.

Statements in the complaint are referred to as allegations. Almost all jurisdictions require that they be in some paragraph form, in numerical order. Some jurisdictions specify what each paragraph can contain. Again, it is imperative that you refer to and be familiar with the rules of civil procedure not only in your state (or the federal rules if in federal court) but also the local rules that each court may issue.

Before any allegations as to facts and events, a complaint should identify the parties and set forth the basis for jurisdiction. The basis for personal jurisdiction will often accompany identification of the parties. An example would be:

> The defendant John Doe, an adult individual, is a citizen and resident of the State of…, County of…..

Each party should be identified. Following that there should be statements that allege the basis for jurisdiction. These set forth why the case is filed in that particular court and why the court has jurisdiction of the subject matter as well as over the parties. In other words the complaint must allege both that the court has subject matter and personal jurisdiction, as well as the basis for it. Also included in this section will be allegations as to venue. If in a court of general jurisdiction, that court will almost always have different locations. Some states have defined judicial circuits, or areas. Others are based solely on county. Nonetheless the rules or statutes will always define in what location the case must be filed. This is usually, but not always where the defendant resides or where the events giving rise to the case occurred. There should be some allegation in this section regarding venue and the basis on which the case was filed in the particular location. Often you will see this whole section labeled "parties, jurisdiction and venue."

The next general grouping from a logical perspective would be allegations regarding the facts of the case. Basically here is where the plaintiff sets forth what has occurred that gave rise to the lawsuit. If the author of the complaint uses section headings this will often be titled something like "Statement of Facts" or "Summary of Facts" or "General Allegations". Here the complaint should set forth the facts, in some logical order that gave rise to the causes of action. These allegations are presented before listing any causes of action to avoid having to restate underlying facts with every cause of action that may be included in the complaint.

If the case is about a contract, there should be a recitation of the relationship of the parties, the reason or circumstances behind the contract, when it was executed and the terms of the contract that are relevant to the lawsuit. If a breach of contract is alleged the complaint in this section should discuss what the defendant did or failed to do that resulted in a breach. Finally, it should allege what consequences the plaintiff suffered as a result.

If the case is about personal injury, say a car accident, the complaint should set forth the facts leading up to the accident, what the defendant did or failed to do that resulted in the accident, and that the plaintiff was damaged

The next section or sections will contain the legal basis upon which the plaintiff contends that it is entitled to recover. These will often be referred to or titled something like: "For a First Cause of Action" followed by the name of the legal cause of action, or, "Count I" again followed by the name of the cause of action. Most rules require these to be set forth separately. And again, depending on the jurisdiction, the detail with which the legal theories must be pled varies substantially. Even if the rules do not require it, the better practice is to set them forth separately if for no other reason than it helps you be sure that you have everything you need, and in the proper sequence.

Understand too that the causes of action work together with, not independently of the statement of facts.

How the causes of action and statement of facts are set forth depends on which of two general types of jurisdiction you are in, known as fact pleading or notice pleading courts. The difference actually reflects an underlying difference in jurisdictional philosophy as to how in a case the facts are developed and presented to the defendant. Fact pleading is the common law norm and all jurisdictions historically were based on fact pleading. Notice pleading, or at least some variation of it, is found in the federal court system, and in many states that have embraced the federal rules.

Notice essentially requires that only the barest facts be actually set forth in the complaint. The theory is that the details will be developed through discovery and at the trial of the case. As the name implies the complaint need only contain enough factual allegations to put the defendant on notice of what acts or omissions gave rise to the suit, and the legal basis for it.

Fact pleading on the other hand requires much more extensive statements and requires that the complaint set forth all the facts necessary to establish the basis for the causes of action, as well as of course, the legal basis for relief.

To give you an idea of the difference in the two kinds of pleading, consider a simple case where the plaintiff is alleging that the defendant breached a contract.

In an actual notice pleading jurisdiction it would usually be sufficient to simply say that parties had entered into a contract, what the contract was for, that the defendant breached the contract, and that the plaintiff was damaged.

In fact pleading, the allegations would be much more extensive, setting forth when and how the contract was formed, that there was consideration for it, that it was written or oral, that the plaintiff performed their obligations, all the specific things that the defendant did in violation of the contract, the specific losses that the plaintiff experienced and how these relate to the breach of the contract and what the plaintiff did to minimize its losses.

Obviously a complaint in a jurisdiction requiring fact pleading will be longer and more detailed that a complaint in a notice pleading jurisdiction.

Regardless of which form of pleading applies, the rules governing civil litigation will always specify what must be plead, either facts or notice, but once again, you need to review all the law, including especially court decisions that have interpreted the rules and statutes.

The issue of form of pleading in federal courts is a perfect example.

Rule 8 of the Federal Rules of Civil Procedure establishes that the form of pleading in federal courts is notice pleading. It states that a pleading must contain "a short and plain statement of the claim showing that the pleader is entitled to relief". This is notice pleading.

A rule requiring fact pleading would read something like: "The material facts on which a cause of action or defense is based shall be stated in a concise and summary form."

At first glance, simple. But as you should have grasped by now, court things are not always as they seem.

The United States Supreme Court in the case of Bell Atlantic Corp. v. Twombly, 550 U.S. 544 (2007) basically re-wrote Rule 8 to some extent, holding that the plaintiff must allege facts that would plausibly support its claim.

With the Twombly and other related decisions the distinction between the two forms of pleading is becoming much more blurred. Courts are requiring at least some form of fact pleading even in some "notice pleading" jurisdictions. This is especially important to bear in mind should you go online to find sample pleadings to work from. What was once perfectly acceptable in terms of pleading in a "notice" state, or in federal court, after the "Twombly" case, may no longer be enough.

It is important here that every legal cause of action be separately set forth, even if different causes of action arise from the same set of facts. There are circumstances where the same conduct, act or omissions can entitle a plaintiff to relief under different legal theories.

An example might be where an officer of a corporation, working under an employment contract commits an act involving theft of corporate funds by making misrepresentations to the corporation. This conduct could give rise to at least four different and distinct claims of the corporation if it should bring a suit. The corporation could sue on breach of contract, breach of fiduciary duty, conversion and fraud. Each of these is a separate cause of action and should, in a complaint be separately stated, or pled.

Likewise, if you are suing for the breach of contract discussed earlier, there are often several different legal theories. In addition to breach of contract, you could sue for breach of an implied contract, breach of fiduciary duty, quantum meruit, breach of warranty, etc.

One might argue that they really only care about one or two of these, so why bother with the rest.

The reason is that there are legal principles which require all causes of action that could be brought to be brought or possibly be waived. And they must be brought in the first lawsuit between the same parties in which they could have been brought. They provide that if a cause of action that could have been raised in a lawsuit is not raised, it cannot later be pursued in a new lawsuit. Put in plain English – you get one shot at it so don't leave anything out!

Why raise only a "breach of contract" cause of action when you could have brought three others as well? What if your breach of contract claim fails? Remember the elements of a cause of action that you have to plead. You have to prove each of those elements in court. If there are multiple elements or parts to a cause of action, and you fail on any one, that cause of action is gone.

In simple terms, why would you want to "put all of your eggs in one basket" so to speak, and rely solely on a breach of contract claim when there are other claims out there, with different elements, that you can prevail on? If the evidence presented does not satisfy all the elements of a contract cause of action, it may easily provide the elements of a different claim.

So make sure you do your homework, research the law and get in all your bullets or in this context, your causes of action. A good way to research that is to think of one cause of action that you might have, then do an internet search on sample complaints for that cause of action. As you read complaints that pop up that contain your cause of action, you will often see that other causes are included. Do another search on new causes of action that you have found and more sample pleadings will come up. Soon you will find yourself with a complaint containing three, four or even more claims when you started with only one.

At this point, where you are setting out any causes of action that might be viable, you should consider a reality check. When you have identified the causes of action that you will want to raise, research the elements of each, and make sure your factual or general allegations actually do include all elements for all causes of action.

The next issue that needs to be addressed by a complaint is to explain how the plaintiff has been damaged. It is possible to have the most egregious conduct possible, but without some damage suffered by the plaintiff, there is no cause of action. A defendant can be guilty of going a hundred miles an hour down a residential street, running three stop lights and five stop signs. Certainly outrageous conduct and certainly conduct that would make the defendant liable if an accident occurred. But unless a plaintiff can show how this conduct resulted in harm to him, there is no viable civil lawsuit.

In this section you should be prepared to set out what has happened to you, but this can usually be expressed in general terms. For example, if you are suing over a breach of contract you can usually allege that because the defendant breached the contract you have lost profits. It is usually not necessary at this point in the complaint to state that as a result of the actions of the defendant you have lost profits in the amount of "X" dollars.

An exception to this principle is that if you are in a court with a dollar amount ceiling or floor, you must allege that your damages fall within that range. An example is a lawsuit filed in the Circuit Court in Florida. Because cases with amounts in controversy of less than $15,000 must be filed in the county courts, you must allege in your complaint that the amount in controversy is greater than $15,000. But this can still be a general allegation.

Finally, in this section you must set forth in your allegations that the damages you are complaining of were caused by the defendant.

The last element of a complaint is to request relief. Put simply, you have to tell the court what is it that you want it to do for you. Do you want a monetary award? Do you want the court to interpret a contract and make a ruling as to what it means? Do you want the court to issue an injunction or a restraining order? You can't ask the court to provide relief if you don't specify the relief.

The basic pleading formula in a nutshell then is:

- these are the people involved

- this is what happened

- this is why I should recover

- this is how I've been damaged

- these damages were caused by the defendant

- this is what I want the court to give me

The importance of correctly preparing the complaint cannot be overstated. It forms the core and basis for the entire lawsuit. Everything that follows is determined by what is alleged in the complaint.

The Response

What is required when a defendant has been served with a summons or summons and complaint occasionally varies, but with a few isolated exceptions, requires the filing and service of some form of written response.

The rules always provide a time limit in which a response to a summons and complaint must be served and filed and that time limit is stated on the summons.

The response can be in one of four forms.

The defendant can respond with an answer, addressing the allegations of the complaint.

The defendant can answer and add to the answer a counterclaim, setting forth his own claims against the plaintiff.

 The defendant can answer and add to the answer a cross complaint or third party complaint, answering the complaint but setting forth a complaint against another party.

Or, the defendant can respond with a motion (in some places the term demurrer is still used) of one sort or another. Motions are discussed in a section devoted specifically to that topic, so here discussion is limited to an answer, or answer and counterclaim or answer and third party complaint

The Answer

The answer as its name implies, is the response to the complaint. While essentially the defendant goes through each allegation of the complaint, which are numbered, and either admits it or denies it, there are some additional, important considerations.

First, if the defendant has not first filed a motion, that is if the answer is the first response to the complaint, there are certain things that must be included in the answer, or they are waived. Litigation is filled with such pitfalls that you have to be both aware and careful of.

These include legal defenses which may be addressed by a motion to dismiss as well as what are referred to as affirmative defenses. The rules in virtually all jurisdictions specify that these defenses, while they may be raised by motion, MUST be raised in the first responsive pleading or motion or are waived.

This is extremely important and underscores the admonition earlier to stop and take a deep breath before answering or responding to a lawsuit.

The kinds of things that MUST be addressed at this stage, either by motion (including a demurrer) or answer are:

-        issues relating to personal jurisdiction

-        issues related to whether there was proper service of the summons

-      whether the complaint on its face properly sets forth a cause or causes of action

-      In federal court and some state courts whether the case is brought in the proper venue

-      whether all necessary parties are included

-      any affirmative defenses

To show you how important it is to address the necessary issues, consider just one of these – the issue of personal jurisdiction. Jurisdiction has been addressed briefly, and there is a separate section on it in the reference sections, but consider:

Courts have universally held that making a general appearance; that is answering the allegations of the complaint without reserving the issue, waives any objection or defense concerning personal jurisdiction.

What does that mean in real terms?

It means that If you happen to get sued in a court that has no jurisdiction over you, you can really mess up by not responding properly. Consider that you live in New York and receive a summons and complaint from a court in Florida – a state that you've never lived in and in fact have never even visited. You understand that you should respond to this lawsuit, but how you respond becomes critical.

If in this case you file with the Florida court a response in which you deny what the plaintiff is saying, you have probably made a general appearance. You have lost your chance to say "hey I've never been to Florida, I live in New York, and you can't sue me in Florida."

Where you could have forced the plaintiff to come to New York to sue you, you are now in court in Florida. It is you instead of the plaintiff that must travel back and forth throughout the course of the case. It is you instead of the plaintiff that is incurring huge travel expense. It is you instead of the plaintiff that is more likely to want to settle the case because of the expense.

The important thing is if you believe that you have been sued in a court that has no jurisdiction over you, you need to first file a motion to dismiss on that ground. If you simply go ahead and generally answer, you've waived the issue and could end up trying to defend yourself in a court hundreds of miles away.

In addition to matters that can be raised either by motion or answer, some things must appear in the answer, even if a motion has been filed first.

These are referred to as affirmative defense, and will be addressed in more detail below. The most important thing though that you need to understand about affirmative defenses is that affirmative defenses not raised in the answer are deemed waived.

In actually responding to a complaint then, the first thing to do is determine whether any of the defenses addressable by motion in the rules exist.

If so, a decision must be made whether to raise them by answer or separate motion. Rules generally give you the option of raising these issues by motion or in your first responsive pleading (your answer), but generally any issues relating to jurisdiction should always be raised by motion. This prevents any possibility of the appearance of the defendant being deemed a general appearance, possibly constituting a waiver of the jurisdictional matter. With other issues there are some considerations that may make it better to bury things in an answer rather than draw attention to them with a separate motion but not so with jurisdictional issues.

The filing of a motion tolls (stops the clock) on the time to answer. Typically if you file a motion to dismiss a hearing or other disposition of the motion will take place before you have to file any other response including an answer. Only if your motion to dismiss has been denied do you need to proceed with the filing and service of the answer.

Again, the rules will specify how long after a motion is addressed the defendant has to answer, but you do not need to file a motion and an answer at the same time.

After determining to proceed with the answer, each allegation of the complaint must be addressed. Anything set forth in the complaint that is not denied or otherwise addressed is deemed admitted. Once it is admitted, whether by actually being admitted, or by being deemed admitted for failure to deny, it is admitted for the entire case. In other words if you mess up and don't deny something that you should have, you're stuck with it!

By now you can understand how critically important it is to respond to the complaint correctly and properly.

Allegations in a complaint can be admitted, denied, or admitted in part and denied in part. One way or another, they have to be addressed.

Affirmative Defenses

In addition to considering the allegations of the complaint and how to answer them, it is important to raise any affirmative defenses. An affirmative defense effectively states that even if what is alleged by the plaintiff in terms of facts is correct, there is another legal basis, based on additional law or facts which would bar the plaintiff from recovering.

A good example of an affirmative defense is a statute of limitations.

Every jurisdiction has some legal framework that puts a limit on how long after something has occurred, you can go to court over it. Statutes of limitations just as a point of interest also often apply in criminal cases. The theory on both is that after a long enough period of time has gone by, an issue should be put to rest. Almost every jurisdiction has a set of statutes that give specific time limits, usually listed by kinds of cases, in which a suit must be filed on the matter, or it is thereafter barred. By raising the statute of limitations in an answer, the defendant is basically saying "even if everything alleged in the complaint is true, you have waited too long to sue, and the action is barred".

So where a plaintiff files a lawsuit to collect a promissory note three and a half years after it is due, in a state where the statute of limitations is three years, the suit is barred.

That does not mean the money was not borrowed. It does not mean that the defendant did not promise to repay it. It does not even mean that the defendant does not owe the money. It simply means that the court will not now allow a suit to collect it.

In terms of raising a statute of limitations defense there are three important principles to understand and to take into account.

First, most jurisdictions have what is called a discovery rule regarding limitation periods. That means that the time period prescribed in the statute of limitations does not even begin to run until the plaintiff discovered, or reasonably should have discovered that they had a cause of action. This issue arises often in products liability cases. For example, a drug that you were prescribed could be on the market for years when finally a study showed that it caused seriously detrimental side effects. Even if the time during which you took the drug was long before the case would normally be barred by the statute of limitations, the time in which you could commence a suit would not begin to run until you knew of the dangers and how they had affected you.

Another issue is that the statute of limitations does not run against an incompetent plaintiff. Remember incompetent has a special meaning in the legal world. It means in this case competent to bring suit. A minor (otherwise relatively sane) is deemed incompetent to commence a lawsuit. With respect to a minor the period in which to commence suit does not even begin to run until the individual has reached eighteen. That means if you are in a jurisdiction with a three year statute of limitations for personal injury and a six year old child is injured in a car accident, that child effectively has fifteen years in which to commence the lawsuit – twelve years to reach age eighteen and three years beyond that.

Other affirmative defenses include such things as a legal requirement that a document be in writing, having reached a settlement, negligence on the part of a plaintiff alleging negligence of the defendant, responsibility of a third party and dozens more.

Regardless though, the most important thing to understand is that in most jurisdictions affirmative defenses are to be raised in an answer, or they are waived.

And waiving these defenses inadvertently can have catastrophic consequences!

Think about the promissory note example just discussed. Three and a half years ago you signed a promissory note. You were not able to pay the money and for the last three and a half years haven't heard anything about it. Now out of the clear blue comes a nice little lady and hands you a summons and complaint suing you for the $10,000, plus interest plus costs and attorney's fees.

The simple affirmative defense of the expiration of the period in which to commence suit determines the outcome of this case. Do your homework and know to include it, and you're off the hook. Overlook it or forget it and you owe $10,000.

When responding to these lawsuits, stop, do nothing, take a deep breath. Study, review and research!

Don't misunderstand. The purpose of that "deep breath" is not to get the lawsuit out of your mind by going to the beach. It is to allow you plenty of time to research ALL the issues. To familiarize yourself with what must be done and what must NOT be done. The danger of inadvertently waiving affirmative defenses is just one of many pitfalls and traps in what is a veritable minefield called litigation.

How affirmative defenses are raised is always defined in the rules or laws of civil practice for any particular jurisdiction. For the most part as long as these defenses appear somewhere in the answer you will be ok. But do your homework. In some jurisdictions, they must be set forth separately and clearly designated as affirmative defenses. Sometimes they must even appear in a separate section titled Affirmative Defenses.

Other jurisdictions are even more complex. In Pennsylvania for example these defenses must be raised in a separate pleading entitled "Preliminary Objections" and specifically designated as "New Matter." If in that state you simply file an answer, there is a good chance that all of your affirmative defenses will have been waived.

Finally, determine if there are any counterclaims against the plaintiff or potential claims against other parties. Counterclaims, like affirmative defenses may be waived if not raised in the first pleading. Read on!

Answer and Counterclaim

In addition to answering the complaint, the defendant may also have a claim against the plaintiff. At common law, and in most jurisdictions today there are permissive and compulsory counterclaims. Most are compulsory. As the terms suggest, permissive counterclaims are those that can, but do not have to be raised, while a compulsory counterclaim, if not raised, is lost. Generally compulsory counterclaims are those that arise out of the same facts and circumstances that gave rise to the original lawsuit. Permissive counterclaims are usually those that the defendant may have against the plaintiff regarding unrelated matters.

While a counterclaim can be included in the same pleading as the answer, it is important to understand that a counterclaim is a separate statement of a claim and cause of action that the defendant may have against the plaintiff.

A counterclaim serves basically the same purpose as the complaint. Since the suit is already started, and required allegations already made, it is not necessary to go back into things like jurisdiction and venue.

On the other hand, a counterclaim should state any facts that have not already been alleged, set forth the causes of action that the defendant alleges it has against the plaintiff, allege the nature and extent of its damages and set forth a request for relief.

Sound familiar?

In order to bring a counterclaim the basic requirement is that the defendant must have been able to being a separate suit against the plaintiff had the plaintiff not commenced suit first. Think of it sort of like a lawsuit within a lawsuit.

The important thing to be aware of regarding counterclaims is that some are compulsory. They must be brought if the grounds of the counterclaim arise out of the same facts and circumstances as the complaint. A counterclaim under these circumstances not brought, is a counterclaim waived – as in gone.

This principle has its roots in common law and had been adopted in civil procedure rules. The reason is obvious. If there is a dispute between parties, it makes sense to resolve everything related to it at one time rather than piecemeal. The upshot is that if a defendant has separate claims against the plaintiff, arising out of the same facts and circumstances, those claims must be asserted in the first responsive pleading in the form of a counterclaim. Any compulsory counterclaim not brought when required to be is deemed waived and is barred from being raised in the future.

The Answer and Third Party Complaint

This concept was touched upon it the section on planning. It is a powerful weapon in the defense arsenal and is often available where it might not at first glance appear as a likely option. The third party complaint is exactly what it says. It is a complaint against another party, not part of the original lawsuit. The defendant is bringing new players to the party. While useful, it is not unlimited. The basic premise is that the third party is actually responsible, or has contributed to the facts that gave rise to the lawsuit in the first place. There must be a relationship between the events or facts complained of in the first place.

In terms of how to do it, you fully answer the complaint, including any affirmative defenses. If you are making a counterclaim against the plaintiff, go ahead and set it forth. Then below that you would add another section entitled Third Party Complaint. The caption would be modified to show the original parties, that is the plaintiff with you as the defendant, then below that you would be listed again as Third Party Plaintiff and the new party listed below that a Third Party Defendant.

In terms of preparing the third party complaint, it is just like the original complaint. And unlike the counterclaim where it may not be necessary, in the third party complaint you would need to set forth new allegations as to jurisdiction and as well as factual allegations and your causes of action. It is almost like filing a new lawsuit in terms of what needs to be included. Finally, because you are bringing a new party into the lawsuit, it is necessary to issue or have issued a summons, and have it, together with the third party complaint, served on the new third party defendant.

The Reply

The response to the counterclaim is the reply. It is like the answer except that instead of addressing issues raised in the complaint, it addresses issues raised in a counterclaim.

Like an answer, a reply should raise any affirmative defenses to allegations in the counterclaim, or they are waived. Just as regards answer, any allegations of a counterclaim not denied or otherwise addressed are deemed admitted.

A reply is normally not permitted to be filed unless there is a counterclaim. In other words, the plaintiff doesn't get a second bite at the apple unless there is something to respond to. There is an exception. In some jurisdictions a plaintiff may reply to answers that contain affirmative defenses, but even then, the reply can only address the issues raised by the affirmative defenses.

Amending Pleadings

We're all human and we overlook things. We make mistakes. Then too, things sometimes come to light that we were not aware of to begin with. In any case, there are times when the pleadings may need to be amended.

Basically the rules in many jurisdictions (but but certainly not all) provide a period following the filing and service of a pleading during which it can be amended as a matter of right. In these jurisdictions all that you have to do is file and serve another pleading with the title preceded by the word "amended."

After this period, or for a subsequent amendment, a pleading can only be amended with the permission of the court. The permission can come as a result of agreement or upon motion. If agreement is not possible for one reason or another, a motion to amend must be filed and the matter submitted to the judge. This is addressed more completely in the section on motions. Basically the likelihood of a judge allowing an amendment of the pleadings depends on a variety of factors, including the nature of the amendment, the time that has passed since the original pleading was filed, how far along the case is, the harm that would be caused by not allowing the amendment and the harm caused to the other side if it is allowed. Common sense tells us that a minor change, early on will almost always be allowed. Conversely, a substantial change, such as adding a new cause of action, three weeks before trial, after all discovery has been completed, probably won't fly.

Handling Court Papers – Filing and Serving

There are a lot of papers involved in a lawsuit. The summons and complaint kick things off, but they are only the beginning.

In discussing court papers, after the complaint, there are two terms that are important: filing and serving.

Filing refers to actually having the papers in the file maintained with respect to the case at the courthouse. This usually means giving them to the clerk of court, one of whose main functions is to keep track of all the papers filed in a case. This can be accomplished by mail, by actually going to the courthouse and handing them to the clerk or a deputy or, more and more, electronically. In order to file something it must be identified with the specific case. That is, it must include the name of the parties, the court that it is filed in and a case number. Obviously if paper has a caption, this issue is taken care of, but with other papers, it may be necessary to add that information.

To "Serve" means get something to the other side. The rule, with very few exceptions is that anything - a pleading, a motion or even a letter that is sent to the court - must be served, that is copied to the other side. One sided communication in any form with the court is not permitted.

You've learned about serving the summons and complaint, so now it's time to discuss how to handle all the papers thereafter.

Once the initial service has been accomplished, papers can be both filed and served by mail. Also, in the age of the internet, all federal courts, and many state courts have provisions for electronic filing and service of papers. You must refer to the court rules to understand how this works.

Because date and time are often so important, when filing a paper with the Court, it is generally a good idea to take an extra copy, and ask the clerk to "clock it in" as the original is filed. When the original is time stamped, your copy will be as well, and handed back to you. That way you have a copy of what you filed that bears the stamp of the clerk's office showing the date and time it was filed.

Do this even if you file by mail. If you file by mail, just include an extra copy and a self-addressed, stamped envelope. Request, in a courteous cover letter, that they return a clocked in copy to you. If you file electronically, all this is generally taken care of in that most systems automatically generate an email back to you showing the document name, and a unique document identifier along with the date and time of filing.

Since time limits are so important when you represent yourself in court, be sure to check the rules of the court you are in to determine how time limits are computed, and when something is deemed to have occurred.

There will always be provisions in the statutes or rules that specify the time in which something must happen and how much notice must be given. They will also specify when something is deemed to have occurred. For example, the rules will specify when something is deemed filed (when it was mailed vs. when it is actually received by the court) and when something is deemed served. Typically an item is deemed served when it is placed in the mail, but is not filed until it is actually received in the clerk of court's office.

It cannot be stressed enough how important it is that you read the rules carefully. Even in the case of service by mail, there is usually a difference between using regular first class mail and certified mail where a delivery receipt is signed. Some jurisdictions have caught up with the times and make provision for service by courier such as Fed Ex or UPS. But be careful. Some courts have not made this adaptation and in such a jurisdiction even if you have something delivered personally to the other side by courier, because it was not placed in the mail as specifically provided for, it was not properly served.

Many rules also alter the time for responding where service has been made by mail, automatically adding extra time. Since so many things in a court case have strict deadlines and time limits, it is absolutely critical that you familiarize yourself with the rules and in particular the rules regarding service and filing.

When serving any pleadings, discovery, responses to discovery, notices or other required exchange of documents or information, you establish that it has been served by including a proof or certificate of service. This is simply a statement signed by you5 to the effect that you have served the document or exhibit (naming it in the

---

[5] However, check the rules of your jurisdiction. California for example requires that this certificate cannot be signed by a party. You must have someone else certify that they have mailed items.

proof of service) by placing a copy in the mail and specifying that date and the address to which it was mailed. The proof of service must accompany the pleading or paper that was served. In jurisdictions that do allow for service by courier, it is often permissible to insert the waybill or tracking number.

Electronic Filing and Service

Courts traditionally maintained paper files. A lot still do. Typically a large folder is created for each case into which is physically inserted all the papers, pleadings, orders, notices and what have you that pertain to that case. Whenever anything takes place regarding that case, the file was referred to. If a hearing or trial is scheduled, the entire file is taken into the courtroom and accessed as needed. This is still the procedure in many courts, but technology is making inroads.

Since we do everything else on the internet, or on computers, it was obviously merely a question of time before computer technology and the internet found their way into the legal system. After all, what is the legal system but a huge collection of related papers and documents? Computers are extremely well suited to handle that.

While not every court in the country utilizes the Internet for handling court papers (there are still many courts that do not even have websites), more and more are working in that direction. The leader in this is none other than the federal government. Years ago the federal judicial system launched upon a program to computerize and digitize all pleadings and documents in the entire federal court system. In the federal system, all documents are stored electronically and all case records are maintained the same way.

The federal system uses two interconnected modules or systems to accomplish this and through which attorneys, parties and litigants gain access. They are PACER (Public Access to Court Electronic Records) and the ECF (electronic court filing) systems. Pacer is available to anyone though it is fee based. Users must establish an account and are charged for each report generated or document retrieved. The allure of the PACER system is that anyone, anywhere can access in pdf format any document filed in any United States Court anywhere. Cases can be located by searches on a variety of criteria including things like case number, party names, attorney names, etc.

The second portion of the system is the electronic filing or ECF system. Unlike PACER, it is court specific. A username and password for example in the Southern District of New York, does not allow you to file papers in a federal court in Utah. This portion is open only to those who have registered, and usually, have completed a course on how to properly file materials. If you choose to represent yourself in federal court, you will probably not be able to electronically file, but will be allowed to file in person or by mail.

Other systems at the state level allow registration and use of electronic filing by a party as well as attorneys. No matter what system is in place, there will always be a mechanism for you to file your papers when you represent yourself.

With respect to service of electronically filed documents, you need to refer to the rules and procedures in your jurisdiction. On some systems electronic service is automatic, with everyone listed as related to a case automatically receiving a copy of what is filed. Other systems allow you to create a service list of individuals or parties to whom copies are to be sent. In either of these two kinds of systems, any pleading or paper, when filed is automatically served and you do not need to do anything else. Other systems require you to serve other parties, but make provision for doing so by email. Use of technology by the courts is constantly evolving so you need to stay on top of the local rules.

When documents are filed electronically they are generally immediately available. So as soon as you file something, you can retrieve a copy that will reflect the date and time of filing and will have a unique number assigned to that particular document in the court file for the case. In the federal system you do not even have to do that. The system automatically emails a link to every filed document to everyone appearing in the case. This takes the place of taking an extra copy to be clocked in when you file in person

While you're probably tired of reading it, all of this is rule driven. If you represent yourself you will be expected to know and follow these rules. Moreover, rules addressing electronic filing or service are almost always found in local rules or even administrative orders issued by judges. Finding local rules requires research beyond the Rules of Civil Procedure for any jurisdiction. Often there will be court websites that will contain, or have links to local rules or orders that you must be aware of.

In a nutshell, you should have a basic understanding of the kinds of court papers you are likely to encounter, or have to create, and how they must be handled. While court personnel are precluded from giving you legal advice, they are allowed to, and almost always will give you whatever assistance you might need in order to file and get papers properly served on the other side.

Motions in Court Cases

If you become involved in the trial of a civil case, you will become familiar with motions. The term motion, like other terms you will encounter is a legal term, but as with everything else, once you understand it, it need not be intimidating.

That's right, jargon can be simplified and in the legal setting, a motion is nothing more than a request, sometimes in writing, sometimes verbal, to the court for something, or some kind of relief. A motion will always by responded to by the court with some kind of order.

Think of it as a formalized request and response interchange.

There are all sorts of different motions through the course of a civil case, and of course they pop up at different times. There are motions for summary judgment, or motions to dismiss. There are motions related to discovery. There are even motions to limit evidence (motion in limine). Deciphering the magic words is easy. Just substitute "ask for, or request" the court to do something for the word motion and it becomes crystal clear. A motion for summary judgment becomes, I am asking the court to grant me summary judgment.

Motions will be filed and argued throughout the case, but because motions to dismiss, or for change of venue occur very early, often as the first response to a complaint, the entire topic is presented here, right after the section on court papers.

So what is all this about motions? Why do we need a motion system? Why even in some busy courts are there separate "motion courts?"

The legal system in the United States is predicated on an adversary system that is supposed to work through the steps according to prescribed rules. There is a judge to resolve issues that come up along the way, and of course to preside over the final trial of the matter, with or without a jury. Caseloads are heavy, and judges have to carefully schedule their time. It's not as though either side can just waltz into the judge's office and say, "hey, Judge, they're not answering the interrogatories", or "we need to amend our complaint".

As a result, we have what is known as motion practice. Familiarize yourself with the procedures, because it is unlikely that you will be able to represent yourself in court without encountering, or even yourself filing motions for various things.

Since a motion is nothing more than a request to the court for something, and because you are by necessity communicating to the court, you must always send the other side a copy of whatever you send the court. Judges are extremely concerned about what is called ex parte communication. That is where one side communicates with the judge without the outside the presence or without the knowledge of the other. The whole U.S. judicial system is predicated on fairness and openness and even a hint or suggestion that one side is talking to the judge without the other side is a serious matter.

Consequently, while it is mentioned here, it is relevant to many other topics as well. Anything that goes to the court or to the judge gets copied to the other side. This is such a stringent requirement that anything that you file with the court should be accompanied by a statement that you have sent the other side a copy. You will hear this referred to in this book and elsewhere as proof of service or a certificate of service.

So now you know that to get the judge to consider whatever it is that you're asking for you need to file and serve a motion.

Rules, Rules, Rules

Before embarking on the task of filing or responding to a motion, read the rules. All of them! This cannot be emphasized enough. Every court that you may find yourself in has one and probably more than one set of rules that govern how it operates, and how you must conduct yourself in the handling of your case. If this point was not made sufficiently clear in the section on Rules, please allow this to be a wake-up call. And if there is one arena in which knowledge of and adherence to rules is more critical, in is in the realm of motions. You may be in the right on an issue, but unless you comply with the rules on such things as when and how to present it, chances are good that you will lose regardless.

Where to find the rules you need to deal with motions depends on the court that you find yourself in. In a federal court, there are three main areas that you need to consult.

First, the Federal Rules of Civil Procedure. This is the bible for federal courts. Be aware too that you need to familiarize yourself with all the rules through trial. Why? Because there are parts of various rules that specify how something is to be done, even though rule itself does not specifically refer to the topic at hand. For example, there is no single rule or section of the rules that applies specifically, just to motions. Section III is titled "pleadings and motions", but does not limit itself to types of motions and the specific procedure for bringing or defending them. Before filing or responding to a motion, there would be (depending on the kind of motion) probably a half dozen different rules to consult. Motions are referred to in Rule 12 and there is a separate rule for Summary Judgment Motions – Rule 56. To get the whole picture, you need to familiarize yourself with all the rules.

Next, each federal district court has local rules which supplement the federal rules, but are just as important. The local rules generally go into more detail and are more specific. These can always be found on the individual federal court websites. The local rules may impose different requirements than the federal rules and complying with the federal rules is not an excuse for failing to comply with the local rules.

In addition to the local rules, in most federal courts there are standing administrative orders issued by the chief administrative judge, which dictate issues specific to that court. Individual judges likewise may have standing orders addressing a variety of issues, and if there are such orders, they will almost always have some reference to motions.

State courts are more varied. All states have the equivalent of the federal rules of civil procedure, either in the form of rules promulgated by the Supreme Court of a state, or appearing as part of a statutory scheme governing the administration of courts within that state. Like the federal system, there will often be local rules for the court that you find yourself in. All of these may impact to some extent the bringing and defense of motions. Within this smorgasbord of rules you will find such things as how to determine whether your motion requires a hearing, how to schedule it, how long you have to respond, how much time you have to allow the other party to respond, whether your motion requires a memorandum of law, if so, if there are limits to length, and so forth.

Motions in General

Once you grasp and appreciate the rules, actually filing or responding to a motion is not difficult.

First, if you're the one bringing a motion, decide what it is you want. Sounds simple, but people get hung up on simple things. If you find that you need to amend your complaint, after the time to amend as a matter of right has passed, then that's what you ask for. If the other side has not answered your interrogatories, or has given evasive answers, then that is what you ask for.

If the motion is brought by the other side, decide whether you need really need to oppose it. Here you need to bear in mind that there are separate and distinct reasons why attorneys bring motions. First, they bring a motion because they are actually seeking to resolve something. Second, the motion is a formality required by the court rules. An example of this kind of motion would be a motion to amend a pleading when the time to amend as a matter of right has expired. Many courts will require a motion to be filed even if the other side agrees, so that an actual order in response to the motion can be filed. In such a case, you may not really need to oppose the motion at all. If you have discussed with the other side amending a pleading, and you are in agreement, the actual motion to amend is not something you are going to be vigorously fighting. Since unopposed motions are generally granted, you can either just ignore a motion in such a case, or file a brief response saying that you do not object. The third category of motions filed by attorneys is filed simply to provide a basis for billable hours. While not all attorneys are guilty of this kind of practice, far too many are, justifying the time by insisting they are being thorough and covering all possible contingencies. This kind of conduct is seen most frequently with motions to dismiss and motions for summary judgment. Attorneys will inevitably file, brief and argue a motion to dismiss based on the pleadings, knowing full well that the case will not be dismissed but instead, the judge will allow the non-moving party to amend the complaint. At first glance it is beyond understanding why an attorney would file such a motion, knowing full well the outcome in advance. On the other hand, when one considers that a motion to dismiss, with supporting memorandum and the time required to go to court to act out the charade, can require between ten and twenty hours of billable time, it becomes more comprehendible. And most clients, unaware of the nature of the proceedings or the actual intent of the motion remain clueless, actually believing their attorney has their best interests at heart.

Unfortunately, just asking for something, or saying you don't agree with something is often not good enough. Judges are not psychic (though they've seen the same things over and over again). You need a little more than to say "hey judge their answers to my interrogatories aren't right". You have to give a legal reason and basis, which will vary in complexity based on what it is you are asking for or opposing. In other words it's usually not enough to ask for something because you want it. You need to show how and why you are entitled to it, or the other side should not be entitled to it.

Sometimes this can be very simple. Using the discovery example, say that you have served interrogatories on the other side, the time limit to respond has passed, and they have not answered. In the case of the other side presenting a motion to amend, it can either be to do nothing, or to file a one line response saying you do not oppose the motion.

Some motions can become more complicated. If you are asking for something which the other side could legitimately oppose, such as amending a complaint or an answer well into the litigation process, you will have to justify your motion (request) both in terms of legal issues as well as factual issues. In the case of a discovery issue, the other side may have responded, but objected. There could be a genuine dispute as to what is or is not a proper response.

Now you will have to reference not only the applicable rules, but will have to refer to law, usually in the form of court decisions, that supports your request. You will also have to cite a factual basis for the request you are making. Using the same examples, if wanting to amend late, you generally must show a good reason for not amending sooner, and will usually have to show that other side will not be unfairly taken advantage of or prejudiced by allowing the late amendment. In a discovery dispute, you will have to justify why the other side should be required to respond.

When a motion becomes more complicated in this way, many courts require that it be accompanied by a memorandum of law. Some jurisdictions require a memorandum of law with EVERY motion, others with only some, and in others it is left to the judgment of the party filing the motion. They are required virtually as a matter of course in federal courts, and more and more state court judges are requiring them.

A memorandum of law is a concise presentation of the law that applies to and supports what you are asking the court to do. It can be as simple as referring to rules, or as complicated as referring to cases decided by appellate courts where the issue is addressed. Continuing with our discovery example, which is a realm ripe with dispute, assume that you've served interrogatories on the other side and the response has been nothing but objections to the questions asked. The memorandum of law that you add to your motion to compel discovery will have to address the questions and the objections, showing how, based on prior decisions and the rules themselves, your questions were proper and the objections not valid.

Even if it is not specifically requested or required by any rules, it is a good idea, in all but the most simple and straightforward motions, to submit a memorandum of law with the motion.

First, it improves the likelihood that your motion will be granted. Judges are human and they are often overworked. If in what the judge directly has before him he can see that your request is reasonable, that you have gone through the effort to present and argue the legal issues, and that there is a legal basis for your request, he is far more likely to give you what you are asking than if he has to drag every nuance of the motion from you in a painful question and answer sequence.

Second, as surprising as it may sound, the judge may not be familiar with the law, especially if the issues in the motion are somewhat complex. In a motion to dismiss for example it may be helpful to set out clearly, with supporting authority the requisite elements of a cause of action, followed by a showing that they are missing in the complaint.

Finally, in representing yourself in a civil case one thing that you will always have to do in order to maintain credibility is to show that you are both conscientious and knowledgeable. Judges are often not enthusiastic about pro se litigants because so many of them think that all they have to do is wander into a courtroom and announce that they are representing themselves. Many pro se litigants incorrectly assume that because they are pro se, and because they are not attorneys, all those pesky rules and requirements will be waived for them. One of your biggest hurdles is to convince the judge early on that this is not you. It is important that you make it clear that you are aware of the rules, have done your homework, have prepared, and have researched the law in order to present your position. You can be assured that the first time the judge in a case sees a motion that you have filed, that complies with the rules and is accompanied by a memorandum of law that correctly supports your position, he will breathe a sigh of relief and you will be welcome in the courtroom.

There is also a requirement in most jurisdictions that attorneys confer, either in person, by mail or by telephone about the issues in at least some motions before they are filed. These jurisdictions require as part of the motion a written certification that the attorneys have actually communicated with one another and made and earnest effort to resolve the dispute before filing the motion.

Whether this requirement applies to you is determined by the wording of the rule. Some rules specifically state that "attorneys" or "counsel" shall confer. Others refer to communication by the "parties" before filing. Obviously if the rule specifically mentions "parties", it applies to you. On the other hand, if the reference is to "attorneys, it probably does not apply to you.

First determine whether there is such rule that applies to the motion you are contemplating filing. Next determine whether it applies to you as representing yourself. If it does then obviously you must comply.

Even if it does not apply to you it's probably not a bad idea to comply anyway. It's not difficult. A phone call or an email to the other side saying in effect: "hey, here is a motion I'm getting ready to file. Is there something we can work out or agree to?" This will accomplish two things. First, it lets the judge know, if the motion has to be heard, that you have done your homework and are trying hard to comply with the rules. Second, it lets the other side know that you are prepared, know the rules, and know how to take care of yourself in court.

The final thing that many judges will look for, and is often required by the rules, is a proposed order. This is as the name suggests, an unsigned order that you submit to the judge. Whether this is required will generally be found in the local rules for whatever court you find yourself in.

Again, even if not required, including a proposed order is a nice touch. If the rules don't require it, there is nothing to prevent you for submitting one anyway. It lets the judge know that you have done your homework. More important, it makes it easy for the judge to give you what you want. A lot of judges will want to think about a motion (take it under advisement), or will waffle a bit. Judges are human too. With a proposed order right in front of him, it is easier for the judge to decide and just sign the order, for a ruling in your favor.

Serving the motion is not difficult and usually (there are a few exceptions) does not require personal service. Mail is most often the preferred method, and all you do is make a copy of the motion (including the memorandum of law and any cover letter that you send to the court), prepare a certificate or proof of service and drop it in the mail to the other side. Your proof of service will show that you mailed it and to what address.

As more and more courts are moving toward electronic filing, you can often serve motions and other papers electronically. You need to check and review the local rules. Some require a proof of service showing that you have sent the papers by email. Other systems automatically send copies of everything filed to every recipient on a service list. In these jurisdictions, you do not even need a proof of service, since as soon as you electronically file, everyone else receives a copy.

Some Specific Motions

Since motions are basically asking the court for something, there are all sorts of different motions that could be filed and if filed by the other side, need to be addressed.

Here some of the more common motions that you can expect to encounter, or even to file yourself.

Motion to Dismiss

In the progress of a case there are certain issues that must be raised early on, either in a motion or in the first responsive pleading, usually the answer. If they are not, they are often waived.

There's a reason for this. The issues we're talking about are all basic and often go to the legal technicalities as opposed to the facts of the case itself. These are issues that the law, and for the most part common sense tells us should be resolved early on, not brought up later in the case. If the case has no merit, if it's going to get dismissed on legal issues, or if the court has no jurisdiction over a party, why let it clog up the docket and waste everyone's time?

An extreme example of such a case would be a citizen suing the President of the United States for squandering their tax money. Can such a lawsuit be filed? Of course! The clerks' offices don't have the authority to screen cases for merit. If the proper forms are there; if it's put together in the right format; and the filing fee is paid, it's filed. Of course it has no merit because there are uncountable constitutional and legal elements that do not allow for each individual citizen to bring such a suit. Lawsuits that have no legal merit need to be disposed of quickly. This kind of lawsuit will be disposed of with a motion to dismiss.

A motion to dismiss asks the court to issue an order dismissing the complaint, and therefore the case, before it gets any further. These motions never go to the truth of any contested matters since in considering such a motion the judge must generally assume that everything alleged in the complaint is true. The motion is based on the face of the complaint.

Obviously, these motions are usually centered on legal issues, or the manner in which the complaint is worded. If you are the plaintiff and have filed the complaint, you absolutely have to address such a motion. Failure to do so will likely result in your case being dismissed.

Motions to Dismiss are not new and while they today are addressed in the Rules of Procedure, their basis is in common law. They are an offshoot of the common law concept of a demurrer. While the concept of a demurrer has in most jurisdictions given way to a motion to dismiss, in some states it is still used. Since the motion to dismiss embraces the demurrer concept and adds a few twists to it, when motions to dismiss are discussed, it also applies to a demurrer in those places where it is still applicable.

To get an idea of some of the areas that a Motion to Dismiss might address, consider the applicable federal rule and go through it. It's not that the federal rules are better than other rules, but Federal Rules of Civil Procedure were one of the first comprehensive efforts to make sense out of court procedures, and many states have adopted them to some extent, even to the point of using the same rule numbers. The federal rule of civil procedure that governs motions to dismiss is Rule 12(b). It is stated here in its entirety because there are different potions that need to be addressed.

Here is Section "b" of Rule 12 of the Federal Rules of Civil Procedure:

(b) How to Present Defenses. Every defense to a claim for relief in any pleading must be asserted in the responsive pleading if one is required. But a party may assert the following defenses by motion:
(1) lack of subject-matter jurisdiction;
(2) lack of personal jurisdiction;
(3) improper venue;
(4) insufficient process;
(5) insufficient service of process;
(6) failure to state a claim upon which relief can be granted; and
(7) failure to join a party under Rule 19.

A motion asserting any of these defenses must be made before pleading if a responsive pleading is allowed. If a pleading sets out a claim for relief that does not require a responsive pleading, an opposing party may assert at trial any defense to that claim. No defense or objection is waived by joining it with one or more other defenses or objections in a responsive pleading or in a motion.

Let's take a look at this rule. There is a lot here. And it is potentially confusing.

The first part of the rule simply states that every defense to a claim for relief must be asserted in the responsive pleading which will usually be the answer. The operative term is: "every defense". If you contend that something in the complaint is not true, you have to say so. If there is an affirmative defense (Pleadings and Papers) you have to say so.

Since this section is about motions though, you need to focus on the next part of the rule. The rule goes on to say about certain defenses: "But a party may assert the following defenses by motion". This is the basis for the motion to dismiss. Finally, the rule provides that if you raise these issues by motion, the motion must be made before any responsive pleading.

It is potentially a bit confusing but if you read the rule carefully, it will make sense. Considering all the parts of the rule together yields the following summary:

- Your answer must include every defense you have, or even think you might have. This includes denials, affirmative defenses and specific issues enumerated in the rule.
- Subject to that requirement, you have the option of raising several specifically listed defenses by motion.
- If you do choose to raise them by motion, you must do so before you answer.

Basically, with respect to the listed defenses, you can file a motion, or you can include them as part of the answer. The one thing you cannot do is file a responsive pleading that fails to include any a required defense, then raise them later. If they are not raised in the first pleading or motion, they are waived to the extent that they can be waived.

The next question to be addressed is whether or not, if the motion to dismiss is denied, to include these defenses again in the answer. Yes. Definitely reassert any of these defenses in your answer if your motion has been denied. Here's why. A motion to dismiss is limited to the face of the complaint. For the purposes of the motion all the factual allegations in the complaint are deemed to be true. Remember, this is taking place at the beginning of the case. There has been no discovery and no evidence has been presented. Therefore the judge in ruling on a motion to dismiss simply takes the allegations of the complaint as true. Later, those allegations may be shown to be false. Many of the issues in a motion to dismiss, for example personal jurisdiction, can be raised again but they must be preserved. It is questionable whether having raised them in a motion that was denied is enough. To avoid any risk that a judge may rule that you failed to raise the defense or preserve it, reassert in the answer. It's painless, and there is no downside to including it again.

So let's look at the some of the grounds for a motion to dismiss and the things that must be raised or are waived.

(1) Lack of subject matter jurisdiction. This refers to the jurisdiction of the court in which the case is pending to handle the case at all. An example is federal jurisdiction

since after all this is a federal rule. In the United States we have a federal judicial system, and of course we have state courts. The cases the federal courts can handle are defined by the United States Constitution and by federal statutes. If neither the Constitution nor a statute give federal courts the authority to handle a case (jurisdiction), then the federal court has no authority regarding that case. Subject matter jurisdiction is in some cases referred to as an exception to the often misstated premise that a matter not raised by answer or motion to dismiss is forever waived. That is often simply not true. It is not a question of whether it has been waived, but instead it is something that cannot be waived. But again, the objective of a motion to dismiss is to get rid early of cases that have no merit. If there is a question of subject matter jurisdiction, early is the time to address it.

(2)   Lack of personal jurisdiction. This is the flip side of subject matter jurisdiction and in it one contends that the court cannot assert jurisdiction over the person being sued. Courts are limited as to who they can assert authority over. This is discussed in greater detail in the section on Jurisdiction. There are limits imposed both by the statutes that created the court to begin with as well as state and federal constitutions on the extent of a court's authority. Except as provided in specific statutes (Long Arm Statutes) a court cannot reach beyond the borders of the political entity in which it sits. The courts of the State of Georgia for example usually have no authority impose their orders or judgments on a citizen and resident of the

State of Maine. The United States has no authority to impose its orders and judgments on the citizens and residents of Brazil.

If you have been sued and believe that the court in does not have jurisdiction over you, it is absolutely imperative that you raise that issue in the first responsive pleading, and preferably by motion. Unlike subject matter jurisdiction, which can often be raised again later, the issue of personal jurisdiction once waived can never be raised again. And unfortunately it is incredibly easy to inadvertently waive objections to personal jurisdiction. Basically, if you do anything other than object to jurisdiction, there is a possibility that you will have waived your defense of personal jurisdiction. Some courts have held that even asking for an extension of time in which to answer or respond constitutes a general appearance and waives the defense.

(3)   Improper Venue. Dismissal for this reason is more likely to occur in federal courts than in state courts. Remember, jurisdiction goes to the power of a court, while venue merely refers to whether the location is proper. While it of course depends on how statutes and rules govern venue, generally the remedy for improper venue in state courts is simply to move the case. Rarely will venue affect the merits since even if a case is dismissed it is not on the merits and therefore can simply be re-filed

(4)   Insufficient Process. This refers to whether the summons itself, which is the document by which the court

actually acquires jurisdiction of the defendant, was proper. It is not the same as whether or not the summons was properly served, which is addressed in Rule 12(b)(5). Since it refers to the validity of the summons, which is often only valid for a specific amount of time (Rule 4 FRCP specifies 120 days), it can also refer to the failure to serve the summons on time.

(5)   Insufficient Service Process. This basically refers to those situations where there is some question as to whether the summons and complaint have been properly served. It of course relates indirectly to the issue of jurisdiction. Without proper service the court has not acquired jurisdiction of the defendant. This is usually not a major issue, since the remedy is to go serve the papers properly, but in instances where the statute of limitations on a case is close to expiration, it can be critical.

(6)   Failure to state a claim upon which relief can be granted. This is the most common ground for filing a motion to dismiss. The thrust of motion to dismiss for failure to state a claim upon which relief can be granted is basically that even assuming that all of the allegations of the complaint are true, there is no basis for recovery as a matter of law. There are a number of different scenarios that would apply.

In some instances it is an issue of there being a legal bar to the lawsuit. In the example set forth above where someone tried to sue the president, it would be issues of sovereign immunity. There may be conditions that must be satisfied before a lawsuit could properly be commenced. An example might be a discrimination case of some sort. These cases usually require that some agency investigation be initiated and pursued to a certain point before filing suit. Some require the agency to issue what is called a suit letter. Bringing these cases without going through these steps is not permitted and doing so would be grounds for dismissal. The motion to dismiss in such a case would basically be saying that even if all of the allegations of the complaint were true, the lawsuit cannot proceed as a matter of law. The prerequisite steps must be taken first.

Another instance of reason to file a motion to dismiss would be if a complaint fails to set forth all the essential elements of a cause of action. This goes back to the section on planning and doing research. The complaint, on its face must set forth the required elements of a cause of action. While the requirements are more relaxed in those states that still adhere to notice pleading and have not adopted the enhanced pleading requirements established in recent cases, in other states as well as in federal courts, the complaint must state facts such as will allow a court to discern a cause of action. If the complaint does not contain these required elements, it will be subject to dismissal.

(7)   Failure to Join a Necessary Party. This motion recognizes that there are times when a lawsuit cannot resolve the issues in dispute without another party participating. An example of this is in what is commonly referred to as a derivative shareholder action. The law

allows a shareholder of a corporation to pursue a cause of action or claim that would otherwise belong to the corporation, but that the corporation for one reason or another is not pursuing. The statutes creating this cause of action generally hold that while a shareholder is allowed to bring such a suit, the corporation is a necessary party. A lawsuit that failed to name the corporation as a defendant would be subject to dismissal. If a court determines that in fact a necessary party is missing from the suit, the remedy may be as simple as amending the complaint to add the party. On the other hand, it may be fatal to the lawsuit if, for example the missing party is beyond the jurisdiction of the court.

Discovery Motions

Discovery in a civil case, covered in a section devoted to that topic, is by and large intended to be engaged in between the parties, without involvement of a judge. The rules set forth what must be divulged and the procedures to be used.

Of course it doesn't work that way. The discovery process generates far too many issues that often can only be resolved by a judge. One side is seeking information from the other side that does not want to divulge it. As a result, the responses to discovery often include objections (some meritorious, others frivolous) and evasive answers.

Obviously, with all the rules and court decisions involving these issues, you can expect at least one if not several motions concerning discovery through the course of litigating a case.

In the discovery process you will encounter two general types of motion: motions to compel and motions for protection. Motions to compel are those filed by the party seeking discovery. They argue that that other side has either not responded to discovery requests at all, or if they have, they have not responded completely. Motions for protection are filed by the party from which discovery is sought. They argue that they should not be required to provide certain kinds or specific items of information, or that the other side is abusing the discovery system by requesting overly broad and burdensome information.

Motions to compel discovery come in three flavors.

The first is filed when the other side simply does not respond at all. Interrogatories or requests to produce are served, and nothing happens. In this case a motion is filed which requests an order requiring responses to the discovery. A court also has other options available. It can fine the non-responding party. If the non responding party is the plaintiff it can dismiss the lawsuit. If it is the defendant it can strike the answer which puts the defendant into default. This version of the motion to compel is rare, because, it is clear to the parties that they must participate in discovery, and the outcome is certain.

The second variety occurs where responses have been provided but it is felt they are not proper responses. Let's look at an example.

A common set of interrogatory questions asks that anyone who is expected to testify at the trial of the case be identified. It further asks for a summary of what the witness is expected to testify to at trial. Often attorneys will provide a response such as "Witness 'A' will testify as to the facts and circumstances of the matter in dispute".

This answer is of course totally meaningless. Attorneys present these responses hoping that they can get away with them. You can fully expect responses such as this if you represent yourself. Attorneys will assume that you do not know any better and will simply accept such a silly response. Responses like this require a motion to compel, so that a judge can issue an order requiring an appropriate answer.

The third variety of motion to compel is where the other side has objected to specific interrogatories, or requests for production, or has refused to answer certain questions at a deposition. This is an area that often involves a genuine dispute between the parties as to whether or certain information is subject to discovery.

A motion to compel discovery is one of those motions that almost always requires either the attorneys or the parties, regardless of whether represented or not to attempt to resolve the issues before filing. To accomplish that is easy because it is by and large an exercise in futility. If a party or their attorney was going to respond to the discovery in the way that you are expecting, they would already have done so.

While a somewhat on the cynical side, the observation must be made that the realm of discovery is cherished by attorneys. The potential to bill almost limitless hours of time bickering about the technicalities and niceties of privilege and scope of discovery is often irresistible. Suffice it to say that it is an often abused area of the law for less than scrupulous attorneys whose main objective is to bill as many hours of time as possible.

So in communicating with the other side as a precursor to filing the motion, you might as well just be preparing the motion and send them an abbreviated version in a letter or an email.

The manner in which a motion to compel is prepared is governed by the rules, but very often for motions such as this there are unique requirements in local rules. For example, some local federal districts require that in any motion to compel, each interrogatory or request in dispute be set forth verbatim, along with the response, if any, in the motion. Read the rules. All of them!

The most common areas of dispute in the discovery realm is whether the request is within the scope of discovery, whether the request or question is subject to some form of privilege, and whether the question or request is overly broad or burdensome under all the circumstances.

The good news is that discovery being such a ripe area for litigation, it is never difficult to find case law or authority to support your position regarding any of these questions.

On the other side, the party from which discovery is requested may file a motion for a protective order. The rules providing for discovery are usually pretty general and allow for liberal discovery but there are some things that are often asked or requested that are not included in that scope. While some rules, such as the Federal Rules of Civil Procedure limit things like numbers of interrogatories, or requests to produce, others contain no limits. So there is plenty of potential for overly broad or excessive discovery requests. The problem is that you cannot simply refuse to answer or respond. This just sets the stage for a motion to compel to be filed by the other side. You are far better off, and not on the defensive if you take the initiative and request a protective order.

Motion for Summary Judgment

A motion for summary judgment is one that you will see frequently in the course of litigation, and may consider filing yourself. It is a request to the Court to grant judgment in favor of the moving party and against the other party either as a matter of law, or because following development of the case, there is no genuine issue of material fact that would enable to the nonmoving party to prevail. A motion for summary judgment and a motion to dismiss have some similarities, but in the end are substantially different. A motion to dismiss concerns itself with the adequacy of the complaint, while a motion for summary judgment goes beyond that and encompasses factual matters.

A motion for summary judgment basically says that with the evidence developed as of the time of the motion, and with evidence that can be developed, there is no genuine issue of material fact, and the moving party is entitled to prevail on the issue as a matter of law. That is the party making the motion is entitled to win before the matter ever gets to the jury.

A motion for summary judgment can address the entire case or part of it.

The key things to be aware of about motions for summary judgment are:

Unlike a motion to dismiss, which must be filed at the beginning of the case, a motion for summary judgment can be filed at any time until trial unless some other time limit is specifically imposed.

Unlike a motion to dismiss, where if a pleading has some problems the result is to allow amended pleadings to address the issues, an order granting summary judgment is final with respect to those issues. There is usually no going back and fixing it.

A motion for summary judgment can be based on purely legal issues, or it can include factual issues.

If a motion for summary judgment includes factual issues, these can be presented to the judge in the form of affidavits, depositions, exhibits, other documents, or basically anything that is in the court record.

The standard for a judge to use when considering a motion for summary judgment is that all factual issues and all inferences from factual issues must be assumed to be in favor of the party opposing summary judgment.

What the last two points taken together mean is that if there are factual issues to be considered they can be presented to the court in several ways. They always have to be attached or referred to in the motion itself so the party opposing summary judgment has a chance to address them. A party moving for summary judgment can attach affidavits (sworn statements before a notary or other officer) or all or part of deposition testimony or answers to interrogatories and responses to requests to admit.

The party upon whom the motion is served has a reasonable amount of time, which varies from jurisdiction to jurisdiction to respond to the motion, after which a hearing is held. That means the other side gets a chance to gather its own evidence in the form of affidavits, etc. to counter what is in the motion for summary judgment. The rules are always very specific and require that any factual issue be resolved in favor of the party opposing the motion for summary judgment.

That makes perfect sense when you go back and look at the motion itself. A motion for summary judgment basically says that there is no genuine issue of material fact. If there is conflicting evidence presented, the requirement has not been made. There IS a genuine issue of material fact and summary judgment cannot be granted.

The important thing to keep in mind is that the difference must be of material fact and must be demonstrated by at least some evidence. Virtually all rules pertaining to summary judgment specify that a party opposing summary judgment cannot simply rely on the pleadings, but must put some evidence forward. In short, if a motion for summary judgment asserts "X" by some of the things listed above, the party opposing the motion cannot simply say "X" is not true. There has to be something backing that assertion.

That means if you are served with a motion for summary judgment you cannot just point to your complaint or answer and say "See Judge it's right there in the answer. We disagree with that."

You will lose.

Summary judgment motions are very serious in that potentially, if you lose the motion you could lose your whole case before it ever gets to trial. But, just because they're serious does not mean that you cannot deal with them. It does require a lot of work and research. You have to fully understand the law as it applies to the case and how it applies to the facts at issue.

As a case progresses toward trial there may be other motions. Remember, a motion is nothing but a way to get an issue in front of the judge so that he can make a ruling.

Some other motions that you might expect to see:

Motion to amend pleadings.

All civil procedure rules have provisions for amending pleadings. Most (but certainly not all) provide some period of time in which the right is automatic and no motion is required. If you want to change your answer or complaint you just file and serve an amended answer or amended complaint.

Later on it's not so easy. It really gets down to a question of fairness. Early on it's no big deal. No one has done anything in reliance on pleadings being as they're originally filed and served. No depositions have been taken and probably any other discovery has been generic. No one is going to be prejudiced, and the trial of the case will not be delayed if the complaint is amended. That changes as the case goes along. Once a defendant has answered, once a defendant has served and responded to discovery, identified and interviewed potential witnesses and gone through all the work involved in moving toward trial, it could be too late to allow the complaint to be amended to add a new cause of action.

So after the initial automatic amendment period, in order to change pleadings a party must file a motion asking for permission to do so. The motion must of course state the reasons why the amendment is needed, why it is just now being amended, whether whatever is creating the need to amend could have been discovered earlier with a little effort, and how the party seeking to amend would be harmed if the amendment was not allowed. The other side must file a response (assuming they object to the amendment) pointing out the converse of these issues. They will try to establish to the judge that with a little effort and diligence the pleading could have been amended much earlier. They will point out the time spent and expense incurred in reliance on the pleading before amendment, and how they will be unfairly taken advantage of should the amendment be allowed. The judge will of course take these factors into consideration and make a ruling. Obviously, if a pleading is amended, the other side is allowed time to file and serve new responsive pleadings. The general rule of thumb is that the later in the case, the more work that has been done, and the closer the case is to trial, the more there had better be a very good reason for amending pleadings.

Motions in Limine

A motion in limine means to limit testimony. Sometimes in a case there are things that one side or the other just does not want to have brought out. Often these are things of an embarrassing or personal nature that the other side may want to introduce to embarrass someone. Often they are the kinds of things that while possibly relevant, would tend to prejudice a jury. A motion in limine can be filed at any time prior to trial, or sometimes, even during a trial when it appears that testimony is going to create problems, which makes it a very versatile motion.

What the motion asks the judge for is an order directing that certain evidence may not be used, or must be disclosed ahead of time. These are very handy motions. Don't be afraid to use them. One example, depending on what jurisdiction you are in, would be the use of charts, drawings or exhibits. As technology advances, many courtrooms are equipped with things like computer terminals at the counsel tables, video display equipment and so forth. The rules on things like power point displays, graphics and similar things have not kept pace with technology. The rules regarding exhibits and displays are very sketchy. As long as they merely summarize evidence that has already been admitted into evidence, or merely present it in a different way, they are allowed. Bottom line, do you really want to be in court and see for the first time as it is presented to the jury, a power point presentation?

Probably not.

The problem is that since it is not evidence, nor a discoverable document, the other side is under no obligation to share it with you ahead of time. Unless that is, you've filed a motion in limine and gotten the judge to issue an order saying that nothing along those lines will be presented to the jury unless you've seen it at least twenty-four hours ahead of time. With a little experimenting, you'll find that these motions are great tools.

Conclusion

Motions are an inevitable part of litigating a civil case. You should not fear them or be apprehensive, with one caveat: be prepared. As with anything else, presenting or defending a motion to a judge requires research and organization. Once the case is filed there are facts to be dealt with, even if they consist of nothing more than what the pleadings say or don't say. There is law, in the form of rules and court decisions to be applied to those facts.

As long as you do your homework and are organized you will be fine. Just remember that judges will hold you to the same rules and same law as the attorney on the other side. You cannot waltz into court on a motion and play the "gee I don't have a lawyer so I didn't know" game. You will lose.

Discovery – the Nuts and Bolts

The term "Discovery" in a lawsuit has nothing to do with finding new planets or inventing things. It has to do with what is often an extensive phase in a lawsuit where the parties are required to exchange information.

The ways this information is exchanged, and how to navigate your way through the process is the topic if this section. The most important thing to remember is that it is not optional! Discovery is one of the realms of litigation that creates opportunities for those who understand it, and traps for those who fail to appreciate its importance. Knowledge is power someone said, so the more you understand about your opponent's case the better.

Discovery takes various forms that accomplish different things. All are important.

The concept of discovery has evolved over time and the purported purpose of this exchange of information is twofold.

First, it argued that the free exchange of information will expedite the litigation process.

Second it is believed that if each party is more fully aware of all the available information, it is more likely that a case will settle. While there is merit to both arguments in theory, the reality is that discovery as it has evolved, seldom accomplishes or even contributes to either objective.

As with many legal issues, a little understanding of the underlying principles will make it easier to understand what you really need to know about discovery.

First let's look at how discovery originated and how it evolved to its present state.

The History of Discovery.

The early history of discovery in litigation is simple. There was none.

In the early days of civil trials, going back to England, there simply was no mechanism for what we now know as discovery. Of course there were no rules of evidence, or written rules of procedure either. The lack of predictability made early civil trials intriguing to say the least. The premise back then, and in early America was that you went to court to resolve your differences. Everybody knew what the facts were, so let's get on with it.

In America, even as late as the early twentieth century, there was very little formal discovery. In "the old days" the trial of a lawsuit was generally trial by ambush and pretty risky for the litigants. You walked into court without knowing what evidence the other side would be presenting, and they of course did not know what you would be putting up.

That system probably actually worked in its day when facts underlying lawsuits were not all that complex. There were of course no computers or electronic records. People dealt with each other face to face. In short, when you went to court, there really weren't a lot of surprises.

Then too, viewing discovery in the context of legal procedure "back then" also sheds some light on the rationale for no or limited discovery. America began as primarily a rural legal environment. When it came time to have a term of court, planning was easy. The judge and all the attorneys for any pending cases simply got together to talk about them. And do not believe for one second that we are referring to something that disappeared at the end of the "way back when". These "roster meetings" were conducted well into the latter half of the twentieth century. These involved all the attorneys with cases pending meeting with the judge. Everybody just sort of lounged around the courtroom and talked about their cases. If the meeting ran into lunch hour, it was adjourned to the café across the street. When lunch was over, everyone wandered back to the courthouse. The meeting was over when the judge and the attorneys agreed what cases would be tried, and in what order during the next term of court.

At these meetings the attorneys would be called upon to discuss their respective cases, let the judge know if they were ready for trial or if not, what else remained to be done, and most relevant to this discussion, tell the judge how many witnesses they expected to call and how long the trial could be expected to take. This, early on, was the extent of discovery.

As litigation developed and became more pervasive and complex, it soon became apparent that the trial by ambush system was not all that great for a lot of reasons.

First, the old roster meeting arrangement which worked well when there might have been a few hundred cases on the entire roster, and all involving a couple of dozen attorneys who all had offices within shouting distance of the courthouse, was found lacking when the roster contained thousands of cases and hundreds of attorneys. Absent a formal system, there was no guarantee the attorneys or parties would exchange information, or provide meaningful information to the court. The result was a clumsy and unwieldy system. The court clerks had no way of knowing if a particular case would take one day or three weeks when it came to trial. So when it came time to schedule cases, everyone was groping in the dark.

Beginning with strides in a few of the larger court systems, and in the federal system, courts began to require that attorneys and parties exchange information that would provide basic information about the cases, and give the court itself a better understanding of the cases it was dealing with. This exchange provided courts with important information such as how many witnesses could be expected, how long it would take for the trial, and if there were any potential problems that might delay the trial.

This was the beginning of the evolution and development of the modern system of discovery in civil litigation.

The second theory supporting discovery is that exchange of information promotes settlement. And while there are some things that sometimes detract from that concept, by and large, it has some merit. A party is far more likely to settle a case if they realize, from discovery that there is a good chance that they could lose. Likewise, knowing what the other side's damages are gives a party a much better idea of what a reasonable settlement might be. If the other side has a strong case in a contract dispute and has lost a million dollars, offering to settle for fifty thousand dollars is probably not a great strategy. On the other hand, if the amount in dispute is much less, which you've learned through discovery, it is much easier to extend an offer that is likely to be accepted.

Like everything else in life, discovery in civil cases has evolved from the simple and basic to the complex.

At first discovery was limited to a few interrogatories6, often specified by the courts, and the taking of

---

[6] Interrogatories are written questions sent to a party which must be answered in writing, usually under oath.

depositions7. There are versions of specific court rules published as recently as the 1970s and '80's that provided for only four interrogatories that were printed verbatim in the rule. No other written questions could be asked. But as time went on, more forms of discovery were added. The rules were modified and expanded, until we now have extensive discovery and court systems where before a case ever gets to trial, the parties often spend months exchanging information.

Not only have there been changes in the kinds of discovery, but the extent of discovery has been dramatically expanded over the years. We now have completely broad discovery. The scope of allowable discovery in federal courts and most state courts includes anything that is in any way relevant to a claim or defense, or may lead to the discovery of admissible evidence.

How much discovery will you have to deal with when you represent yourself? Impossible to say because the kind of discovery and how much it is used will vary quite a bit depending on the kind of case involved the amount in controversy and the issues presented.

For example, if the case involves a contract dispute where the issue is interpretation of a contract term, the parties probably know a lot to begin with about the case. Both parties will be familiar with the contract, how it came into

---

[7] A deposition is a form of discovery where a witness (who can also be a party) is put under oath and asked questions which are stenographically recorded.

being, the problems that arose and discussions that were had regarding the matter before the suit was filed. There won't be all that many surprises and discovery may be more limited.

On the other hand, if we are dealing with a case in which a party is alleging that another business used confidential information to solicit its customers, things will be different. Here there may be dozens of witness and thousands of documents. Discovery will be far more extensive.

Methods of Discovery.

So far we know that discovery in a lawsuit is the exchange of information between parties, but that's rather vague and general. Let's look at the methods or modes of discovery available in modern litigation. This will both provide a better overall understanding of how to not only deal with, but use discovery to your advantage. While there are some other techniques sometimes used there are four types of discovery available to be used between parties. They are Interrogatories, Depositions, Requests for Production and Requests to Admit. They may have different technical names in different jurisdictions, but they will always be essentially one of these four.

Interrogatories.

Interrogatories are basically questions that are answered in writing.

Questions are written and served upon the other side, and in turn must be answered in writing, usually under oath. Interrogatories are probably the most basic form of discovery in that they are generally the first discovery that you will see or use it a case. In fact, as is often permitted by court rules, interrogatories are sometimes served upon a defendant at the same time as the summons and complaint. Likewise, very often when an answer is served, it is often accompanied by interrogatories. Think of interrogatories as a way to get things started and as a discovery tool that will more than anything else lead to more discovery.

The types of questions asked in interrogatories will of course vary considerably from case to case. Clearly different questions will be posed in a case involving a contract dispute as opposed to one involving personal injury. There will though be some things common to all interrogatories.

First, they will almost always include a request that witnesses as well as people with knowledge of the case be identified, usually requesting name, address and telephone number. There will probably be a subsequent interrogatory asking for a summary of what each witness has knowledge of or may be expected to testify to. Almost all interrogatories will ask for the names of all persons who have participated in the preparation of the responses, or who have provided information used in preparing the responses. If interrogatories are directed to the plaintiff, they will generally include one or more questions as to damages and how any dollar amounts claimed to be due were calculated or arrived at. There will often be one or more questions asking a party to disclose and describe any other litigation of any kind that they have been involved in, to include the specifics of each case.

The number of interrogatories that can be served on the other side is usually limited by the court rules, with different jurisdictions allowing different numbers of interrogatories. Even then, the court can, and will in cases that merit it, allow additional interrogatories.

While they have definite benefits, the usefulness of interrogatories is limited to information that is fairly basic. The major problem with trying to get information by using interrogatories is at the root of the whole discovery. It has evolved into separate area of conflict where on the one hand both parties want to gain as much information as they can, but conversely, want to divulge as little as possible.

Interrogatories can though be important in another regard in that later, when it comes time for summary judgment motions, answers to interrogatories are deemed part of the record and can be used in support of, or to oppose a motion for summary judgment. And too, as with everything a party signs, they can be used at trial to impeach a witness if he suddenly tries to testify in a way that contradicts his interrogatory answers.

So while they probably won't yield you awe inspiring mountains of information about the other side's case, they have some value. There are very few cases when you should not be sending out interrogatories early on in the case.

Requests for Production

"Producing Documents, Electronically Stored Information and Tangible Things, or Entering onto Land for Inspection and Other Purposes" is the title of the rule in the Federal Rules of Civil Procedure that governs what is commonly referred to as a Request for Production.

Rules in different jurisdictions will refer to it in different ways, but the gist is that it refers to a mode of discovery where documents and records are produced to the other side.

For the most part we will discuss this mode of discovery in the context of documents. To be sure, the various applicable rules make provision for the inspection of tangible things and objects, but what we are really talking about in almost every instance, is documents. Just understand that this topic could also include things like inspecting a machine alleged to be defective, the site of an injury and so forth.

The nature and extent of document production requests will depend on the rules of the jurisdiction, kind of case, and nature of the parties.

Obviously a case involving a boundary dispute between two adjacent landowners will not involve nearly as many documents, and therefore document requests, a dispute in a business setting involving computation and determination of income or profits over a several year period.

The rules of the various jurisdictions vary in how documents must be produced or sent to the other side in response to a production request. Some impose specific limits while others do not. Usually, but certainly not always you will find that while there are limits on the number of interrogatories, few limits are placed on the number of document requests8. The general approach seems to be that while there should be some limit on questions, and that a party should be able to get the information it reasonably needs in a limited number of questions, a party should be entitled to any and all documents as long as they fall within the allowable scope of discovery.

Document productions requests if at all possible should be sent very early. If you are going to take a deposition of the other side, you definitely want to have an opportunity to

---

8 There are exceptions. Utah for example has a staggered set of allowable document requests based on the amount in controversy.

have reviewed all the documents you can before the deposition. You don't want to have a deposition of a witness scheduled before you've had a chance to obtain documents that will help you, so serve Requests for Production on parties and serve subpoenas requesting documents out to non- party witness as soon as possible.

Request to Admit

The federal rules of civil procedure and virtually all state rules make provision for serving and responding to Requests to Admit.

Requests to Admit fall into two general categories: requests to admit that a document is authentic, or that a copy is a correct copy of the original, and requests to admit or deny the truth of factual statements.

Requests to Admit are in a strict sense as much a method of narrowing and simplifying issues in anticipation of trial or settlement discussion as they are a discovery method. To that extent they are actually a hybrid form of discovery.

If both sides will agree and admit that certain documents are authentic, or that copies provided are in fact true copies of the originals, then for the purpose of discussion at a mediation for example, these issues as can be accepted as true. Likewise, in preparation for trial it will not be necessary to locate and arrange for witnesses who would testify concerning the authenticity of a document since it has been established.

The same goes for admissions concerning fact issues. If a party admits that a certain factual statement is true, then for all purposes, for the rest of the case, that fact is deemed to be true. No evidence to establish it will be required, and no evidence to refute it later will be allowed or considered. That means that as far as an admitted fact is concerned, there is no need to have witnesses testify. It is already established.

A big advantage of Requests to Admit is that there is often no limit on the number of requests that can be served.

Requests to Admit are of course good discovery tools as well. By seeing what the other side is prepared to readily admit, versus what they deny, you can get a lot of insight into the posture and theory of their case.

Requests to Admit are plagued by the same issues surrounding other forms of discovery, and then some. Attorneys will make every effort to avoid directly responding, and will always look for ambiguity in the way in which the request is worded as an excuse. If a request regarding a fact is not precisely worded, it can be denied. If it is vague it can be denied or objected to.

Requests to Admit have two factors which mandate close attention when dealing with them.

First, any admission not answered within a defined time limit is deemed admitted.

That means exactly what it sounds like.

If you are served with Requests to Admit a series of facts, and do not timely respond, all of those facts are deemed admitted. It doesn't take a lot of imagination to see that the whole case could be lost by failing to respond.

Second, as with all discovery, the rules require good faith responses. With respect to Requests to Admit, failure to admit the authenticity of a document or the truth of a fact that is later proven to be authentic or true, may result in being required to pay all costs incurred in proving same, including the other side's reasonable attorney's fees. So obviously, you can't just go down a list of Requests to Admit and deny everything across the board.

Requests to Admit are a great tool. Use them. They cost you nothing while running up legal fees for your opponent. Serving them on the other side can't hurt you in any way. If the other side denies something you just have to prove it in court. That's no different than if you'd never served the request. If requests are admitted you've made your own life easier.

Serving Requests to Admit is truly a no-lose proposition for you, yet it's amazing how little this discovery method is used on in litigation.

Depositions

Depositions are probably the most powerful single tool in the discovery arsenal. As you learn how depositions are taken, and how they can be used, you will understand why.

Law firms and lawyers love depositions because they usually get paid by the hour. Any lawyer worth his or her salt can with a little ingenuity, considering time needed to prepare for, take, and later review the deposition, easily manage to bill ten hours or more on one. Of course this is one of the times that you can chuckle and enjoy representing yourself. The other side is dropping three to five thousand dollars while you sit there knowing it's not costing you a dime!

First, let's talk about what a deposition is.

It is sworn recorded testimony of a witness or a party taken outside the courtroom.

As with most things, short definitions like this are deceptive in that the whole picture is not nearly as simple as the definition suggests.

A deposition is a formal question and answer session between the person taking the deposition, who is asking the questions, and the person being deposed, who is answering the questions.

It is basically an interrogation of a party or a witness, differing from a criminal setting only in that in a criminal setting you can decide at any time that you don't want to answer any more questions, while in a deposition, you generally cannot. So under no circumstances should a deposition be taken lightly.

Typically you will find depositions taken in attorney's offices, generally around a conference table. Less often, as when taking the deposition of an expert, or someone suffering a disability, a deposition may be taken in places like a doctor's office, a conference room made available in a courthouse, a hospital room, or even someone's home.

In addition to the person giving testimony, a deposition may be attended by any party to the litigation, an attorney for the person giving testimony if not a party, and any attorney for a party. Otherwise, a deposition is not a public proceeding and attendance may be refused to anyone else.

Several factors make depositions a very powerful discovery tool.

The fact that the person being deposed is under oath, just as in a courtroom and subject to sanctions for refusing to answer, or penalty of perjury for lying, is one of three things that make a deposition such a powerful tool.

The second important thing is that unlike other forms of discovery, where the responses are prepared in consultation with a party's attorney or other helpful people over an extended period of time, answers to questions at a deposition must be given immediately. The person giving the deposition does not have the opportunity to contemplate the ramifications of a response and does not have an opportunity to consult with anyone, attorney or otherwise, regarding the question or the answer. A question is asked and an answer is required.

The third important thing is that the questions and answers are recorded. The deposition is recorded in a number of ways, depending on the jurisdiction and the rules that apply. It is almost always recorded by a court reporter or a verbatim reporter, but is usually also electronically recorded as a back-up and may be video-taped.

So that you understand the distinction, and are not confused, a court stenographer is a reporter who takes the testimony down using a stenographic machine. The testimony is set forth on paper in a type of shorthand, to be transcribed later. A verbatim reporter actually repeats what is said into a special noise canceling microphone. The result is that a recording of the actual testimony as well as a recording of the reporter's repetition is preserved.

Finally, if the rules permit and the parties agree, the deposition may be videotaped. Note that even if a deposition is electronically recorded, or videotaped, it will almost always be stenographically recorded as well.

By way of observation, with modern technology, many court reporters have available at a deposition an instant transcription that any attorney or party with a laptop computer can connect to and see in real time a written version of what is being said and recorded.

Regardless of how recorded, the end result is preservation of the questions and answers, and transcription of that testimony into written form. The original of that testimony, or transcript, is preserved in accordance with rules of the jurisdiction in which you find yourself. Copies are made and are available to anyone who wishes to purchase a copy from the court reporter.

Depositions, as with all discovery, are addressed in the civil procedure rules for the particular jurisdiction. The rules will specify how they are to be taken, how they may be recorded, how the original transcript is to be handled, and what the depositions can be used for. It is the latter topic that makes depositions so important, since almost all court rules now provide that a deposition, once taken can be used for any purpose. What does this mean?

The most common uses of depositions are:

To Learn what a Party Knows and Will Testify to.

This is the most straightforward use of a deposition and what it in fact was originally devised to accomplish. Remember interrogatories will disclose the names and addresses of potential witnesses in the case. Depositions of these people can give you a very good idea of what they will testify to at trial, and what they know about the case. Depositions are far more useful in this regard than interrogatories because they are dynamic. If you ask a question in an interrogatory, you will, within the specified time limit (usually thirty days) receive a written answer.

Unless the answer is so vague or misleading so as to be objectionable, you are stuck with it. In a deposition you ask a witness a question and receive an immediate answer. You can ask a witness to explain a confusing answer, you can rephrase a question, you can ask follow up questions. Clearly a deposition is going to give you a wealth of information in a relatively short amount of time. Interrogatories will give the broad kind of information. With depositions you can get down into the details.

To Expound Upon other Discovery.

Because the legal establishment has made a science out of making discovery as difficult and protracted as it can possibly be, other forms of discovery can be viewed as at best, a good starting point, to be followed up with deposition questions. Vague answers in interrogatories can be asked again in depositions. If they are still vague follow up questions can narrow the issues. If documents have been stated in response to a Request for Production to be unavailable, a witness with knowledge can be asked point blank where the documents are, who prepared them, when they were last seen, who had access to them and so forth.

To lock in testimony.

Once someone gives testimony under oath at a deposition, it will be very difficult later for them to change that testimony.

If you establish through questioning the other side that for example on the day of an accident the road was not wet, it will be difficult for him later to testify that in fact it had just rained and the road was wet. In the eyes of a jury if he does this at trial the best the witness can be perceived as is confused with a bad memory. It is possibly he could be perceived as a liar.

How to Handle Discovery

Discovery is such an important part of a civil case that it begins almost immediately. The only thing that might take place sooner once a civil case has been commenced is a motion to dismiss. Some jurisdictions allow the first discovery to be served along with the complaint while others impose a short waiting period. Virtually all jurisdictions allow the defendant to serve discovery along with the answer.

Most people that represent themselves don't realize what discovery consists of, or how important it is. Attorneys will always serve discovery on the other side. First, it has a legitimate purpose and perhaps just as important, because it is time intensive, it is a great revenue generator for attorneys.

Now that you've got an idea of the different forms of discovery that you will most often encounter let's see how this thing is really done.

How discovery works in whatever court you are in is always spelled out in detail in the rules of that court. Usually you will find it in a separate section of the rules entitled discovery. For example, if you are in federal court your will find what you need to know in Title V called appropriately enough "Disclosures and Discovery". It includes Rules 26 through 37. In California you will find what you need in Part 4, Title 4, in the California Code of Civil Procedure. Obviously where discovery rules are found varies from state to state. In many cases you will find that states have adopted, either verbatim, or in some hybrid form the federal rules of civil procedure. In those cases, it is easy. The discovery provisions are broken out just as in federal courts.

Wherever you find the rules, you must read them carefully. They will prescribe everything from when you can initiate discovery, to how long you have to respond, to how many interrogatories can be propounded and so forth.

The next thing that you have to understand is the scope of discovery - what it can include. In general, in keeping with the intent and purpose of discovery, accept that it is very broad. It is important that you understand that the range of areas that can be delved into in discovery is much broader than what might be allowed at the trial of the case. The most often stated rule concerning the scope of discovery is based on Rule 26 of the Federal Rules of Civil Procedure, which states:

"... the scope of discovery is as follows: Parties may obtain discovery regarding any non-privileged matter that is relevant to any party's claim or defense—including the existence, description, nature, custody, condition, and location of any documents or other tangible things and the identity and location of persons who know of any discoverable matter. For good cause, the court may order discovery of any matter relevant to the subject matter involved in the action. Relevant information need not be admissible at the trial if the discovery appears reasonably calculated to lead to the discovery of admissible evidence."

If you read that rule carefully, you will see that it is quite broad. The matter being sought does not have to be admissible at trial. It just has to appear to be reasonably calculated to lead to the discovery of admissible evidence. That leaves the door wide open.

Techniques for Interrogatories

Preparing

Sending the other side interrogatories is a little more complicated than sitting down and firing of some written questions. Two factors involved require that interrogatories be carefully worded.

First, as we pointed out, the number of interrogatories is often limited. You have to make your questions count.

Second, the other side will pick the language of your questions apart, using every variation of the possible interpretations of the language to avoid giving you any more information than absolutely necessary. An attorney truly skillful at the discovery game will be able to generate answers to interrogatories that while arguably complying with the rules will provide absolutely no meaningful information.

To understand, let's look at an example. Let's say we're asking questions about a car accident that took place, and we want, by serving interrogatories to know who might be witnesses. Let's say that there was a person, call them Mr. Doe, who did not actually witness the accident, but arrived shortly afterward and heard statements made by both drivers. He will obviously be an important witness and you need to know about him. The other side would just as soon that you didn't because his testimony will be to the effect that the other driver admitted the accident was his fault.

Here are three versions of an interrogatory for you to consider:

> Identify by name, address and telephone number all persons who you may call as a witness at the trial of this matter.

> Identify by name, address and telephone number all persons known to you or your attorney to be witnesses to the accident, the subject of this litigation.

> Identify by name, address and telephone number all persons known to you or your attorney who may have knowledge of the facts concerning the accident, the subject of this litigation or any other matter related to or associated with such accident.

While the intent is the same, and in good faith any one of those interrogatories should produce the name of Mr. Doe, the reality is that only one in fact will. Only the last version, in this day of discovery gambits, will likely get you in response the name and address of Mr. Doe.

They will not include Mr. Doe in response to the first version since they have no intention of calling him as a witness.

They will not include Mr. Doe in response to the second version since he did not witness the accident.

Clearly the intent and spirit of the interrogatory calls for disclosure of Mr. Doe. Perhaps with an explanation that he did not actually witness the accident but arrived later, but clearly common sense tells us that he is an important witness and should be disclosed. Nonetheless based on the way the interrogatory is worded they can and will omit Mr. Doe and moreover, no judge will be able to sanction them, since all they need to do is to point to the wording of the interrogatory.

Remember, any weakness or vagueness in a discovery request will be pounced upon to allow evasiveness, and to prolong the discovery process. Attorneys love discovery. They bill by the hour and discovery is a goldmine!

Bad questions will give bad or even no answers, but will count against your total allowed interrogatories. Careful drafting is important.

The best way to regard interrogatories is a good place to start. They can give you an idea of who potential witnesses might be that you don't already know about. They may also identify witnesses that the other side may not be aware of. Failing to include a witness to a broadly but well worded question is not something that an attorney is likely to do intentionally. Not because they are ethical or moral, but because the consequences of getting caught at it are not pleasant. So, far from being a sure thing, but at least an indication, if you are aware of a witness that does not appear in the other side's interrogatory responses, it may be that they are not aware of them at all.

Interrogatories will help you identify documents to be requested later, and may point you to other sources of documents. For example, if you have asked for names of banks, accounts numbers and other information pertaining to any financial accounts of the other side, the response will give a great source from which you can issue subpoenas for bank statements and records.

Interrogatory answers will help you define questions to ask at depositions. For example, with respect to every witness listed in a response, you can ask the other party at a deposition how they know that person, how long have they know them, when did they last talk to them, what was the conversation about and so forth. This is especially useful when the other side swamps you with witness names. It lets you figure out by questioning the other party who is really a significant witness and who is not, without going to the expense of taking depositions of insignificant witnesses.

So in this context, your interrogatories should be designed to get as much preliminary information as possible. At the same time be aware of the limitations of interrogatories and accept that they are really nothing more than a good starting point.

Answering Interrogatories

Here of course the shoe is on the other foot. You are served with interrogatories which you must answer in writing. The most important thing to do is take your time. You usually have thirty days to answer, and unlike Requests to Admit, which are addressed later, nothing really bad happens if you don't answer on time. So remember the advice early on for answering a lawsuit. Well, the same holds true for interrogatories. Sit back and study them.

By looking at the interrogatories you can sometimes get a feel for where the other side is going with the case. Not the basic interrogatories; the ones that ask about witnesses and so forth. Those are always there. What you want to take a look at is the ones that are further down. What is the other side after? What are they interested in? You can sometimes get clues from the kinds of questions they ask.

The next thing to bear in mind is that you do not have to answer things that you do not know. The court will only require that you respond to things that you are aware of, or with respect to which the means to become aware are within your immediate control. You are not required to go out and do research in order to answer these.

There is actually a surprising amount of information that you might assume that you have to provide, but in reality, are not required to. You are required to provide answers based on information readily available to you, but you are not required to go and find that information, especially if it is in the hands of a third party, equally available to the other side, or readily available as public information. Of course you cannot take this to an absurd extreme either. To illustrate, let's look at an example:

You are asked for your business bank account number and to identify all persons who have or who have ever had access or signatory authority with regard to that account.

The bank account number is obviously readily available to you and must be provided. The second part though is different. If several people over the years have been authorized on the account, and you do not have in your possession or records all the names, you can answer that you do not have that information. The key here is that even though it is your account, you are not required to request information that only the bank has. You are only required to provide what you know or what is readily available to you. Of course you must provide the names of people that you are aware of, but you are also leaving a big hole in the response.

When you actually answer the questions, read them carefully. You are required to answer the questions. You are not required to expound or go beyond the questions as stated. Answer as briefly as possible. This is not the time to go into story telling mode.

Be as vague as possible without becoming absurd or silly about it. Here some examples:

Set forth what each person known to the party to be a witness to accident will be able to testify to.

You could go off in great detail, and with respect to each witness set forth what they saw or heard, explaining where they were, why they were there, who they talked to, etc., etc., or, you could simply answer...

Mr. Doe is expected to testify as to his observations at the time of the accident.

Both answers are technically acceptable. The first gives them specific information, some of which they might actually not have. The second response, fully compliant with the rules and discovery requirements, gives them absolutely nothing.

Also, be sure to read the introductory comments and definitions that will always accompany discovery requests. For example, if you are in business, those comments and definitions might define "you" as meaning you personally as well as any employees. The problem is that many attorneys have taken this to an absurd level, with "instructions" and "definitions" to a set of interrogatories often being longer that the interrogatories themselves.

In answering interrogatories you can and should make clear that you do not accept their instructions and definitions. Simply state that all interrogatories will be answered to the best of your knowledge at the time responses are generated, that all terms or questions will be interpreted and responded to in their normal and customary usage and sense and that you refuse to accept any obligation to respond other than that set forth in the rules of court.

One point to note in responding to these interrogatories is that the instructions to the interrogatories will often have a provision indicating that they are ongoing, that is, that if additional information becomes available, you are expected to supplement your responses. Ignore these. The rules govern, period! Some jurisdictions provide that discovery responses are deemed ongoing. Conversely, some jurisdictions specifically provide exactly the opposite. Attorneys, as much as they would like to believe otherwise cannot supplement or modify the court rules.

Requesting Documents.

The art of requesting documents is very similar to asking questions in interrogatories. It is a compromise between phrasing the request to include as many things as possible, while at the same time not being vague or so broad that the request is objectionable.

Your objectives here are twofold. First, in the stated spirit of discovery you want to get your hands on as many documents as possible. Second, you want to give the bad guys as little as you possibly can.

In a case that is detail and record oriented, such one having to do with the operation of a business, documents are a not only gold mine, but without them you simply can't win. Use document production requests freely and liberally and take advantage of the benefits.

So here are some thoughts and ideas on requesting documents:

Avoid relying on blanket definitions in your requests. This is as we've said regarding interrogatories a popular practice among attorneys, and if addressed correctly, by and large useless. It may be cumbersome, but our recommendation is to include the definition of what you want and from what sources in each request.

In making the requests, even though it may be wordy, make your request broad enough to include every conceivable document or version of a document that you want. An example would be:

> All documents of any kind in your possession or under your control, pertaining to, arising from or relating directly or indirectly to any conversations, whether in person or by telephone or other electronic media, between "X" and "Y"

occurring at any time
between (date) and (date)
including but not limited to
correspondence, letters,
emails, electronic notations
of any kind, handwritten
notes, diary entries or
written or electronically
stored materials of any kind
whatsoever.

Use multiple requests, just as in the case of an interrogatory to make them specific and less likely to be objectionable or evaded due to lack of specificity being vague or over-broad.

In the foregoing example, assume that we are looking for documents in a case involving confidential business information and are looking for documents that pertain to conversations with officers or employees of a business. Rather than just use a broad request such as "any conversations to or from any employees, officers or directors", we target specific conversations involving specific people. That way the inevitable objections of being too "broad, vague and cumbersome", as well as the "private, confidential (possibly privileged) and beyond the allowable scope of discovery", are avoided. You can always include another general, catchall request, but the specific requests are far more likely to get you what you are looking for.

As with every other kind of discovery, you have to keep it within the scope of discovery that was discussed above. You also have to know your jurisdiction's rules of proportionality and difficulty in terms of obtaining documents. That is, there may be a comparison of the degree of difficulty to the requested party to produce the documents versus from some other source. For example, under the federal rules a court when making decisions on what must be discovered will consider if what is being sought "can be obtained from some other source that is more convenient, less burdensome, or less expensive".

This can be a factor in how you word your discovery requests. Don't ask the other side for example to produce records that you can just as easily get from a public source.

Responding to Requests for Production

The way to respond to requests for production is very similar to answering interrogatories. For each request, a written response should be made indicating if you are responding to the request, or objecting to it. Do not hesitate to object and even if you respond and produce some documents9, be sure to include any objections as discussed below.

---

[9] Most jurisdictions allow you to produce some documents while still objecting, others require you to objection and have he objection ruled on by the court first.

If responding, be careful of how you answer. As with so many things in the litigation process, you will be stuck with your answer.

You would for example never want to simply state that "all requested documents are available for inspection" or something to that effect. To begin with, given that the request you must respond to will be broad and all encompassing, it will never be possible for you to produce everything being asked for. So don't say that you will!

Instead, you might indicate that "all document in your possession and not objectionable, responsive to the request will be made available."

Remember that you normally only have to produce what you have. You do not have to go to other sources to obtain documents. At the same time, realize that there is an element of common sense to this and "what you have" will include what you would normally keep and what you can readily get your hands on. An example of this comes up with regard to bank statements. In this day and age of online banking, many people do not actually keep copies of bank statements. They rely on the fact that the bank keeps they and if needed they are readily accessible. If you are asked to produce copies of your bank statements, an objection or failure to produce them on the grounds that you do not have them will not fly. First, you are the only one that can get them. Second to the extent that you can access your documents online at the bank at any time is tantamount to them being in your possession.

On the other hand, if you are asked to produce a log or record of every entry into your safe deposit box at the bank, you could object or refuse. You do not have ready access. This is a record kept by the bank and under the bank's control.

No matter what, make it clear in your responses that you are producing what you have and what is under your control, and that you have no knowledge of the whereabouts or existence of other documents that may be covered by this request.

To make Copies or Not

Another decision that you have to grapple with is how to produce the documents to the other side. While the discovery request is called something to the effect of Production of Documents for Inspection and Copying, as a practical matter these are often addressed by just making copies and sending them to the requesting party.

There are of course two ways that you can respond. You can make the copies and send them. Or, you can follow the letter of the request and make the documents available in your office or place of business and let the other side come and inspect or copy.

Both options have advantages and disadvantages. Obviously, making the copies is more work for you. It is likewise less work for the other side, thereby reducing the costs to the other side – not one of our favorite things to do. On the other hand, it keeps the other side's attorneys, and possibly even the other party out of your office or place of business. Second, it requires you to at least cursorily go through what you are sending. There might be something in that box that you set in front of them that you really do not want them to see and they really have not requested. While you cannot destroy evidence, you do not have to give them "extras".

Of course if you are agreeable to the other side having access to everything in a group of records you can definitely run up their costs by letting them sort through a box (or several) of bank statements, cancelled checks, receipts, invoices and what have you. In addition to costing you less and them more, this also allows you to argue to a judge, if they accuse you of not complying with the document request, that you gave them free access to inspect and copy everything you had. Finally, it insures that the documents, which may be important, never leave or office or your control.

It's a decision that will vary from case to case. Take your time to think about it. Remember, you normally have thirty days from the time that you receive a request for documents to respond to it. Your response can specify a day even beyond the deadline for them to come to your office or place of business and inspect.

Making Requests to Admit

Requests to admit the authenticity of a document, or to admit the truth of a matter are potentially powerful discovery tools, but just like Interrogatories and Requests for Production, you have to take the time to word them carefully. They can be useful for identifying documents or qualifying copies as well as for potentially narrowing the issues for trial.

Here are some examples:

Admit that the document attached as exhibit "A" is a correct and true copy of the contract executed by "X" and "Y" on or about (enter a date).

If there is some question about where the original contract is, but everybody has copies, this can be a way of avoiding the question later on of whether a copy is correct.

If you are trying to place a party at the scene of an accident, a Request to Admit might be phrased something like:

Admit that on June 3, 2002 at approximately 10:00pm you were operating a 1998 Ford automobile in a northerly direction on U.S. Highway 1 in or near the city of....

If the party will admit this Request to Admit, you have eliminated a lot of other questions and issues. You can move on from the fact that the person was driving on a specific road at a specific time in a specific direction.

Make the requests specific rather than broad. It is easy for a party to deny the request if it is too general and covers too many things. There is usually (there are exceptions) no limits on the number of Requests to Admit that you can propound, so make them more specific rather than a general. Don't be afraid of using several requests, chipping away at any issue rather than one request that attempts to encompass the whole thing.

Responding to Requests to Admit

Of course when you are answering these requests, the caveat is to be very careful. If you admit a request to admit, or even fail to deny it, it is admitted and whatever it stated, you are stuck with for the rest of the case. Cases have been lost for failure to respond to Requests to Admit.

Read the requests carefully and do not assume any hidden or implied meanings. You do not have to admit what you think the other side is getting at if the request is not clearly stated. At the same time, don't be ridiculous about it. Most jurisdictions have provisions in the rules that failure to admit something without cause or justification may expose you to the costs of proving it to be true.

So if you are asked to admit that a copy of a contract is a correct copy of the original, and it clearly is, don't waste everybody's time and effort by denying it.

At the same time if you get a request in a contract dispute to admit that you breached the contract, you would object in that it calls for a legal conclusion and you do not believe it was you who breached. Attorneys will slip stuff like this in, especially if you are unrepresented and they think that they can take advantage of you. If they can get you to admit this issue, or even not respond to the request, they've effectively just won their case.

Some of the things that you need to be careful of are probably much more subtle and require much more thought and consideration. Let's revive the ABC Roofing case and assume that when the roof was not completed, you refused to pay the balance. Let's assume that you get the following Request to Admit:

> Admit that you refused to pay the balance of the amount required by the contract

This request is a veritable minefield. If you admit that you refused to pay the balance due, you have admitted to breaching a term of the contract. All the rules permit you to explain a refusal to admit, or allow you to admit in part and deny in part. The way to handle this Request is to deny it, then go on to explain that because the other party failed to perform, there was no payment amount required by the contract.

This keeps your denial intact. You have not given them the element that you did not make payment. It was never necessary to address that specific point, and you have preserved your position in terms of legitimately not admitting the request.

Taking Depositions - Planning

First, don't be in a rush to take a deposition. Why schedule a deposition if the other side will do it for you? Remember, even when you are not the one who is taking the deposition, as a party you have the right to attend and when it is your turn, to ask any questions you would like. That means you can ask a witness the same questions you would if you had scheduled the deposition.

Even in a case with numerous witnesses, you should at worst, when all is said and done, need to take only a few depositions. Those should be limited to the adverse party, or if your opponent is a company, its key witness, and any witnesses closely aligned with and probably loyal to your opponent. The rest of the depositions, if you respond to their interrogatories properly, you can expect to be taken and largely paid for by the other side.

This is great from your perspective. They set the deposition up, arrange for a place to conduct it, and arrange for the court reporter. Usually they'll even provide donuts and coffee. They will also, since they start the questioning, do most of the work for you. All you have to do is make sure you ask any questions to cover any ground that the other side did not, and to address any testimony they may have elicited from the witness that might be damaging to you. We'll talk more about that later.

Finally, letting the other side schedule a couple of early depositions lets you see what a deposition is, what happens at one, so that you can see how it's done. It will also let you see how the other side's attorney conducts the questioning. This can be a big help for you when your own deposition is taken.

Preparing to take a deposition, or to ask questions at a deposition scheduled by the other side, is very similar to preparing for a trial. Think of it as weaving a story through questions that you ask and answers that you receive.

So the first thing you have to so is to define the "story". What are the issues and where do you need the questions and answers to take you? You start with the goal and work backwards to define the areas of questions that need to be asked to get there. Specifically how you do that depends on the kind of case and the witness whose deposition you are taking. Defining what you expect from a deponent depends of course on the kind of witness they are. Deposing your opponent is going to be entirely different than deposing a witness that has no interest in the case.

The best technique to preparing for a deposition is not necessarily to write out all the questions ahead of time, but to use instead a fairly detailed outline of what information you expect to elicit from the person you are deposing.

By using an outline instead of carefully scripted questions, you retain the flexibility to deviate from your outline into other areas of questioning when the responses of the witness give you that opportunity. The outline gives you a place to pick up when your diversion is completed.

If you are taking the deposition of the other side, you will of course have to deal with the fact that he or she will not be cooperative and, if their attorney possesses the slightest degree of competence, has prepared them for the deposition.

Nonetheless, proceed with an outline of the areas you want to cover, broken down into logical parts. What those parts are will depend on the witness, the kind of case and what you are trying to accomplish with the deposition.

Here are some thoughts on taking and giving depositions.

Taking a Deposition

Once everyone is present, there may be some preliminary discussion. One thing that you need to be aware of is the other side side's attorney may, even though you are not represented attempt to ask you to agree to "the usual stipulations". Since you don't know what these are (and actually quite a few attorneys don't either) your response is no, you're not familiar with the stipulations counsel is referring to and the deposition is being taken in accordance with the applicable court rules.

The next step is for the court reporter to swear the witness. This of course is what distinguished the deposition from a friendly chat around a conference table. The witness is under oath, just as if sitting in a courtroom. The court reporter will then go "on the record" which means that everything that is said from then on, while on the record is recorded and transcribed.

You should begin my introducing yourself. This is true whether you are taking the deposition, or whether someone else is taking it and it is now your turn to ask questions. Nothing fancy is needed here. Just your name and whether you are the plaintiff or defendant, but be sure you get on the record that you are appearing pro se.

If you listen to other depositions you will hear a lot of attorneys blather on about the procedure, and taking breaks, etc. Disregard that silliness and don't try to emulate it. The only thing that you should be sure to get across to the witness on the record is an understanding regarding the questions and answers. Again, nothing fancy. You can just state that you are representing yourself, you are not an attorney, and will be asking some questions. Simply state: "so that there will be no misunderstanding, or later confusion, let me know if you do not understand a question. If you answer a question I

194

will assume that you understood it and that your answer is in response to what I have asked".

The reason this is an important point is that it helps reinforce later, should an issue arise that the witness is bound by their testimony at the deposition and it will be difficult at best to use the excuse that they did not understand the question. Also it helps, especially with a witness opposed to you or your side of the case, from the outset that you are in control of the deposition. Of course if you are being deposed you won't want to agree to this.

A lot of attorneys try to make that sound like a cooperative effort, asking the witness if they can agree to that, of if they think it's fair. There is obscure amateur psychological theory at work in that approach, but it is not necessary. Moreover, most people are smart enough to know that nothing the attorney is suggesting is really in their best interests, reinforcing their inherent and well deserved distrust of attorneys.

You're much better off making it clear that even though you may not be an attorney, you are taking the deposition and are in control. So just tell them the way it's going to be and their agreement or acquiescence is neither needed nor asked for.

Actually Asking Questions.

First you want to get as much general information about the person as you can. Remember, unless it becomes ridiculous, time is not a factor. Ask about the person's occupation, marital status, family members, how long they have lived at their current address. Ask about their educational background and work history.

Ask open ended questions rather than specific. You are likely to get more information. Here is an example of the differences:

In this deposition you are asking questions pertaining to someone's work history.

The version to avoid:

Q. Is it true that you went to work
for XYZ Company in 2003?

A. Yes

Q. How Long were your there?

A. Two years.

All you have gotten the witness to
say is that he worked at XYZ for
two years starting in 2003.

Now try this:

Q. Did you ever work for XYZ Company?

A. Yes

Q. Tell me about it.

You've asked a completely wide open question. The witness may or may not bite. If he's been carefully prepared by his attorney, he will come back with. "I'm not sure I understand your question. What is it you would like to know about my employment at XYZ?"

If that happens, you'll have to ask more specific questions. But chances are pretty good, he'll start rambling on. You can ask him how he found the job, how he liked working there, how his co-workers were. Every broad answer from him gives you more questions to ask. And remember, most people enjoy talking, especially about themselves

The flip side of rambling is that you have to be sure that you get your question answered. Don't be afraid to cut a rambling witness off and require him to answer the questions asked.

Using our "XYZ" company example, an issue may be the reason the witness was terminated from "XYZ". The witness may have been well prepared for the deposition. If you are trying to nail down specifics, question by question, you might find that in response to the question "when did your employment with XYZ corporation end", he starts going off on a diatribe about what a jerk his supervisor was, and how they were unfair and so on. This technique is briefed by attorneys and it essentially lets the witness hijack your deposition to get their own version of the facts across. You do not have to allow this. Let everyone there know you are in control of the deposition. Interrupt this story-telling if it's not what you want and instruct the witness that you want an answer to your question and nothing more. Remind him that if he doesn't understand the question to let you know and you will rephrase it, but make it clear that you are not going to tolerate the story telling.

Your remedy if it persists is to stop the deposition and make a motion to the court for sanctions or a motion to compel the witness to properly answer the questions.

Depositions may go on for a while. That's ok. You have a right to have your questions answered. Use your outline as a checklist and don't quit until you've gotten all the way through everything you wanted to.

Giving a Deposition

Remember that the person taking your deposition is your enemy! No need to whitewash things or immerse ourselves in the fiction that this is part of some noble effort to discern the truth. That's a bunch of nonsense. This is a lawsuit and there will be only one winner. Coming in second is not acceptable. Everything he is trying to accomplish is to your detriment and his advantage. The job of the person taking your deposition is to win the case which means it is to make sure that you lose. Don't lose sight of that at any time. Don't be beguiled or swayed by the apparent pleasantness of the environment. But do indulge freely in the coffee and snacks that law firms always provide in an effort to be civil and appear gracious. Your opponent is paying for them so enjoy. Don't let your guard down because everyone seems relaxed and friendly. They're not. They will pounce on you given a chance.

First, the most important thing to understand is that while you can never win your case at your own deposition, you can certainly lose it!

So here are some techniques and thoughts for the inevitable time when it is you that is sworn and have to answer the questions.

Do not agree to anything.

You do not have to. The rules require you to give a deposition. They require you to answer the questions put to you unless there is a legitimate reason for not answering. They do NOT require you to be pleasant, agreeable, amiable, friendly, or anything of the sort. Basic civility and generally acceptable decorum are all that any judge will ever require.

Make it clear from the outset that you recognize the deposition for what it is, an adversarial environment. There is little advantage to you to agree to anything.

Do not agree to things that you do not understand. An example of this is what was discussed in taking a deposition. You are not required to agree to any "regular or normal stipulations" or to reserve any objections. Let's be real. If they're asking for it, it's to their advantage. Even if it does nothing more than shorten the proceedings, why would you do that? Why make things easy for them?

Set the mood and relationship of the deposition from the start.

The apparent and inevitable pleasantries of attorneys at depositions are a facade. They are intended to convey the impression that the deposition is nothing more than a pleasant conversation around a conference table, intended to get to the bottom of the case. Make it clear from the outset that you're not buying into that line.

One of the best ways to do this is to attack head on the inevitable transparent attempt to get you to agree (and presumably become a participant in the deposition process as opposed to an adversary) to the wording or framing of the questions. This is your chance to fire a shot across their bow right out of the gate. Here's a sample colloquy that will let them know that you recognize the deposition for what it is and recognize their games for what they are. It will set the tone for the rest of the deposition and will almost certainly end the silly little games that lawyers like to play:

> Questioner: (during introductory portion of deposition)   If I ask a question that you do not understand, please ask me to rephrase the question. If you answer a question I will assume that you understood the question. Can we agree to that?

> Your Response: No.

> Plain and simple, you do not have to agree to any such thing!

> Questioner: (who may be a little surprised since everyone always agrees) Excuse me? You don't agree?

> Your Response: That is correct. I am required to be here today and to answer your questions to the best of my ability. I will do so. I do not agree to any assumptions. I do not agree across the board that by answering a question I confirm that I understood it. There is always the possibility that I may misunderstand your questions, and if that proves to be the case, it will have to be dealt with later.

While this may appear to be a little unnecessarily contentious, it is not.

First, you have made it very clear that you are not absolutely locked in by your deposition testimony. You have preserved, if it is legitimate of course, your ability to address any damaging testimony by suggesting that you did not understand the question. If you agree with the questioner as they request, count on having that agreement brought out to your detriment. Why give them ammunition when you are not required to?

But you have done more. You have made clear that you understand the deposition for what it is. You have made clear that you see through their attempts to manipulate you with amateurish psychological ploys. And finally you have made clear that you understand the applicable rules and are well prepared. All in all, a pretty good return for at worst irritating a lawyer whose apparent courtesy and friendliness were a facade to begin with.

By the way, remember in the discussion on taking depositions, I suggested that you make this principle clear when you were the one asking the questions. Remember, I did not suggest that you ask the witness to agree as in the foregoing exchange. That's because the witness was probably prepared for the deposition and told by his attorney to respond exactly as we suggest you do. By making it a statement:

"When I ask a question unless you let me know otherwise I will assume that you understood my question and have answered it."

You don't give them the chance to refuse to agree. You just tell them how it's going to be.

Don't run at the Mouth

People like to talk about themselves and you are not immune. Resist the natural urge to wax eloquent.

Answer the questions as briefly and simply as possible. It is doubtful that a competent questioner will limit questions to those that can be answered "yes" or" no", but when such a question is posed to you, take advantage and stop with the "yes" or "no".

When asked a question that permits an explanation, almost always resist that urge. You can explain later, at trial, but why educate them now to any explanations or additional information that you might have. This is not the time to explain your case or argue your position. They don't care and it will not sway them. It will only provide them with the advantage of more information that they may not have had.

Answer the question that is asked

This is along the same lines as "Don't run at the mouth". Listen to the question. Take your time. When the deposition is transcribed, at no point will the transcription read: "deponent pondered the question for thirty seconds". It will read "Question:", "Answer:"

So don't feel compelled to try to answer a question as quickly as possible. Remember, you're stuck with the answer when you do give it, forever. Be sure it's the answer you want to give. Answer the question that was asked and no more. If you're not sure about the question, ask that it be repeated. If a question can be answered with a long answer or a short answer, the short answer is almost always better.

Do not Guess.

For some reason people in a deposition environment begin to believe that they are obligated to provide answers to questions. This has to do in part with the psychological gambits employed by the questioner setting the stage to appear as in control. We are raised and imbued with a tendency to want to please those we perceive to be in authority. It's a subconscious thing. A skilful questioner will go to great lengths to establish himself as an authority figure and ingrained behavior will make you want to "please" him by giving favorable answers to questions. Recognizing this makes it easy to resist.

Another part of it is that being knowledgeable equates with prestige and authority. We get a good feeling when we can provide information to people and answer their questions.

A deposition is not the place to give rein to those human foibles.

To put it as simply as we can, if you don't know, for sure, don't guess. Probably is not good enough. Most likely doesn't cut it. If you know for sure, answer the question. If you do not know for sure simply state that you do not know.

Just as important, do not allow yourself to be pressured into guessing. If a question is asked that you do not know the answer to and so state, the questioner will usually ask you to give your best estimate. Decline. Just tell them bluntly that you refuse to speculate.

Remember, your deposition is being recorded. You will be stuck with your answers. It is far easier, and is far less damaging to your credibility, to have to deal with not knowing the answer to a question than having to somehow correct a wrong answer.

Remember too that part of a deposition is a fishing expedition. Questions are asked in the hopes that they will lead to other questions and information.

"I don't know" is pretty much a dead end of, while answers like, "I think", or "so and so might know", do nothing but lead to more questions.

Do not be afraid to simply not know the answer to a question.

Be Aware of Questioning Techniques and Games

The other side's goal in taking your deposition is to get as much information as they can from you and to lock in your future testimony to the greatest extent possible. Giving short, direct answers only to questions asked, and stating that you do not know answers to questions that you don't, does not get them very far in their goals. There are techniques that will be used to try to get (for them) better answers. You need to be aware of some of these.

Hypothetical questions. If you have stated that you do not know about something, a questioner technique is to ask you to assume certain things and to answer based on those assumptions. The way to address this is absurdly simple – don't. Simply state that you refuse to speculate. You are not required under the rules of any jurisdiction to deal in "what ifs" and "maybes". You are not required to, so don't. Simply make it clear when these questions are asked that you are neither required, nor inclined to speculate.

Narrowing Questions. When you are asked a question that calls for a date or quantity and answer that you cannot recall, the technique that will be used is to narrow the possible range of responses. The defense to this is to stop the narrowing at a point that is still meaningless. You can't

206

stop it entirely. There will always be a range into which you will have to admit that the answer lies. Every time you answer that you do not know, the range is expanded until not admitting the correct answer to be within a range is absurd and abusive.

The way to respond is to admit to the obvious ranges, but to fail to recollect when it gets to a meaningfully specific level.

For example, assume you are being asked for the number of people attending a party.

> Q.   How many people were at the party?

> A.   I do not recall.

> Q.   Do you have an estimate, a range?

> A.   I'm not going to speculate, I don't remember how many people were there.

> Q.   Well it was more than one correct?

> A.   It was more than one.

> Q.   Was it more than a hundred?

> A.   No, not likely that there were a hundred people there.

Q.   So we can agree that it was more than one but fewer than a hundred right?

Here's where you just slam the door on what you know will be a series of questions narrowing the range.

A.   Sir, the number of people could have been in a very broad range. People were talking, moving from room to room, some were outside at times. It could have been any number of people — twenty, thirty, fifty -- I just do not recall and I'm not going to speculate.

If he continues now to ask questions attempting to narrow the range, simply repeat that you refuse to speculate. He will quickly realize that you are not going to be drawn into the game.

General Speculative Questions. Since one of the purposes of a deposition is to gain information, do not be surprised if you are asked vague questions about other people and their actions or motivations. Many people are drawn into this gambit if they perceive that the information they can give will help their case or vindicate them.

A glaring example: you are in a contract dispute case where the other side refused to pay you money owed. Their attorney is questioning you:

208

Q.   You allege in your complaint that my client, Mr. Tightwad owes you $10,000 and refuses to pay you, is that correct?

A.   (Assuming that that is what your complaint says) yes that is correct.

Q.   Have you asked him for payment?

A.   Yes (resist the temptation to go into details here just answer the question)

Q.   Has he refused to pay you?

A.   He has not paid me.

Q.   Why do you think that he has refused to pay you?

Stop! How tempting it is at this point to launch into all the reasons why Mr. Tightwad is an SOB and a cheat and a crook! This is your chance to be heard right?

Wrong!

Don't forget, you cannot win your case at a deposition. If Mr. Tightwad was going to pay you, he would have already done it. Whatever you say at the deposition won't change his mind. So what is the correct answer to this question? Simple:

A: I do not know and I decline to speculate as to Mr. Tightwad's reasons for doing or not doing anything.

The door to a multitude of possible subsequent questions has been slammed shut. You have made it clear that you are not going down that road.

Finally, there may come a time when for a variety of reasons a deposition should not continue. Though it happens only rarely, a questioner may become abusive or threatening. They may persist in asking you questions that you feel are inappropriate or beyond the scope of discovery. The deposition may be going on far too long. If any of these things happen, you have a remedy. Simply tell the questioner that you are terminating the deposition so that you can move for a protective order. Ask the court reporter for an expedited a copy of the transcript because you will need it when your motion is heard by the judge.

Objecting to Discovery

Just because you have been served with interrogatories, requests to admit or requests to produce, does not mean that you have to answer every question, admit to everything, or produce every document.   Attorneys routinely ask for far more in terms of discovery than they are entitled or, or in fact realistically hope to receive. This does not mean you have to provide any information or documents beyond what is legally required.

If an interrogatory or a request for production exceeds the scope of discovery, really is overly broad or burdensome, or requests information that you should not have to divulge, such as privileged material, you should object. There are two ways to handle this: objections to specific discovery requests, or a motion for protective order.

The way to address these issues through objections to the discovery requests is spelled out in the rules. Normally they state that every interrogatory or request to produce must be responded to or objected to. This is more important than it sounds because as with so many things in legal proceedings, an objection not made is waived. That would leave you later in the event of a discovery dispute with nothing to resolve but whether you had responded completely or not. Not a good place to be if they have requested information that you neither want, nor should be required to divulge.

There are numerous potential objections to discovery, but among the most common are that the request is too vague, broad or burdensome, that it exceeds the scope of allowable discovery or that it requires the production of private, personal or confidential information not related to the litigation and intended only to harass, embarrass or unduly burden you. There is another objection and that is that the information requested is equally available to the party requesting it. The federal rules and many state rules of civil procedure specifically make this "proportionality" a basis for determining whether discovery is appropriate. If there is a discovery dispute that results in a hearing, a judge is far less likely to order you to produce something if it is obvious that the requesting party could just as easily get it elsewhere.

This will also serve as your introduction to the concept of a privacy/privilege log. To excuse you from producing documents which you deem private, confidential or privileged, the courts will often require that you provide a basis for the privilege, setting forth a description of what you are trying to protect, what kind of privilege (attorney-client, doctor-patient, etc). Where there are numerous specific documents that may be subject to such a privilege, this is usually done by producing this information in a list form, often referred to as a privilege log. Courts always lean toward allowing full discovery, but at the same time, there are many instances in which they will not allow invasion of privacy or the use of discovery for purposes unrelated to the litigation.

A privacy or privilege log can be done on a spreadsheet, or similar document. Simply list the documents, either individually or by group that you do not want to produce with a brief explanation of why. Also helpful to getting any documents excluded is if you can show along with the description, that they information they are seeking to obtain from the documents, is easily available from other sources.

To illustrate how and when to object let's look at just one hypothetical request to produce and possible responses.

The case is one involving real estate and you receive the following request to produce:

> Produce all deeds (or copies) of deeds whereby you obtained or acquired any interest of any kind in real property.

First, this request is objectionable in that it is overly broad and vague, it is beyond the scope of discovery and the documents requested are readily available for the deed recording agency in your jurisdiction.

So the first thing you would do is refuse to produce any documents at all in response, instead objecting to the request for those reasons.

Later, if the other side narrowed it down to a more specific time period and properties relevant to the lawsuit, you would still object on the grounds that they can trot down to the courthouse and get copies.

Finally, if you have one or two deeds, you would respond by saying that you are providing documents that are in your possession but are without knowledge as to the existence of any other deeds or documents that may be encompassed by the request but not in your possession or immediately available to you.

If a requested document is subject to a privilege you can assert that privilege, but remember that you will be required to identify the document and state how and why it is privileged.

What you would NEVER do is respond by saying that you are providing the deeds requested. First, you have no way of knowing how many deeds are out there. Second if there are deeds and you are not providing copies (because you don't have them) you are putting yourself into a bind.

Bottom line is that you need to read the requests carefully and thoroughly think through your responses.

Another Technique – Motion for Protective Order

The federal rules and the civil procedure rules of all states make provision for a court to limit the extent or nature of discovery on a case-by-case basis. In the Federal Rules of Civil Procedure this is found as part of rule 26. States organize their rules differently, and some even refer to it differently. The point is though that there is always a remedy, if the discovery is too intrusive, too burdensome, or simply irrelevant, for you to go before a judge and ask that the discovery be limited, or that you not be required to provide specific information or documents. The procedure is to move for a protective order. Moving for a protective order is also appropriate where there is an issue concerning a deposition.

If you are objecting to producing documents, or even from answering interrogatories that are too invasive or touch on areas well beyond the litigation you are in, it is almost always best to file a motion for a protective order rather than simply not respond or refuse to answer specific questions. Merely objecting or refusing to produce the documents, answer interrogatories or answering questions at a deposition will only give rise to the other side filing a motion to compel, which will put you on the defensive.

By filing for a protective order you are taking the initiative and sending a message to the judge. You are making it clear that this is not a question of you simply not wanting to cooperate in the discovery process, but is instead, your good faith effort to produce what is requested, but limited by overly broad, invasive and irrelevant requests.

Again, you are far more likely to prevail on such a motion if you properly prepare by having a privilege/privacy log ready before being asked to create one, and if you can show that the requested documents are not really necessary because they either have little to do with the case or the information asked for can be obtained in another way.

The court may grant your motion in whole or in part, or it may grant some qualified relief. For example, if you are objecting in a business dispute from producing your customer list, knowing that the other side could use it to steal your customers, a court may order that it be produced, but used only by the attorneys and not shown to your opponent. There are all sorts of possible variations, but the key is not to simply refuse to produce documents. The result at a motion to compel will be an unsympathetic judge and the likelihood that you'll be required to produce a great deal of materials that might have been protected.

Third Party Discovery

All the discovery discussed so far has addressed information and material in the possession or under the control of the other side. In addition to getting information from the other side it may be necessary to obtain information from third parties – that is, people or companies that are not involved in the lawsuit.

Obviously, if the person with the knowledge or documents you want is friendly, or will cooperate, then all you have to do is ask. If you want to take their deposition, just discuss it with them and ask them to appear at the designated time and place. More often than not though, either the person you are wanting testimony, documents or other evidence from will not be quite so cooperative, and may in fact be hostile, that is aligned with the other side.

The way to address that issue is with the use of a subpoena. A subpoena is an order, issued by the court requiring a person or company to appear at a certain place or time and give testimony. It can be directed to a named person, or, if to a corporation or other business entity, can require that entity to designate a person who will appear and give testimony. There is also a document known as a subpoena duces tecum. This document requires the person or company to produce documents or other physical evidence.

So to be clear, there are two separate forms. One the subpoena commands the presence of the person or representative. The other, the subpoena duces tecum commands the presence of documents or physical evidence. To be sure, the two can be used together. A person may be issued a subpoena requiring them to appear for a deposition and at the same time, be served with a subpoena requiring them to bring with the certain documents or other items.

There is a variation of the subpoena duces tecum and that is requesting the recipient to produce the requested documents by mail, or simply having them delivered to a certain place. The distinction is that the person actually receiving the subpoena is not required to actually be at the designated location. As long as the requested documents are there, even if by mail, the subpoena has been complied with.

The form of the subpoena varies from jurisdiction to jurisdiction. Some courts have printed subpoena forms that must be used. In others you simply type the subpoena language on a regular pleading, bearing the caption of the case and titling it subpoena or subpoena duces tecum.

Issuing the subpoena requires you to go to the clerk of court and have it issued by the clerk who will countersign the subpoena. Before you issue the subpoena, it is critical that you review the rules for your jurisdiction.

Some jurisdictions require that before you can issue a subpoena duces tecum (for production of documents) that a copy be served on the other side. Pennsylvania is an example. In Pennsylvania you cannot issue a subpoena duces tecum without serving a copy on the other side with a notice of intent to issue subpoena. The other side must, if it is going to, object within a defined time limit. If there are no objections you must file a certificate with the court to that effect but are then free to issue and serve the subpoena. If there are objections, the court will schedule a hearing.

Once issued, you are generally responsible for seeing that the subpoena is served upon the recipient. If for some reason it becomes necessary for the subpoena to be enforced, you will not be able to do so unless you can show the court proof that the subpoena was properly served upon the recipient.

How the subpoena must be served is defined by the rules of your jurisdiction. Some allow for service by mail. Others require that the recipient be personally served.

Finally, again, checking the rules carefully, it is often a requirement that the subpoena be accompanied by a check for payment to the recipient of specified witness fees. The rules of civil procedure in your jurisdiction will specify how much, and when any witness fees need to be paid.

The Trial of The Case

Finally!!

You've diligently done all the research. You've carefully drafted your pleadings. You've gone through the discovery and you've dealt with motions. You finally get the letter in the mail from the Clerk of Court. Your case is set for trial.

Suddenly it hits you that this is real. All the months of work on the case, all the hours spent are finally coming to the point of decision. Your case is going to be resolved, either by a judge or a jury!

Before you get all flustered, relax! If you've done everything properly, if you've put together your case in an orderly fashion and laid it out as a story, the trial of the case is nothing more than sharing your story with the judge or the jury.

True there are rules about how you tell the story. There are rules about what can be in your story and what must be left out. But there's nothing insurmountable there. Nothing you can research and learn so that you can tell your story as it should be told.

That's what this section is about. For the sake of clarity this is presented from the perspective that you are the plaintiff. Obviously if you're the defendant, just switch things around. The principles apply equally.

What Kind of Trial

In the beginning of the planning section the issue of the option for a jury trial was touched upon. As the trial date approaches it is time to revisit that issue. This is one of the first things you should do in terms of trial preparation because there are differences in the way a case is presented to a jury as compared to a judge.

All jurisdictions have some provision for a trial of cases by jury but not all cases end up in front of a jury.

Whether a case is tried before a jury, or just a judge, depends on the kind of case, on the laws of the local jurisdiction, and on the court rules. You will need to research the law in your jurisdiction and specifically for your case to determine whether it can be tried by jury. The law is very complicated on this issue to the point that in some cases certain issues in the same trial can be submitted to a jury, while others are decided by the judge.

Once you've determined that a jury trial is an option, and that you haven't inadvertently waived a jury trial early on, you need to make a decision as to whether you even want a jury trial.

You can still waive a jury trial if the other side agrees. The right to a trial by jury belongs to both sides. You as the plaintiff for example cannot waive the defendant's right to trial by jury, and vice versa.

This determination is far from automatic. There are certain kinds of cases that lend themselves well to being resolved by a jury. Cases in this category are personal injury cases as well as other negligence claims. Another great class of cases for jury trials is essentially any case where the plaintiff is an individual and the defendant is a large corporation. Juries almost universally will favor the underdog against the perceived mighty, impersonal corporation. A jury is far more likely to be swayed by emotional appeals and more likely to be able to relate to subjective issues like pain and suffering than is a judge. Let's face it; judges have heard hundreds of these cases. They are human too and tend to take in stride things that might inflame a jury to be extra generous.

On the other hand, there are certain things that juries are not well suited to. If a case revolves around a lot of legal issues, or highly technical issues, you are often far better off having a decision from a judge without a jury.

How to make this determination depends on a number of factors. There are resources available that will give you a statistical breakdown of the verdicts that juries in your jurisdiction have returned as compared to other areas or even nationally. A review of these resources clearly demonstrates that juries in different areas tend to be more conservative or liberal than in others. A very general rule of thumb is that juries in predominantly conservative areas will be less likely to be generous in awards than juries in areas with a larger liberal population and orientation. Translated, you are far more likely to receive a generous jury award in a place like Los Angeles than you are in a small rural community in the middle of the Bible belt. Obviously, this is not etched in stone and there are exceptions, but across the board, this sort of analysis will help you decide if you want a jury or not.

If you are thinking about going with just a judge, many jurisdictions now have online filing systems that will let you retrieve decisions, sometimes even broken down by similar cases of the judge you are dealing with. This information will show if the judge is conservative or liberal, generous or stingy. Likewise, research the background of the judge. Many judges, especially in the federal system served as prosecuting attorneys. These are usually very conservative and have a strong mental bent, from years of dealing with criminal cases, that there is right or wrong, black or white and not much gray in between. Likewise, if you're the plaintiff, you do not want your car accident case tried by a judge that worked for years as an insurance company attorney before becoming a judge.

Of course these are generalizations and you need to do your own research into the way things are in your jurisdiction.

Trial Preparation

If the trial of a case is the telling of a story, then the complaint is the table of contents. Consequently, that is where the preparation for the trial begins. And something that is very important to understand is that this trial preparation does not begin when you get that letter from the clerk's office giving you the trial date. This preparation begins the day you decide that you are going to litigate a civil case.

This is a possibly fatal error that many people, including attorneys, often make. Because court dockets are crowded and it can take a year or two from date of filing to date of trial, they view the trial of the case as some distant, far off thing to be worried about later. Many attorneys settle into smug assurance that the case will never get to trial because it will be settled along the way.

This kind of reasoning and procrastination is exactly what you don't want to do. As the case progresses, every pleading that you prepare or respond to, every interrogatory you ask or answer and every question at every deposition must be in the context of getting the case ready for trial. You should always be asking yourself the question "how will this affect the trial of the case?"

So often people do not begin trying to get ready for trial until the case is looming on the trial docket, then they scramble. They try at the last minute to get organized, to find witnesses, to gather up documents. This is nothing but a train wreck in the making. Don't allow it to happen to you. With the proper groundwork along the way, trial preparation is nothing more than bringing out and putting the final touches on what has already been done.

In undertaking this preparation hopefully throughout the case, follow the table of contents. The complaint.

If you are the plaintiff, you need to work through your allegations to see what you will have to prove at trial.

The section on pleadings and court papers told you about causes of action and essential elements. Well, here's where the pedal hits the metal! You prove through evidence and testimony those allegations.

The difference between the pleading stage and the trial stage of a case is that in the pleading stage you state those allegations. At the trial stage, you prove them. You enter into evidence the proof to support the allegations. Trial preparation is organizing the way in which you will do that. In preparing for trial you will weave together what needs to be proven and how you will prove it.

What needs to be proven is determined by the pleadings in the case and the discovery that you've suffered through for months.

While it sounds complicated, it really is not. Think of your story and your table of contents. What things do you have to prove? What has been admitted or denied? What has been established during discovery? What remains to be proven? How do you prove it?

Let's take a simple breach of contract case as an example of how to lay this out. The elements of the cause of action in your complaint are the roadmap.

The elements of a breach of contract are a contract, including all the elements of a contract, a breach, and damages to the plaintiff.

There is potentially a lot to prove to establish a case – or perhaps, not so much. Think about it.

The first element is that there was a contract and to establish that all of the elements of a contract must be shown. Those include an offer, acceptance, consideration, lawful purpose and so forth. It can get quite technical. In the real world though, where contracts are a part of life, the existence of the contract will probably not even be in dispute.

How do you determine that? Go back to the roadmap, and the response and the discovery.

In the complaint you will have alleged that the plaintiff and defendant entered into a written contract. What did the defendant have to say about that in the answer? If they admitted that yes, a contract existed, move on. You've got the first element and the issue of whether a contract was formed has been resolved. Move on to element two.

On the other hand, if in the answer they denied that a contract had been entered into, you will in discovery have established that a written contract existed, will have gotten the defendant to admit that they signed it, and will have elicited from the defendant the basis for denying the contract, or in the alternative an admission that a contract really did exist.

Think of it is a checklist, where you have to make sure that each item is completed. It is not necessary that you complete each item – just that it is completed. If the defendant admits in the answer that there was a contract, you haven't done it yourself, but it has been done for you. You can check off a major check-box and probably a bunch of "sub" check-boxes in one batch!

If you are the defendant you will need to have formed your theory of how to address the allegations of the complaint. Again, if this is a contract case, was there a contract? If yes, move on. If you signed a contract and didn't have a gun to your head, don't waste time and make yourself look stupid by suggesting otherwise. Focus on the things that matter and that will probably be who did what to breach the contract and why.

Once you have identified what you need to prove the next step is to determine how to do it. Ideally as you've worked your way through the "checklist" you will end up with an outline of what you need to show the jury, or the judge by way of proof.

Here is where you will lay out the witnesses or evidence that will establish what is required.

Remember our ABC Roofing case? The roof never got installed and you did not make final payment. What do you need to prove? Primarily that you paid the initial payment and that the roof was never completed. What things would you get together to prove those elements?

Go back to the checklist. The contract has been admitted. You've got your copy of the ABC Roofing contract and ABC Roofing has admitted in its answer that there was a contract. The next item on your checklist is the breach of that contract. Your checklist should show, in order to prove a breach, what was required versus what happened. That is after all what a breach is.

In this case the contract required you to pay a certain amount of money and for ABC Roofing to install a roof of certain specifications. The contract provided for payment of an initial amount, followed by the balance at various points of work progress.

To prove the breach In this case you would demonstrate that the roof was never installed. How to do that? Easy. Put yourselves in the mind of a judge or a jury sitting in a sterile courtroom. What would it take to make them understand that the roof was not completed?

You could enter into evidence time sheets that you obtained from ABC Roofing in discovery showing the last day that they worked on your project. You could then subpoena the workers that worked on the roof and make them admit that on the last day they were on your job site the roof was not completed.

You could ask your neighbor to testify about the condition of the roof, the fact that workers were present for a while, but then never returned and she has not seen anyone working on the roof since a certain date.

At the same time, bear in mind that witness testimony is not always the best way to get the jury to see things your way. For some reason lawyers are hung up on putting witnesses on the stand and working through hours of direct and cross examination.

If you are trying to prove that the roof was defective, close up photographs of the roof showing the shingles curling up are great. Better yet, bring in a shingle to show the jury. Don't ever forget that human beings are very much visual creatures. We believe what we can see. Touching, smelling, even hearing are of course strong senses. But there is reason that people cling to old adages like "a picture is worth 1000 words", or "seeing is believing". You can put a dozen witnesses on the stand to testify about the appearance of the roof, or you can put two or three good pictures along with a curled up shingle into evidence. Which will have the greatest impact on the jury?

Without going into excessive detail, this should give you an idea of how to organize this material, and it should underscore the point that this preparation begins on day one.

If you haven't defined what you will need to prove at trial, how could you possibly know what questions to ask of people in depositions? Or what interrogatories to set forth? OR what documents to request?

The way to organize and prepare for a trial is to start preparing at the beginning, but use as your goal the end. That is when all the shouting is over, all the motions made and testimony given, what do you want to have in the minds of the jury, or the judge? That goal is what you should be working toward from day one.

Staying ahead of things will leave you much better organized in other aspects as well. For example, by setting all of this out ahead of time you will know what witnesses you will need to subpoena and which ones will show up voluntarily. Getting witnesses to the courtroom is your responsibility. If a witness is not going to appear voluntarily it is your responsibility to be sure that a subpoena is issued and served upon that witness in plenty of time to appear.

The Trial Begins

The big day has come. You've gone through all of your notes

The trial of a civil case is a choreographed presentation of law and evidence. The extent of the choreography varies to some degree from a case before a judge only, to a case before a jury, but in both cases, there is a process and protocol that you must follow.

While there will of course be minor differences from court to court, the general outline of the process is as follows:

1. The case is called. This officially puts the matter before the court.

2. The judge will ask both parties if they are ready and ask parties to enter their appearances. If the other side is represented by an attorney you will hear him state his name, the name of his firm and who he is representing. You will just identify yourself by name, indicate whether you are the plaintiff or defendant and say that you are appearing pro se.

3. The judge will ask if there are any preliminary matters, such as motions, requests for a postponement or factors that may delay the case either at the beginning or as it progresses.

4. If the trial is by jury, the jury is selected. This is discussed in a little more detail below,

5. The judge will instruct the jury on procedural matters.

6. Opening statements will be made by both sides

7. Plaintiff will present its case by witness testimony and evidence.

8. Following plaintiff's case court will consider motions. Typically a motion to dismiss or motion for non-suit will be made by the defendant.

9. The defendant will present its case.

10. Following presentation of the defendant's case the court will consider motions. Plaintiff may make a motion for a directed verdict arguing that the case does not have to go to the jury at all.

11. The plaintiff will usually be allowed to reply.

12. Final motions will be heard by the court, typically the defendant will renew its motion to dismiss and for non-suit.

13. Both sides will make closing arguments to the jury

14. The judge will charge or instruct the jury

15. The jury will return a verdict

16. The losing side will make a motion for judgment notwithstanding the verdict of the jury.

Obviously, where the case is tried before a judge without a jury, the parts referring to the jury are not applicable. Also, while a judge will almost always allow opening statements, for this is where the parties outline their cases, they often will not want closing arguments, taking the position that they understand the law and the facts and do not need to hear the arguments.

Some of these steps are pretty obvious. Some merit a little more explanation. Here are some more things you need to know, or be thinking about.

Preliminary Matters

At the beginning of the trial, once the case is called, the judge will ask if there are any preliminary matters. As this point what is being referred to are any of the following:

- unresolved motions

- motions that need to be made such as motions in limine

- any logistical issues, such as a witness having travel or scheduling problems, the need to take the testimony of a witness out of turn for some reason, any physical limitations of any witness, such as the need for an interpret and so forth.

The point here is to resolve all outstanding issues that would impact or impede the trial and to let the court know of any anticipated problems or issues that might have to be dealt with.

Jury Selection

When you try a case with a jury, there will always be some mechanism for jury selection that provides for some participation by you.

The process is divided into two phases. Information and research before trial, and the actual selection process at the trial of the case.

Potential jurors are selected from a pool, always by some sort of random selection method. The pool can be registered voters, holders of drivers' licenses or state issued identification cards, or some other grouping that is designed to include as many qualified individuals as possible. Usually, as part of the final stages of getting the case to trial a list of potential jurors will be available. This list will in one form or another, be available to you. If you do not receive it as part of the trial notification process, ask the clerk about it.

Some jurisdictions make two lists available. One with the bare minimum of information at no cost, and another, with more information about each juror, available at some modest cost. It is important that you get this list as soon as it is available, and if affordable and available in your jurisdiction, the more detailed list.

Now you have the list what to do with it? Jury lists will contain varying amounts of information, depending on your jurisdiction, but should always give you some idea of who the juror is. They will contain things like name, address, gender, age, occupation and marital status. Now is the time for you to do as much research as you can, given the time available, the amount in controversy in your case, the kind of case and the size of the jury list. Bear in mind that if there is a substantial amount of money involved in a lawsuit, the other side will be doing the same thing. There are even companies out there that do nothing but jury research to the extent that if the case is important enough, they will provide a complete background check on each juror.

Fortunately in the age of the internet, it is fairly easy for you to get a decent picture of the potential jurors without spending a fortune or making a career out of it.

The problem at this stage is that all you have is a list of prospective jurors. You know that your jury will be selected from this list, but of course you have no way of knowing which twelve (or other number) will actually be selected. The objective here is to glean as much information as you can about all the people in the pool. The more information you have, the better off you will be when it comes time to actually select the jury.

At the trial of the case, the actual selection process occurs. This process varies tremendously from jurisdiction to jurisdiction. Almost all jurisdictions provide for some random selection of the requisite number of jurors from a selected jury pool. But from here the process can vary and it will be up to you to learn the procedures in your jurisdiction.

Generally though the jury you end up with will be what is left from a jury pool after potential jurors are eliminated. In courtroom parlance, jurors are stricken.

Usually each side is allowed a specified number of strikes. That is a potential juror can be stricken by either side without requiring a reason Jurors can also be stricken for cause. If a juror is for one reason or another completely unable to render a fair verdict, a judge can strike a juror for cause. A juror stricken for cause does not require either side to use one of their strikes. An example would be in our ABC Roofing case if in examination of a juror it was revealed that he had been involved in a lawsuit with ABC Roofing. Obviously this juror could not possibly be fair or impartial.

Some states allow for complete voire dire – that is questioning the jurors - while others allow for virtually none, leaving the parties to rely on their own out of court research. In any event, at trial is where you will see the jurors face to face and can make your decision as to which ones you want to determine the outcome of your case.

So what are you looking for when you are in the actual selection process? In a nutshell, you are looking for jurors that will be favorable or at least sympathetic to you and your cause. How that is determined is by and large common sense. It depends on you and the kind of case you are involved in. And here, quite bluntly, political correctness needs to be dispensed with in favor of you getting every advantage you can in the trial of your case. If you doubt for one second that the other side is not doing the same thing, you are being naïve.

Consider two different cases and how you might select jurors from the same jury pool, depending on the case.

Let's assume that your case involves an automobile accident in which you were injured.

Jurors you would want:

Lower income, less advantaged, less educated. These groups are more likely to sympathize with "sticking it to" the fat cat insurance companies.

Jurors you don't want:

Middle to upper middle class, especially retired. These people have attained some degree of financial security and resent anyone they perceive as trying to take advantage of the system. It will be easy for the other side to turn them against you by suggesting somewhere in the trial that you are just a money grubbing opportunist. Also, they will resent payment by an insurance company, knowing that this is what is likely to make their own rates go up.

Different case – same jury pool:

You own a large tract of land that has been damaged by periodic run-off of water from your neighbor's property caused by the fact that he has decided to construct a pond. The case involves testimony by experts in various areas concerning the reasons for run-off, ground contouring and so forth.

Here the potential jurors that you want are exactly the opposite.

The low income, uneducated jury will have no interest or sympathy for the problems of some rich guy with lots of property. The money that you or your neighbor spend on aesthetics related to this issue would probably feed such a juror's family for a year. They will resent both parties and are unlikely to be sympathetic in terms of any kind of verdict. If the issues are at all technical, they are less likely to grasp or even be interested in what the evidence and testimony means.

In such a case you definitely want the educated, middle to upper middle class juror. They understand and appreciate the concept of property rights. They understand and appreciate what it means to work for something over the years, and the need to protect what is yours. They are more likely to understand and pay attention to the technical testimony.

For the most part let common sense prevail. If you're the plaintiff in the ABC Roofing case, you do not want another roofing contractor sitting on the jury. Likewise, your opponent does not want someone sitting on the jury that has been cheated by a building or construction company. If the president of ABC Roofing is in the Glenn Oaks Country Club, you don't want the club pro from that country club sitting on the jury.

Red flags like this can be discovered through your jury research and from questions that you are allowed to ask the potential jurors.

One important note about jury selection. You cannot use your strikes to remove jurors for reasons of race or gender. If there are other legitimate reasons for striking a juror, that is fine, but it cannot be based on race or sex. In our example if the plaintiff was a woman and ABC Roofing used its strikes to remove only women form the jury pool that would be improper.

Opening Statement

This is the actual beginning of the trial. You are in the courtroom. If it is a trial with a jury, the jury has been selected and seated. The judge has instructed the jury on all the necessary details. If you are the plaintiff it is at this point that the judge will turn to you and say, "You may begin"

Assuming that you don't have an anxiety attack, it will be time for you to deliver your opening statement.

Many people, attorneys included let themselves be intimidated by this part of the trial, complete with sweaty palms and nausea. Don't do this. Calm down. And no, it's not an "easier said than done" issue. True, you will have visions of stumbling through your opening statement only to see your opponent stand and give an oratory fitting of Clarence Darrow. That's actually not likely to happen. Attorneys spend a lot of time in law school studying the law and rules, but rarely does anyone ever take them aside and teach them basic public speaking and people skills. They are not likely to do any better than you. The way to handle this is just as if you were going to give a speech at your civic club. Practice it. A sure way to exact retribution on your son or daughter for some transgression is to require them to sit through three or four practice runs of your opening statement. By the time you get into the court room you'll find that it is quite easy. You're simply standing there telling he jury the story you want them to hear. If you approach this properly, with the right mindset, you will do fine.

First, you will have done your research and homework. You will know all about the case and you will have planned carefully how it will unfold. Think of this not as a painful challenge, but as an opportunity to finally tell your story to someone that can do something to put things right. This is what you've been working for and waiting for.

Making an opening statement is no more or less than telling the jury your story. Of course you have to tell it in the context of what you will be able to prove, but it is still telling your story. Obviously the opening statement will be substantially different for a jury than for a judge sitting without a jury. This discussion will focus on what you would say to a jury.

Talk to the jury. Explain to them who you are, why you are here, what the case is about. Remember, these are not lawyers. Within the framework of the rules, the very best way to talk to a jury is as if you were telling someone your story. Many people feel that they are at a disadvantage because they are not attorneys. There are actually times when you can turn that to your advantage and exploit it. The opening statement is one of those.

First, when you begin your opening statement, you introduce yourself. Let them know right up front that you are representing yourself and are not an attorney. Tell them that you will probably make mistake because you unfortunately don't have the education and experience that all those lawyers have, but not to hold it against you.

You're actually accomplishing two things. First, no matter how much you study and research, you will make some mistakes and sooner or later the judge will call you on it. You've just let the jurors know that this will happen, that it's not intentional, and that you're trying the best that you can.

This is important. Psychology is much more important in a trial than most people, including attorneys realize. Jurors relate and respect authority, which in a courtroom is the judge. They will subconsciously resent what they perceive as challenges to that authority. If the judge has to continuously admonish you, if objections from the other side are constantly sustained, the jurors will begin to have negative feelings toward you. By addressing this upfront and letting the jurors know that you are not doing anything wrong intentionally, you minimize this problem.

The other big thing that you are doing is to get the jurors to associate with you as opposed to the other side. You have begun laying the basis for the "us and them" framework with "us" being you, the jurors and all other ordinary people and "them" being "all those lawyers".

Tell them about your house and how it needed a new roof. Explain how you found ABC Roofing and discussed the kind of roof you wanted and how much it was going to cost. Tell them what was promised. Then tell them what happened. Let them understand the case from your perspective.

Your opening statement should take the jury right down the roadmap you have laid out. Tell them what they will hear in the trial and what you will prove. Tell them that they will see the contract and the proof that you paid the initial payment. Let them know that you will show them pictures of the uncompleted roof, and that they will hear from your neighbor who saw it. Explain to them your frustration and irritation at making repeated calls to ABC Roofing to try to get the roof completed. Tell them about the excuses you received and finally the rude responses. Press home again the "us and them" point whenever you can. A statement such as "everybody (obviously that includes them) gets frustrated and irritated when you (us) try over and over again to talk to these people (them) and are ignored."

Always look for ways to get the people on the jury to associate with you. Any time the other side is a large corporation this is remarkably easy to do, and it is extremely potent. One reason large corporations shun jury trials if they can settle is because they realize that in any dispute between an individual and a company they will never be able to select a jury that does not include at least one person that has had a similar adverse experience with a large company.

Finally, tell them what you want. Make it clear that you're not after a windfall. You're not out to make a profit. You just want what you paid for, what is fair. This is important. Most people have an innate sense of fairness. We're brought up that way. It is much easier to get a jury to be sympathetic to you if they perceive that what you are asking for is reasonable... "Come on ABC Roofing, just give me my money back or finish the roof. That's all I'm asking". Conversely, they will resent you if it appears that you are overreaching or trying to get something that you are not entitled to.

An opening statement is your opportunity to get the jury on your side. It is your chance to let them see that they could be in the very situation that you find yourself in. At the same time, don't make outlandish or ridiculous claims, or promise evidence that does not exist. Juries are made up of people and like all people they don't like being misled. Once you lose the trust of the jury, it will probably not be regained.

Witness Testimony

Once the opening statements are completed, it is time for the jury to hear the evidence of the case. Now is when you put up the testimony of witnesses and the documents that will prove the items in your checklist.

One of the primary ways that evidence comes into a case (is admitted) is by witness testimony. One thing to bear in mind is that whatever you may have seen in movies or on TV about courtroom scenes has little to do with reality. The hostile witness never collapses and confesses to all under a blistering cross examination. The mystery witness with the key testimony does not magically appear at the last minute. It just doesn't happen that way.

Here's what will really happen.

Witnesses get facts into evidence by being asked questions and giving answers. How the questions are asked depends how well you've prepared, on the kind of witness and what the witness will or can testify to.

When witnesses are questioned by the party calling them, it's called direct examination. When the other side gets to ask them questions, it's cross examination.

There are exceptions, but for the most part a party puts up a witness and asks them questions, the other side cross examines. The party calling the witness has another opportunity to ask more questions, which is call re-direct, and of course the other side gets the final crack at the witness with re-cross examination.

How questions are asked of a witness, what can be asked and what cannot be asked is unfortunately a rather complex area of the law. The section on evidence introduces you to the basics. You will have to do more research based on the kind of case that you are dealing with. Once it is clear that a case is going to trial, it is very important that you go beyond the brief reference section and study in depth how evidence is presented paying particular attention to the kinds of evidence that you know will be used in your case.

For example, if you are dealing with a case involving an estate, you will have to get into a lot of research on the rules that pertain to hearsay (what someone else told the witness) because sooner or later, whether you ask the questions or the other side did, the issue of whether what a decedent told someone is admissible will come up.

If you are dealing with a case where a lot of documents will be introduced into evidence, you need to study up on the rules that pertain to business records and the particular exceptions to the hearsay rule that pertain to documents.

And remember it is just as important to anticipate what kind of evidence the other side will try to get in and be prepared for that too. You can count on the fact that if the other side is represented by an attorney they will assume that you do not know the rules of evidence and try to slip in otherwise inadmissible evidence. Do not count on the judge to help you if you don't object.

This is part of doing the research and study to represent yourself. If the other side objects to a question that you've asked on the grounds of hearsay, you will get more respect points than you can imagine from them and the judge if you can respond with the applicable exception to the hearsay rule, pointing out why the question is proper.

Likewise, when the first time the attorney on the other side, believing that he is dealing with someone who has no clue as to the rules of evidence, tries to slip something improper in and you object, you will have promptly put an end to that nonsense.

If you are calling a witness, your first questioning will be direct examination. For this discussion let's will assume that you are trying the case in front of a jury. If there is just a judge, some of the principles will be relevant, some relevant but less so, and some not relevant or applicable at all.

Direct examination, or questioning of the witness actually accomplishes several things. First, the order in which you present witnesses often helps define the "story" you are telling the jury. Just as most people reading a book get a feeling for the progression by the way the chapters are organized, so too the order that you present witnesses will in part lay the foundation for your story.

Second, and most obvious, it gets important facts in front of the jury.

Third, more subtle but just as important, it lets the jury get to know your witnesses and you.

Presenting a case to a jury is often as much a psychological drama as it is regurgitation of facts. Juries are made up of people. They are driven by their emotions and prejudices just as everyone else. With a little work, you can garner the jury's sympathy, or at least their empathy. If you get them on your side, the battle is half won!

In putting up your witnesses, you should focus as much on rapport as with facts. If you put up a hostile or rude witness, the jury will remember that he was hostile and rude, and will be less likely to remember what it was he actually said. On the other hand, if you put up a witness with whom the jury can relate, they will be both more likely to remember the testimony and will give it more credence. It's just human nature. If we like someone, we're more likely to believe what they say.

So take your time. There's no rush. Before you ever get to the facts of the case with your questions, introduce the witness to the jury in a way that makes them like him or her. How do you do that? It's not nearly as hard as it sounds.

First, you paint the witness as a person. There is nothing in the rules that requires you to ask the witness only questions directly related to the case. Ask questions that will let the jury know your witness as a person. Where are you from? Where do you work? Are you married? Do you have any children? What do you like to do?

While you are not permitted to ask leading questions – that is questions which suggest the desired answer - you can certainly ask questions that will allow the witness to understand the direction you're going. Just think of it as an interview and ask questions that will lead to the testimony that you are seeking from the witness. In your trial preparation you will have outlined what the testimony should be. No mystery here. Why have you put this person on the stand? What is the purpose of their testimony? What is it you want them to say? Just ask the questions in that direction and build from simple, introductory questions to get to where you want to go.

The kind of witness will have some impact on the way that you phrase your questions. If the witness has a lot of knowledge about something, or is a favorable witness, you can let them go with general questions. If the witness is neutral, or even hostile, you will need to stick to specific questions that can be answered without a lot of explanation or divergence.

To give you an idea of how a witness that is either favorable or at least not hostile would be questioned, here is an example. Let's assume the trial is about an automobile accident, and you have put on the stand an eyewitness.

Q.   Good Afternoon, would you tell the jury your name please.

A.   My name is John Jones

If this is a favorable witness you want the jury to believe give him a little personality.

Q.   Where do you live Mr. Jones?

A.   Right here in town, 1234 Main Street.

Q.   How long have you lived here?

A.   All my life.

Q.   Wow! Born and raised right here

You've just painted your witness as a local guy, not some stranger, and given the jury someone they can relate to. You can continue along this line for a while, getting to marital status, children, any local social or civic groups etc. You've made him a person, not a "witness".

Q.   Now Mr. Jones I want to call your attention to October 31, 2011 at around 3:00 in the afternoon. Do you remember that day?

This is an important question. It sets the stage and the witness confirms his recollection.

Q.   Where were you on the 31st at around 3 in the afternoon?

A.   I was standing on the corner of Main and Elm waiting for the light to change so I could cross Main.

Q.   As you were waiting there did anything happen?

A.   Yes the light changed and this car.....

Here you may want to interrupt the witness. This is allegedly to clarify, but you actually want to drive the point home that he saw what happened and his recollection is clear.

Q.   Excuse me for interrupting Mr. Jones, but I want to make sure that we are clear on this area. When you say the light changed, let's be specific. When you were first waiting, what color was the light for traffic traveling on Main Street?

A.   Main Street had a green light.

Q.   So of course, Elm street would have had a red light is that correct?

This is technically leading, but no one will fault such an obvious statement, you are building momentum with the witness and the jury is gaining confidence in the witness.

A.   Yes sir that's correct.

Q.   Ok, I'm sorry for interrupting you. I just wanted to be sure there was no confusion. Now I think you had started to say that the light changed....

A.   Yes, while I was waiting the light for the Main street traffic changed from green to yellow.

Q.   Then what happened?

A.   Well this green car going down Main Street started to slow down to stop for the light.

Q.   Ok, let me stop you again. Let me show you a picture of a car so that no one gets confused.

Here you would have, through testimony of the car owner, gotten into evidence (we'll talk about that later too) a picture of his car.

Q.   Is this the car that you saw slowing down for the yellow light?

A.   Yes, it appears to be.

Q.   I'll try not to interrupt you anymore. What happened next?

A.   The blue car behind the green car ran into the back of the green car.

As you can see, you've asked general questions, worded in a way that invites the witness to expound. Even the simple questions give the witness leeway. For example, you ask

"Is this the car that you saw slowing down for the yellow light?" This allows the witness to add, or even correct you. For example, he could say "yes, it's the car, but it had already stopped for the light".

Cross examination is different as you will see a bit later. For now though, just by way of example, if you were cross examining that question would have been broken down into several questions, each designed to not give the witness any leeway.

You can go on and develop questions to get him to testify about where the car was when he first saw it, how far the blue car was behind the green car and so forth, but you get the point. Start with easy general questions, again, just as if we were interviewing someone, then move to ask him questions that get him to testify about the facts you want the jury to hear.

With just the brief sample, you've shown the witness to be a longtime local resident, which implies familiarity with the area and at least suggests credibility. You've put him at the accident scene at the time of the accident and established that he had a good vantage point. Finally, you've established that the saw what happened. Just follow this pattern and getting testimony in is easy.

The key is that it doesn't come magically. If you watch experienced attorneys examining witnesses they seem to just make up the questions as they go along, often they don't even have notes with them. You are not an experienced trial attorney able to formulate questions on the fly, so don't try. You can easily compensate for the difference in experience with thorough preparation and guess what? No one on the jury will fault you if you are holding a legal pad with an outline of the questions you want to ask.

The examination of witness will continue with the plaintiff presenting each of their witnesses in turn. After the direct examination the other side will of course have the opportunity to cross examine the witness.

Following cross examination the party that called the witness is allowed to conduct redirect. This is your chance, if the other side has done damage to your witness on cross examination, to try to address that. For example, if they have found something on which your witness' recollection is not as good as it could be, and have tried to paint your witness as having a bad memory, you can go back over the things that he remembers clearly and drive home the fact that in the things that matter, their recollection is quite good. Bear in mind that the redirect is usually limited to issues that the other side brought up on cross examination, so don't view it as an opportunity to go into everything you might have overlooked on direct examination.

Completion of Plaintiff's Case

When you've worked your way through the whole checklist; after you've had all your witnesses testify; and you've introduced into evidence all the documents on your list, it will be time to conclude your case. Instead of calling another witness, you will simply announce to the judge that your case is concluded and plaintiff rests.

At this point expect a motion from the other side. It will either be a motion to dismiss, or a motion for non-suit. It will be very similar to a motion to dismiss that may have been made early in the case with one important difference.

When a court addresses a motion to dismiss early in the case it is limited to the allegations of the complaint. Since there has been no trial and no evidence presented, there is nothing to consider except the complaint itself. Now, the plaintiff has presented all of its evidence. It has fired all of its bullets and everything is before the court.

What the motion to dismiss or motion for non-suit at this point is saying is that there is nothing to submit to the jury. It is saying that resolving any and every factual dispute in favor of the plaintiff, there still is not enough evidence to establish plaintiff's case and it should be dismissed.

First, do not be alarmed. This is not necessarily a reflection on you. These motions are automatic, because generally, if issues that are problematic are not raised by motion to dismiss or motion for non-suit, they are lost as grounds for appeal. So in reality everyone understands that usually these are just necessary steps – hoops to jump through – to protect positions later if needed.

That does not mean to say that you should take these motions lightly because the consequences are potentially disastrous. Unlike a motion to dismiss early in the case where you are told to go and amend your complaint, a motion to dismiss here if granted, is final. You lose!

The way to address such a motion is to have your checklist ready – the one that shows each and every thing that you have to prove in order to prevail. Go down the list and point out to the judge how each and every element has been established, either in the pleadings (remember the "was there a contract issues") or by testimony. Identify the witnesses and remind the judge of what they said that "checked off" one of your boxes.

Fortunately the standard of proof for these motions is extremely high, and judges are very reluctant to grant them, because it opens the door for an appeal, but you do have to be prepared.

After the motion to dismiss is denied, and if you've paid attention to anything that you've read, it will be, it is time for the defense to present their case.

Cross Examination

The defense will commence the same type of process that the plaintiff did. Witnesses will be called, the order dictated by their own outline and plan of the case. The defense will conduct direct examination and the plaintiff will cross examine.

The objective of cross examination is to counter the testimony the witness gave that can hurt you.

Here is an important point. Pay attention to the last four words of that sentence.

"That Can Hurt You"

It is not necessary to cross examine every witness. This is not Perry Mason! If the witness has not said anything that hurts your case, or could be potentially damaging it is perfectly acceptable to respond when the judge turns to you for cross examination and say "I have no questions for the witness your Honor?"

On the other hand, if the witness has hurt your case, it is important that you address the issue. From a technical perspective, if the only evidence on an issue is what the witness has testified to on direct, then that will be what goes to the jury. So damaging testimony must be addressed.

Asking questions on cross examination is entirely different that direct examination. Since the witness has been called by the other side, unless it is just a necessary formality, such as to introduce documents into evidence, it is general true that you can expect the witness to be at least somewhat aligned with the other side.

Skillful cross examination is an art form learned over years and many trials. It requires not only an understanding of the law, but a complete grasp of the facts and good intuition on human nature. Accept that you will not be able to mount a cross examination attack that will reduce a hostile witness to tears and cold sweats. It's not going to happen. You can accomplish what you need to though by being well organized, and by carefully studying the case, including the pleadings as well as the other side's discovery responses. With all the information available and laid out so that you can easily access it, you will be prepared for the witness.

On cross examination your intent is to either discredit the witness entirely, or at least attack parts of his testimony. On cross examination you get to lead the witness, to frame your questions in a way that forces the answer you are looking for.

Once again don't rely on what you've seen on TV. It doesn't work that way. Even with leading and being able to require yes or no answers, it is very hard to get a witness to say something they don't want to say.

With the example given above – the witness to the car accident - the cross examination might be something like this.

> Q.   Mr. Jones had you ever been at the intersection of Main and Elm before the 31st?

A.   Sure I cross that intersection just about every day to go to the bank from my office.

Q.   So there was nothing special about the 31st. Just another day, and you were taking the same path you'd taken many other days.

A.   Yes

Q.   You testified that you were waiting for the light to change isn't that correct?

A.   Yes

Q.   And you testified that you saw the light change?

A.   Yes

Q.   Are you sure? Are you sure you actually saw the light change?

Here you are making him defend his testimony. Watch carefully as you easily put him in a corner.

A.   I'm sure. I know I saw the light change.

Q.   That's because you were looking at it right?

A.   Well sure I saw it change.

Q.   Well Mr. Jones if you were looking at the light, then you weren't looking down the street were you?

He has no choice here. He's already defended his earlier testimony by being adamant that he was looking at the light. If he had testified otherwise, you could have made him admit he wasn't looking at the light and therefore really didn't know when it changed. You've taken what might have been a very harmful airtight witness and at least given the jury pause to wonder what he was actually looking at and what he actually saw.

But more about the difference in the kinds of questioning. Note that in the direct examination the questions are broader, inviting the witness to answer generally, or even expound.

As you were waiting there did anything happen?

This is the question on direct. It allows the witness to answer in several different ways, explaining as much or as little of what happened on that day.

Now look at the kind of question you would ask on cross examination.

"You testified that you were waiting for the light to change isn't that correct?"

A completely different form of question. The witness is given little if any leeway. He either testified that he was waiting for the light to change or he didn't. This sharply limits any opportunity for the witness to expound or go off on a tangent.

With specific, well planned questions, you will be able to at least cast doubt on the witness' testimony that causes you problem.

You won't be able to decimate a witness who has given testimony that you don't like, so don't try. It will only blow up in your face.

There are two bits of wisdom that will serve you well for cross examination:

First, never ask an unfriendly witness a question that you do not already know the answer to. Chances are better than even that you won't like the answer.

Second, know when to quit asking questions. Every judge and most attorneys have seen countless times when an attorney has done a good job of cross-examining a witness, made good progress and instead of quitting, just had to ask that last question that had the devastating answer.

Get what you want and quit. Let's go back to the questions we were just asking for a great example… you've got the witness to admit that when the light changed he was looking at the light and not down the street. This is where to stop. Watch how the next question, the question you just couldn't resist asking kills you.

Q.   So Mr. Jones since you were looking at the light, you didn't really see the two cars just before the accident did you?

Do you know the answer to this question? Of course not so don't ask it!

A.   Oh yes, I saw it clearly. As soon as I looked back down the green car was slowing down, then I turned and saw the blue car and it was obvious that it wasn't going to stop in time. It was way too close to the green car and going too fast!

You would be blown away at how many purportedly experienced attorneys will do exactly this! It's that desire to get in that last little wedge; that last little bit. Don't! Get what you need, be quiet and sit down.

While the apparent ability to get up and cross examine a witness with brutal effect may be an art form learned over many years, you can accomplish what you need to try your case with careful preparation. The key is the preparation. You should have a very good idea of what a witness will say before you ever get him on the witness stand in a courtroom. While it isn't necessary to write down each question ahead of time, you should have prepared a fairly comprehensive outline of the things you want to question the witness on and the kinds of questions you want to ask.

More Motions

Once the defendant has put up all of its witnesses and rests, it is time for the motions again. This time the plaintiff will make a motion for a directed verdict. What this is asking the judge to do is to determine that after all the evidence is in, and even construing all the evidence in favor of the defendant, no reasonable jury could do anything except return a verdict for the plaintiff.

This motion is very similar to the motion to dismiss or motion for non-suit made by the defendant at the end of the plaintiff's case, made for the same reasons, and just as unlikely to be granted. Later, if the jury verdict or decision by the judge is for the defendant, the plaintiff will make a motion for a judgment notwithstanding the verdict. That is it will ask the judge to make a ruling that the verdict of the jury is completely unreasonable and unsupported by any evidence, or that if it was a ruling by the judge, it was incorrect. The plaintiff cannot make such a motion in most jurisdictions unless he has made a motion for directed verdict at the end of the defendant's case.

So what we have on both sides are motions being made that have no real likelihood of being granted, but are necessary in order to preserve possible grounds for appeal later.

Reply

Once the defendant has presented its case, and the requisite motions have been made and ruled upon, the plaintiff has an opportunity to present reply testimony. But, this is limited to materials that the defendant has raised. It is not an opportunity for the plaintiff to re-present its entire case. Witnesses can be called to be questioned just as in the main case, and of course they will be subject to be cross-examined. They can be new witnesses and the major advantage of reply testimony is that witnesses will seldom be excluded because they were not previously identified. Remember that discovery you did for all those months? Remember the questions about who the witnesses might be? There was a reason for that. The other side wanted of course to know what witnesses they would have to contend with, but just as importantly, absent some last minute revelation, a party is not allowed to call witnesses at trial that it has not identified in discovery. Witnesses called on reply are an exception, the theory being that the plaintiff could not know until the defendant's case was presented, what witnesses might be necessary. As the plaintiff, with some careful planning and study of the defendant's case, you can use this opportunity to get into evidence that the defendant has not had an opportunity to prepare for.

Closing Arguments

Once both sides have presented all of their evidence, each side is allowed to address the jury with a closing argument. Obviously if there is no jury, it will be to address the judge and as already pointed out, if there is no jury, the judge may not even allow closing arguments.

263

Closing arguments are where you get a chance to once again tell the jury why they should return a verdict for you, but this time in the context of the evidence presented.

When you made your opening statement you were telling the jury about the case and what you would prove. Now, they've heard all the evidence. If you've done your job and presented all the evidence that you needed, they know all about the case and you can go over what you've proven.

Now is the time to remind them of what you presented. You can summarize the testimony of the witnesses.

> Remember the testimony of Mr. Doe? He was there. He saw what happened. He saw the light change. He saw the green car, my car slowing down for the light as I was supposed to do. He also saw the blue car – the defendant's car - coming down the road and not slowing down.
>
> Now Mr. Doe testified that he is familiar with that intersection. He testified that he has no relationship and does not know either me or the defendant. He would have no reason to lie.

Each favorable witness can be summed up the same way during your closing argument, and you would also take the opportunity to point out any negative things about the defendant's case. If somewhere during the defendant's testimony in the hypothetical car accident case something was said about a call on a cell phone point it out:

> "Why didn't the defendant slow down? Why did the defendant rear-end my car? Probably because he was distracted by his cell phone"

This is your chance to tell the jury all the good things about your case and all the bad things about the other side's case. It's your chance to tell them why you should win and the other side should lose.

Any don't be shy about it for you can rest assured that when their turn comes the other side will have nothing kind to say about you or your case.

Jury Charge

At the end of the case the judge will instruct – charge – the jury. The extent to which you participate in this varies substantially from jurisdiction to jurisdiction and from judge to judge. Make it a point to find out well before the trial if you are allowed to submit proposed charges to the jury.

Charges are instructions on the law and how determinations are to be made, and it is an opportunity to present things in a more favorable way. Judges will almost always have their own sets of jury charges for just about every kind of case they are likely to try, and in some states, there are even published jury charges that must be used. However, some judges will allow each side to submit proposed charges to be used in addition.

If this is the case in your trial, be sure to have prepared ahead of time what you would like the judge to instruct the jury, and the authority for it.

For example, going back to our hypothetical auto accident, one of the things that you would want the judge to tell the jury is that in your state "a driver is responsible for maintaining a distance behind cars in front of them great enough to allow them to stop." Or, "a driver is responsible for not exceeding a speed, given the conditions then prevailing that is safe and prudent."

You would write these on separate sheets of paper and accompany each one with the case law or statute that supported that principle.

Likewise, if the other side is requesting a jury charge that is not supported by legal authority, or is prejudicial, be sure to object to it.

Once the issue of what charges to use has been resolved, the judge will instruct the jury. There is nothing you need to do at this point except to sit quietly, appear to be interest and not look bored.

When this is completed the judge will usually send the jury back to the jury room but instruct them not to begin deliberating. He will then ask both parties if there are any objections to the instructions or any other matters that need to be addressed. Seldom will there be any issues, except possibly one side or the other may ask that the judge clarify a confusing charge.   •

The jury will be instructed to begin deliberations and of course at some point, will return with a verdict.

Post Trial Motions

Just as at the conclusion of the cases of the respective parties, following the publishing of the jury's verdict expect more motions, at least if the verdict has been in your favor.

The other side, again assuming that you are the plaintiff will renew its motion to dismiss and will move for judgment notwithstanding the verdict. This motion basically requests the judge to intervene as the "thirteenth juror" and hold that the verdict of the jury is not supported by any evidence, or that no reasonable jury could have reached such a verdict. This motion can be as to the verdict itself or to the amount of the award if for the plaintiff. Like the other motions in this category, it is rarely granted. It is a brave judge indeed that would tread on the domain of the jury and disregard a verdict.

If such a motion is granted at all, it usually goes to the amount of the award, where sometimes an award is just so generous that it is not supportable, or alternatively, the verdict has been for the plaintiff, but obviously does not include damages that were clearly proven at trial.

Following these motions the trial is over. For good or bad, you've handled your first civil trial!

Contract Lawsuits

One thing that you will quickly learn when you represent yourself is that all lawsuits are the same in some respects, and different in others. While the underlying mechanism is the same, that is the plaintiff makes allegations in a complaint which the defendant must respond to, the things that must be alleged, and the way in which they are responded to, must of course differ depending on the kind of lawsuit.

If a lawsuit arises out of a contract it will usually fall into one of two areas. Either one party will allege that the other breached the contract, or the parties will disagree on the meaning or interpretation of one or more contract terms.

In an ideal world neither of these two lawsuits would ever exist. Contracts would be entered into between parties that honored their obligations, and contracts would be so carefully worded, with every possible contingency foreseen that there would never be a question as to the meaning of any of the terms or conditions of any contract.

Alas, the world is not perfect. People often reconsider the wisdom of their decisions after the fact, such that the term "buyer's remorse" is a common one. No matter how carefully you sit down and try to anticipate in the language of a contract all the possible things that might come up, there will always be something different that comes up.

Given that it is inevitable that there will be litigation concerning contracts, the best alternative is to be prepared and knowledgeable. To prevail in a lawsuit involving a contract you have to understand not only the mechanic's and principles of contract formation, interpretation and enforcement, but of course the elements of the cause of action, and how to establish them as well.

This section will address breach of contract lawsuits from both sides. The issue of interpreting a contract is a declaratory judgment action, is governed by the principles of declaratory judgments and is better discussed in that section.

Breach of Contract – Bringing the Lawsuit

The first kind of contract case to be addressed is the typical breach of contract case. There is (or you believe there is) a contract, and the other side has failed to perform, or, they are accusing you of failing to hold up your end of the bargain. You need to know how to handle this kind of litigation.

So there you are. You are in court in a lawsuit concerning a breach of a contract.

The whole courtroom is quiet. All the preliminary things have been taken care of. The judge looks at you and indicates that you can begin. "Begin" of course means to present your case. The court stenographer looks at you expectantly, fingers poised over the keys of the steno machine. To take a phrase from the sport of baseball, "you're up!"

Of course standing in the courtroom, trying to figure out what to say and how to say it, didn't happen with a snap of the fingers. It took just about the whole litigation process to get to this point. The filing of a complaint and answer, the discovery, the dealing with the various motions that have been filed back and forth – all culminate here.

So let's rewind the tape a bit and see how this developed.

Going back to the section on contracts, recall the discussion about the contract to buy widgets. For those of you that are somewhat confused because you can't figure out what a widget is, relax. A widget is anything. What it is doesn't matter. It is a term used to identify a product in a legal setting, and what it is exactly doesn't matter.

So you have signed a contract to produce ten thousand widgets from a company that makes them. If the term widget bothers you, they could be brackets, bolts, frames or anything else that you in turn might use in your own construction process. Let's say you are in the business of building wagons, and the widgets, or brackets, or whatever, are used to build those wagons.

You've tried to be very careful when you prepared the contract. You even made it point to carefully read and cross through parts of the seller's "purchase order" form that you didn't like.

Things started out just fine. The first few shipments of widgets arrived as agreed, and you used them to manufacture wagons which you sold to a large department store. Then the phone rings, the widget supplier can't make any more deliveries. One of their suppliers has gone out of business and until they can find a replacement, no more widgets.

You are faced with a major problem. You have workers standing around doing nothing. You have the department store calling because no wagons have been shipped. You have a warehouse full of all the parts you need to make wagons, except widgets.

As the law requires you to do (mitigate your damages) you get on the phone and try to find widgets. Finally, someone will sell you widgets, but at a much higher price, and because they are located much farther away, shipping costs are higher. You order the widgets.

Finally, production with the new widgets starts again and you are able to make and delver wagons. But you have lost a lot in the process. You call the original seller and try to work things out. You explain to him that you and he had a contract for widgets which he failed to produce and that as a result, you've lost production and sales, and were forced to pay a higher price for the widgets. He is not impressed. He points out that the problem is not his fault.

272

He was trying to perform and deliver the widgets and he could not help it if his supplier went out of business.

You have a contract dispute.

The first thing to do is to logically consider and weigh your options. America is a litigious society. The term "sue the bastards" did not materialize out of thin air. Americans file more lawsuits per person and spend more time in court, per person than any other country on the planet. Don't fall into the trap. Litigation is expensive in every respect. Even when you represent yourself it costs money. It is time consuming, and it is incredibly stressful. It is not by coincidence that lawyers enjoy one of the highest suicide rates by profession, in the country. So before you go rushing down to the courthouse, suit papers in hand, think about it and consider options.

One thing that you need to understand before you take any legal action is what a court can and cannot do for you. Generally a court can, if you establish your claim, award a judgment that requires payment by the defendant of your damages. What it cannot do, with rare exception is issue an order requiring a defendant to perform obligations under a contract. So for example, while a court may give you a money judgment for losses experienced as a result of the defendant failing to deliver widgets, it generally cannot issue an order requiring the defendant to actually deliver them.

If you've decided, after trying to work something out with the widget maker that you have no reasonable alternative but to file a lawsuit, your next step was probably to an attorney. In all likelihood they told you that you had an excellent case, but declined to take it on a contingent, or percentage fee basis. The initial retainer they wanted was $10,000, and you were told that you could expect the litigation to cost you in the range of $50,000 (the average cost of litigating a civil case in 2009). Even the hope that your opponent may be required to pay your attorney's fees was dashed. The attorney explained that they would be liable for fees only if you prevailed, and even then, a judgment may or may not be collectible.

Not the news you were expecting to hear.

After exploring options, talking to your opponent, and talking to an attorney you realize that the widget maker has no interest in talking about resolving the problem. If you are going to get any relief you will have to go to court and based on what you've learned from one or more attorneys that you spoke with, you will need to represent yourself.

Getting Started

Long before you prepare your first court paper, and certainly long before you make your first excursion to the courthouse, you need to get a firm grip on your case. What does the contract really say? What are your damages?

What does the law require you to establish to set forth a claim for breach of contract? All of these things must be addressed up front.

The first step sounds almost silly, but it's not! It's amazing how many people make assumptions regarding a contract without ever going back, after it's executed, to look at the contract. Now, before you start drafting pleadings and court papers is the time to examine the contract very carefully.

Look for things like damages, waivers, damage caps, jurisdiction (place of resolving disputes) and attorney's fee clauses. Look for alternative dispute resolution clauses. Many contracts have provisions that require arbitration in lieu of a court action, or, require the parties to attempt a mediated settlement before filing a lawsuit.

Once you have a good grasp of the contract, lay out all of your damages, that is, the losses you have sustained as a result of the breach. Some elements are obvious and clear – others not so much. Certainly you can claim the difference between the contract price and what you ended up having to pay to replace the widgets. Those, by the way, are direct damages. Other damages, referred to as consequential damages, are also recoverable, but may prove a bit more challenging, both to establish and relate to the contract itself.

So, what are consequential damages? Common sense tells us that for every event or occurrence there are consequential events, which also generate consequential events and so on. In a claim for breach of contract a good way to conceive of damages is to put the losses on a sliding scale. On one end are the direct damages, which are so clear that no reasonable person would deny that they resulted from the breach. At the other end are those damages that are so remote in terms of causation that no reasonable person could foresee them occurring as a result of a breach. Here the objective is to be thorough, but realistic. Merely because someone breached a contract with you will not entitle you to recover for every bad thing that happens thereafter.

Likewise, your damages may be limited by the contract itself, or the contract may specify damages that are difficult to determine or compute, known as liquidated damages. All can be found by a careful reading of the contract.

Check the statutes of limitations. This will never be a problem where litigation occurs shortly after a contract has been breached, but in many cases there will be some delay. Be sure that you are still within the time limit in which to file a lawsuit. The time in which a claim can be filed varies from state to state and is also different for different claims. If you run into a problem with one kind of claim (perhaps you want to recover for breach of an oral contract), explore other options (see below).

Finally, do a realistic assessment of what you get if you win. It does you little good (other than perhaps inner satisfaction) to file a lawsuit, go through the trouble and expense involved, and get a judgment, only to find out that the defendant is "judgment proof". That's a nice legal term that means the chances of recovering any money are slim and none!

Going through these preliminary steps should give you a very good picture of whether you have a good likelihood of prevailing on such a suit, what damages you can expect to recover for, and finally, whether the lawsuit regardless of merit, is worth bringing at all.

Pick Your Court

Once you've decided that a lawsuit is the best way to go, and is justified, you need to decide where to bring it. If the court where you will resolve disputes arising from a contract is not specified in the contract itself, you as the plaintiff have some options. This can be an important issue, so don't make lightly of it.

The first decision that has to be made is in what state you want to bring your lawsuit, and what factors need to be considered. In the section on jurisdiction the general issue of how and when a court may exercise its powers over a non-resident (personal jurisdiction) is discussed. Here it will be reviewed in the context of actually beginning a breach of contract lawsuit. How the selection of a state for litigation is resolved can be as simple as where does everybody live, or as complex as analyzing the nature and extent of activities of a non-resident in another state. In the vast majority of lawsuits that you might be representing yourself in, this will not be a major issue. Both parties will live in and conduct business in the same state. It does not however take much to change the landscape so selecting the right state becomes an issue. Taking the example of the widgets, consider that your seller is actually located in a different state. Then things like where were the widgets delivered, where was the contract negotiated, how does the seller advertise its products, does the seller maintain a place of business in your state, where are any meetings to discuss contract performance held, all come into play.

Common sense tells you that there will usually be a tremendous difference in cost, time and expense between going to court in your own state as opposed to one perhaps hundreds of miles away. To the extent that you are able, you should always select a court that is as convenient for you as possible and as inconvenient for your opponent as possible.

Once a state for the lawsuit has been decided on, a court within the state must be selected. All states have some form of hierarchy and structure to their court system. These almost always start with a Supreme (or other appellate court) at the top, with different lower courts that handle day-to-day cases. These courts are frequently tiered on the basis of the kinds of cases they handle and the amounts in dispute. The courts on the lower tiers often handle cases where the amount in dispute is lower, and they often are more relaxed and less rigid. These courts will often have limits on the amount that can be in dispute. All states have what is called a court of general jurisdiction, which means that these courts are empowered to handle all cases regardless of amount in controversy, though they will often decline to take cases within the jurisdictional limit of a lower court. There are advantages and disadvantages with the various courts within a judicial system. Lower tiered courts are often easier to navigate and will resolve cases more quickly. The discovery process may be limited or nonexistent, and many times the rules in these lower courts will allow a principal of a small corporation or limited liability company to represent the company. Recall in the beginning of the book it was pointed out that while you can always represent yourself, you cannot usually represent a company, even if you are the sole owner. Lower courts in many states make an exception to this rule. And make no mistake, it is an important consideration. At its most basic level, if you are operating a business (making wagons) as a corporation or limited liability company, using one of the lower courts may be the only way that you can represent your company. On the other hand, if you are simply representing yourself, and your opponent is a small corporation, forcing them into a higher court will require that they retain an attorney and absorb that expense. One of the advantages to representing yourself is that you can save money while at the same time increasing the cost of litigation to your opponent. The more expensive and uncomfortable you can make things for your opponent, the better. While it may not sound terribly sportsmanlike or "proper", that's the reality of litigation. There are no points for coming in second best or losing graciously.

The last decision in terms of court selection is what is called venue. Within a state, courts on the same hierarchical tier will be organized by geographic location, usually by county. Generally this is not as critical as being in the wrong state, but it can make a difference, and it can confer an advantage, especially in larger states. It's small consolation for example that the court is still in California if you live in San Diego County and have to deal with a lawsuit filed in San Francisco. The important thing here is that venue is governed either by statute or rules, depending on the state, and there are substantial differences. Some states provide that a lawsuit must be brought in the county where the defendant (if a resident of that state resides) while others allow it to be brought in any county where any of the parties reside, or even where the events giving rise to the cause of action occurred. The way these rules and statutes are worded also usually gives the plaintiff a decided advantage because inasmuch as venue may be proper in two or more counties, he will normally have the option of selecting.

Jury or Non-Jury

Along with picking the proper court, you also need to decide whether you want your case tried in front of a jury, or a judge sitting without a jury. Usually in cases such as these, the parties have a right to a jury trial, but it can be waived. The initial preference is usually made by the plaintiff when the case is filed, but the only election that the plaintiff can definitively make is to opt for a trial by jury. That is because both parties have the right to a trial by jury. Even if the plaintiff waives the right, and at the time of filing designates the case as a non-jury trial, the defendant can nevertheless demand a jury trial.

The best course of action is to always request a jury trial, even if you know that you would rather proceed non-jury. You can always go back later (assuming the defendant has not demanded a jury trial) and waive the right. You cannot go the other way. That is, once you've waived your right to a jury, you cannot later request one.

Drafting Your Complaint

Actually starting the lawsuit in a contract dispute is similar in many ways to any other lawsuit. A complaint (in some jurisdictions a petition) must be prepared, filed and served upon the other side. As with any other lawsuit, the complaint is the document in which you state all the allegations which, if proven, will entitle you to recovery. Some of the things that you must consider and include in your complaint are:

Jurisdiction.

Just as with any lawsuit, you cannot successfully sue on a contract if the court lacks either subject matter or personal jurisdiction. Revisit the jurisdiction section for more details, but basically, you must be in the right court and the defendants must be subject to personal jurisdiction in the courts of the state in which the suit is filed. Your complaint must set forth the basis for the jurisdiction of the court both in terms of subject matter and jurisdiction over the parties.

Parties.

Make sure you have correctly identified the parties to sue. If your lawsuit is limited to breach of contract only, then the proper defendant would be the person or entity with whom you had a contract. This is important, especially in cases where there is a small corporation or limited liability company, against which it may do no good to obtain a judgment. By identifying the parties early on you can quickly determine whether you want to proceed solely on a breach of contract claim, or add some additional claims that would allow you to include other defendants. Your complaint must identify the parties and indicate the basis for their inclusion in the lawsuit. Generally from a plaintiff's perspective, the more parties, the better.

Contract.

This is one that many people overlook completely. You have to set forth the contract and the basic factual requirements to establish the existence of a contract. To set out a breach of contract claim it is necessary to show, as the very first element of the claim, a valid, binding contract. Depending on the jurisdiction, the contract must be alleged with varying degrees of specific details. Some jurisdictions will allow a general allegation that the parties entered into a contract, which was breached. The majority however require not only specifics of the contract to be set forth, which can often be done by attaching a copy of the contract, but such facts as will establish the actual elements of a valid, binding contract.

Claims.

Similar to deciding what parties to include, be sure to include all causes of action. Just because you have a claim for breach of contract, don't be afraid to explore other options. Rarely will circumstances give rise to only a breach of contract cause of action without additional options. Some other causes of action that you will often find where a contract has been breached are unfair business practices (most states have legislation that makes unfair or deceptive practices actionable), breach of fiduciary duty (often there will be a relationship of trust and confidence between parties to a contract), fraud, unjust enrichment, promissory estoppel, money had and received, and negligence. Selecting the proper claims will also help you to get other parties into the fray, and may help you with statute of limitation issues as well.

Damages.

You've already identified your damages. Here is where you must, in drafting the complaint, set forth your losses and how you contend they arose from the various causes of action, including of course your claim for breach of contract. There are four kinds of damages that may arise in a breach of contract claim: direct, consequential, liquidated and punitive. Direct and consequential have been discussed. Liquidated damages if specified will be in the contract itself. Liquidated damages are those which are specified by the parties and will arise automatically if a breach of the contract is established. Punitive damages (those intended to punish a defendant for wrong doing) are seldom seen in cases involving only breach of contract issues. In order to entitle a plaintiff to punitive damages there must generally be conduct that is more egregious than simply not living up to deal.

Prayer

This is a legal term for "what do you want?" At some point you have to tell the court just what it is that you want it to do for you. Do you want money? Do you want the court to issue a restraining order? Do you want the court to interpret a contract? Usually this is fairly straightforward and consists of a request for money damages. But even here there are pitfalls. You've specified your damages already, so this request should mirror that, but there are some things to look for. Some jurisdictions require you to set forth a specific dollar amount for which you want a judgment. Others are exactly the opposite and do not want a dollar amount here. Some are a hybrid, wanting an allegation only that the amount you are looking for is above or below a specific amount, or within a given range because of jurisdictional issues. There are few surprises here and checking the rules in your jurisdiction should by now be a daunting or formidable task.

And You're Off and Running!

Filing and Serving

You've done all the checking that you can. You picked what you believe is the right court. You've figured out the right people to sue, and you've meticulously drafted your complaint.

The next steps are to check with the clerk of your court to see about things like filing (paper versus electronic), issuance of a summons, local forms required to be included and whether there are any initial alternative dispute resolution issues. Clerks are not allowed to give legal advice and therefore will not be helpful in that regard. They are however permitted to provide information and advice on administrative matters, and usually, will do so quite freely. After all if something is done incorrectly, they are usually the ones that have to spend time straightening things out.

The clerk's office is where you will file your lawsuit. Most courts, especially courts of general jurisdiction have some kind of website. Don't even think about filing anything until you've had a chance to go over what is usually a wealth of information on these sites. Many courts have gone to electronic filing and document management systems. The most extensive such system is found in the federal court system called ECF/PACER. Many state courts have similar systems. The rules applicable to these systems vary considerably from court to court. In the federal system and some state systems for example only attorneys, and then only after undergoing a training session, are permitted to use the electronic filing system while anyone can establish an account to view documents and case information on PACER. Other jurisdictions may allow pro se litigants to use the system at their option, while still others require everyone to use it. There will almost always be some kind of cover sheet or form you will need to complete before filing. This form requests information on the case, the parties, the matters in dispute and so forth. It is usually for administrative purposes. Finally, given the clogged court dockets and the expense of litigation, most courts have alternative dispute resolution systems that sometimes need to be addressed early on. Some are permissive while others are mandatory. That information is readily available from the clerk's office.

At this point you will also have to decide how you want to complete service of process. You've prepared the complaint, and the summons is either prepared by you or by the clerk, but generally, for non-lawyers it is signed by the clerk.

Now, what to do with it? The original of the complaint, and sometimes the summons, is filed with and kept by the clerk's office. It is up to you to have a copy of these documents served on the defendant(s). In most states, one of the duties of the sheriff of the respective counties is to serve papers. Sheriff's offices often have a separate "civil" division set up to handle this task. So that is an option. For a prescribed fee the sheriff will attempt to find the defendant(s) and serve them (deliver to them) with a copy of the summons and complaint. As an alternative, almost all jurisdictions allow service by anyone over eighteen who is not a party (you can't serve your own papers) to serve process. This opens the door to private process servers who will usually complete service more quickly and be more aggressive in serving a difficult to locate defendant.

While the case is officially begun with the filing of the summons and complaint, it actually kicks off when the defendant is served. You are before the court by virtue of filing your lawsuit. The defendant is before the court by virtue of the service of the summons.

The Response to the Lawsuit

Something has to happen reasonably quickly once the defendant is served. The time to answer varies from state to state and from federal court. It can be as short as twenty days or as long as thirty or more. Check your rules. Within some specified time the defendant must respond or be in default.

What initial response you get from the filing of the lawsuit will depend on a lot of factors.

It is likely that before an answer, a motion of some sort will be filed. The federal rules of civil procedure, and the rules for many states, provide that certain matters must be raised in the first response to a complaint, or be lost, and allows them to be raised at the option of the defendant by motion. This applies to things like jurisdiction and the sufficiency of a complaint. These rules do not allow for successive motions, so if you receive such a motion, it will count as the initial response to the complaint, and must include all grounds that the rules allow to be raised by motion. Even though a defendant has the option of including these issues in an answer, it is more common to file a motion.

You must respond to this motion and respond specifically to each ground for dismissal. Failure to respond may result in the motion being granting and your case being dismissed.

That by the way holds true for many motions. Some courts have hundreds of motions filed weekly. They cannot address all of them and many of them are merely ministerial. That is, they are filed to satisfy a legal requirement with no expectation that there will be any response. Consequently, while hearings will be held on motions that are disputed, undisputed motions are often simply granted as a matter of routine.

If no motion to dismiss has been filed, or if filed it has been denied, the next thing you receive will be an answer. The answer may be accompanied by a counterclaim or even a third party complaint.

The issue of jurisdiction (and other similar issues) can be raised at the option of the defendant either by motion or by answer. If it is raised by answer instead of motion to dismiss it may appear in different forms. It be as subtle as a denial in the answer of the paragraphs in your complaint that refer to jurisdiction, or a single line affirmative defense stating that the court lacks personal jurisdiction, or the complaint fails to state a claim upon which relief can be granted.

While a motion to dismiss must be responded to, whether or not a response to those issues raised in an answer is required, is a little more complicated. Generally the rules will specify when a response to an answer is required or even permitted. Obviously if there is a counterclaim, it should be responded to with a reply. Affirmative defenses (such as failure to state a claim, or jurisdictional issues) can, depending on the court you are in be responded to with a reply, or they may be automatically deemed denied, requiring no specific response. This is one of many areas in which you need to research the laws of your state. If there is any doubt, respond to them instead of assuming them to be denied.

In responding to a motion to dismiss if it is filed, you to need to analyze what the motion is about, and review your complaint in the context of the motion.

A motion to dismiss for lack of jurisdiction requires you to respond with the basis for the court to exercise personal jurisdiction. If the defendant is a non-resident of the state, what is it that the defendant did that would subject it to personal jurisdiction? This needs to be analyzed in the context of the state's long arm statutes and constitutional due process issues. Affidavits and exhibits may be required to demonstrate to the court the conduct of the defendant that makes it subject to the jurisdiction of the court.

If the motion is to dismiss for failure to state facts sufficient to constitute a claim for relief10, the approach will be different. You must re-examine your complaint and make sure it contains everything that is required. If you

---

[10] In federal court and most states the request to dismiss for failure to state a claim is a motion to dismiss. Some states still use a demurrer, and in Pennsylvania for example it is referred to as preliminary objections.

are in a notice pleading jurisdiction it will be easier11. In a fact pleading jurisdiction, or a jurisdiction that has adopted the enhanced pleading requirements established in recent Supreme Court decisions, your analysis needs to be a little more thorough. In the context of contract litigation, remember that in a fact pleading jurisdiction and even in some so-called notice pleading jurisdictions, you have to set forth facts that if true would constitute a cause of action. That means you must allege facts that will establish each and every element of the claim. By way of example, you cannot simply allege that the defendant breached the contract. You have to state that the contract required "X", which defendant failed to do, thereby breaching the terms and conditions of the contract. In other words, making the assumption that the facts in your complaint are true, the court must be able, from the facts set forth to see all of the required elements of the breach of contract claim.

The procedure to respond to a motion to dismiss varies from state to state. Some jurisdictions provide for an automatic amendment of the complaint at your option, which in and of itself takes care of the motion or demurrer12. In those jurisdictions, once an amended complaint has been filed it is up to the defendant, if he feels the problems remain, to file another motion. Other

---

[11] See the Section on Pleading and Court Papers to understand notice and fact pleading.

[12] In California the filing of an amended complaint automatically disposes of a demurrer. In Pennsylvania the filing of an amended complaint automatically negates Preliminary Objections, the equivalent in that state to a motion to dismiss.

jurisdictions require the motion to be addressed by the court. In these jurisdictions it is critical that you file a detailed response, including a memorandum of law as to why the motion should be denied; in other words why your complaint is adequate and proper.

Motions to dismiss are not favored and are usually denied. The purpose of the courts is to resolve disputes on the merits rather than technicalities. Consequently, if you have not already amended your complaint, most judges in the face of a motion to dismiss will allow you the opportunity to amend so that the complaint sets forth the necessary allegations.

Of course, some things cannot be fixed and your lawsuit will be dismissed. An example might be if you working under a void or voidable contract. If you are suing to recover under a contract under which you are paid a commission for the sale of real estate, but do not have a valid real estate license, the contract is void. This can be raised in a motion to dismiss if you have not alleged in your complaint that you were properly licensed. When the motion is heard, and you cannot demonstrate that you in fact had a license, your lawsuit will be dismissed.

At some point you will receive an answer. If motions are filed first, it will be after they are resolved. If no motion is filed by the defendant, it will be the first thing that you get. It may be an answer by itself, or it may be combined with a counterclaim, a cross claim, or a third party complaint.13 If the answer includes a counterclaim, you must respond in accordance with the rules of your jurisdiction. The counterclaim, just as your complaint, sets forth claims that the defendant asserts against you.

The same principles apply as for the complaint. Failure to respond with a reply may result in you being in default and the defendant obtaining a judgment against you. The answer will almost always include affirmative defenses (see the section on Pleadings and Papers). Whether you need, or are even allowed to respond to these in a reply varies from state to state.

Discovery

Just as in any lawsuit following the disposition of early motions and exchange of pleadings, efforts will focus on discovery. A review of the section on discovery will help you to recall the various forms of discovery. This section will address those modes of discovery in the context of contract litigation.

So what is it that you seek to accomplish through discovery in a contract lawsuit? To begin with, since you are alleging that the defendant breached the contract, you want to know why. It is highly unlikely that the defendant just decided one day that it was tired of producing the

---

[13] A cross complaint a defendant complaining of another defendant; a third party complaint is the defendant complaining of a someone not a party to the original lawsuit, but who he brings in.

widgets it had promised to deliver. Discovery will help you find out what went on to cause the problem. Was there a shortage of some component that the defendant needed to produce widgets? Or, did the defendant get a better offer for his limited supply of widgets and decide to sell them to someone else instead. Who will the defendant call as witnesses if the case goes to trial? What will those witnesses testify to? Does the defendant have other contracts for widgets? Who has the defendant sold widgets to? Where does the defendant get the materials to produce the widgets? Has the defendant breached other contracts? Has the defendant been involved in any other lawsuits?

All of this information can be requested in the form of interrogatories and requests for production of documents. Just as with any lawsuit, one of the reasons to engage in discovery is to get a complete (or as complete as possible) picture of what is going on and how it is that you got from happily using widgets to make wagons, to a lawsuit.

Of course if a counterclaim has been filed against you, you will also want to focus your requests for information concerning that as well. What is it you believe that I did wrong? How have you been damaged? What did you do to minimize your damages? Who will be the witnesses to attest to what I did wrong? Did you notify me of any problems as they occurred or as you noticed them? The information that you get in response to these questions will help you determine if the counterclaim is really viable (or just a smoke screen) and the best way to defend it.

Remember, interrogatories are questions that you ask, requests for production are where you ask for documents and records. Used well, these can provide you with a wealth of information about the other side's case, condition, and motivation.

With Requests to Admit, you can easily address a lot of the things that you must prove and establish to prevail. For example, in a contract case, one of the things that you must establish is the existence of a contract between the parties. Use requests to admit to establish that your copy of the contract is in fact a copy of the contract that the parties entered into. You can establish that it was signed by a specific individual and that that individual (if the defendant is a business entity) had the authority to sign the contract. All of this can be done through discovery without the necessity of calling a single witness.

Finally, if you want more specific answers, you can take the deposition of the other side (or its key people) to go through things that were not covered or adequately responded to by other discovery methods.

Discovery however, like many things in the law, seldom goes smoothly. Attorneys in the never ending quest for billable hours have turned the discovery process into a major realm of conflict. Interrogatories and requests to produce will be objected to. Interrogatories will be answered evasively and requests to admit will be denied on technical pretexts. Just because an attorney on the other side elects to complicate things, don't give up. Just file motions to compel. Several if necessary, and sooner or later, because judges get tired of the discovery games as well, you will get the information and documents that you need.

Summary Judgment

In addition to the motion to dismiss, a motion for summary judgment is another step that can end the case. Discussed in more detail in the section on Motions, summary judgment is a tool used by the courts to dispose of cases where either one party is clearly entitled to prevail as a matter of law, or there is no genuine issue as to a critical material fact. If you are served with a motion for summary judgment it is essential that you carefully read the motion, and research the law of your jurisdiction. While virtually every state has some form of summary judgment, the legal requirements for granting such a motion vary. In the federal courts, Rule 56 of the Federal Rules of Civil Procedure applies. In states that have adopted or track the federal rules, the rule number will probably be the same but be careful. Simply because the rule is similar does not mean that the courts of any given state have embraced the same standards or requirements as the federal courts. And this is another example of an issue that must be researched in the case law of the state.

The rule itself will not give you enough information to successfully make or defend a motion for summary judgment. The meaning and significance of the language of the rule can only be found in the case law. The most important thing is to understand the summary judgment motion, and if you are served with one, to understand that it must be responded to.

To bring or defend a motion for summary judgment depends on the basis for the motion. Remember, there are two broad categories of summary judgment motion.

The first is very similar to a motion to dismiss except that additional facts and information have been developed through the course of the case, especially through the discovery process. This form of summary judgment motion basically asserts that even assuming that everything that the party opposing the motion alleges is true, they still cannot win. An example would be a statute of limitations issue.

Let's assume that for one reason or another you did not file your lawsuit for a while. Maybe you hoped things would work out. Perhaps you had tried to hire an attorney before you realized that it would cost more than you had. Regardless of the reason, assume that you waited three years and a month after the widgets were not delivered before filing your lawsuit, in a state where the statute of limitations (the time in which a lawsuit must be filed) is three years. You admitted the date on which the contract was breached in some form of discovery, perhaps a deposition, or requests to admit. The defendant files a summary judgment motion in which he contends that even if everything you allege in your complaint is true, you cannot win as a matter of law because more than three years passed before you filed your lawsuit.

This motion, under these circumstances will be granted. Because the claim is barred by the statute of limitations, it does not matter what witnesses you call, or what evidence you can muster, the lawsuit is barred.

The second form of summary judgment motion deals with factual issues. Here the party asking for summary judgment will rely on facts developed in the course of the lawsuit to allege that on a specific issue required to establish your claim, there are no facts in dispute and that therefore there is no need for a trial. This is a little different in that while the party asking for summary judgment may argue that there is no genuine issue of material fact, that is far from a given and the motion can be opposed with the presentation of factual issues.

An example of this kind of summary judgment motion would occur in the hypothetical if the defendant contended that even if it breached the contract, you suffered no damages (remember this is an essential element of the claim), because widgets were readily available at the same price from other vendors. He submits a motion for summary judgment, accompanied by an affidavit from company "Y" that says that on the date the defendant breached your contract, they had plenty of widgets available for you to buy at the same price your contract with the defendant specified. If this is in fact true, then the defendant will be entitled to summary judgment, because after all, what are you complaining about? If when you were told that the defendant could not deliver widgets, all you had to do was pick up the phone and place another order, what are you doing in court anyway?

Buts things in life and in the law are never that simple. The widgets may have been slightly different. The delivery time may have been excessive. There may have been extra shipping charges, and so forth. In short you disagree with the assertion of the defendant. You can successfully oppose the summary judgment motion, but you must provide evidence to overcome it. You cannot just rely on what you have alleged in the complaint. You cannot just allege in a response to the motion that company "Y"'s widgets were inferior, or could not be delivered in time. You must present concrete materials to oppose the affidavit of the other side.

In deciding this form of summary judgment, a judge (motions are always in front of a judge and not a jury) is required in virtually every jurisdiction to resolve every factual dispute against the party seeking summary judgment, and if there is a genuine issue as to a material fact, then summary judgment cannot be granted. In the hypothetical, once you file a response that includes an affidavit (and it can be from you) saying that widgets from company "Y" were not purchased because you experienced a high number of defects, would have resulted in higher shipping costs, were actually slightly different and thus not acceptable, then a genuine issue of fact exists and summary judgment will not be appropriate.

Summary judgment motions serve a useful purpose in weeding out some cases that should not be in court. At the same time, they are often abused by attorneys eager to bill an extra ten or twenty hours, so not all of these motions will have any merit. Unless your case really is junk and does not belong in court, defending against these motions is not only possible, but especially where there are potential factual issues, fairly easy. It just takes some work and careful organization. The most important thing to remember is that you must respond. Like so many things in the legal arena, a failure to respond and to respond correctly can have catastrophic consequences.

Actual Trial Preparation

In terms of procedure, the trial of a breach of contract case is no different than any other civil case. The pleadings (complaint, answer etc.) provide the structure and outline the content of what will be presented. As the plaintiff it is incumbent upon you to move forward and "prove" your case. That means that the allegations that were set forth in your complaint- the allegations that constitute a claim or cause of action - must now be proven. Until this point they are nothing but unproven allegations. Only if they are proven to be true are you entitled to any relief from the court.

Allegations are "proven" with witness testimony, exhibits, documents and discovery responses. All of these must be properly and correctly presented to the court before the "finder of fact", be it a jury or a judge without a jury, can consider them. The first thing that must be done is to identify just what it is that you will have to prove.

The easiest and best way to plan what you have to present is to get out the pleadings, side by side and decide what remains as an issue and what does not. Some of the elements will have to be proven at trial, others will not.

For example, you would have attached a copy of the contract to the original complaint and would have alleged in the complaint that the parties entered into this contract. If the defendant in its answer (or in discovery) admits this, you do not have to prove it. Therefore if it is already admitted, you don't need any testimony about the execution of the contract, what the parties agreed to, whether the contract is supported by consideration, etc. In fact, presenting this kind of evidence is not optional it is as a practical matter precluded. If you try a contract case in which the contract is admitted and begin to ask a witness details about the formation of the contract, you will quickly hear from the judge or the other side. You will be told that the contract is admitted and to move on because that line of questioning is irrelevant and moot.

What you do have to prove is every allegation that is not admitted. Technically you only have to prove those allegations that are denied, but all attorneys and form answers that are downloadable for pro se litigants, include a general denial. Usually, "all allegations of the complaint not specifically admitted are denied" or something to the effect. To be on the safe side then, as you go through the allegations of your complaint and the corresponding response in the answer, assume that anything not actually admitted is denied and must be proven. Remember, as plaintiff you have the burden of establishing the elements of your claim and until you do, the defendant doesn't have to do anything.

Do not discount or overlook discovery responses. Even if the answer denies some aspect of the complaint, it can often still be established, without the need for additional evidence, from the other side's responses to discovery. If in answers to interrogatories a defendant has indicated that they entered into the contract on such-and-such a date, then you can likely get that answer into the record to establish that the contract attached to the interrogatories constitutes a contract between the parties and was executed. Likewise, if you have asked, and the defendant in response to Requests for Admission has acknowledged the contract, that response too will suffice.

Clearly it is important to identify and lay out in some orderly manner those allegations which remain to be proven.

And this is critical! It is not merely an exercise in trial efficiency.

At the end of the your case, when all of your witnesses have testified and all of your documents have been introduced into evidence, if there is any required element of your claim that has not been proven, the other side will move for, and probably be granted a dismissal of your complaint.

Once you have prepared what will be your basic roadmap of the trial, a list of what you must prove, then you can go about the task of deciding how each will be proven. A good technique to apply to this task is to lay out in table form each fact that you must prove, then a description of how you will prove it. It could be by your own testimony, a discovery response or document or the testimony of a witness. Using this kind of organization will also give you a list of the witnesses you will have to be sure are present at the trial.

The Trial

And all of this is explains the initial question, how you got to be sitting at a table in a courtroom with the judge telling you that you may begin. Because when all is done, when the pleadings and motions have been disposed of, when the discovery is complete, it's time to start the trial of the case.

The first thing that you will do is make an opening statement, though if a trial is before a judge without a jury, this may often be dispensed with. In the opening statement to a jury, this is where you tell the jury about yourself and your case. Various theories of communication and memory tell us that juries will often remember best what they hear first, and last (the laws of primacy and recency). Since you as the plaintiff go first, this is a golden opportunity to get the jury to know you and understand what the case is about before they hear anything from the defendant. In an opening statement you would tell the jury about what you do, how your product is made, and why widgets are important. You would stress that because it is important that you have components you met with the defendant whose representatives assured you that they could provide the widgets that you needed. You signed a contract. You signed a contract to be sure that you would be provided with a sufficient quantity of widgets to manufacture your wagons. You would stress as you speak to the jury that you always did everything that was required of you under the contract, especially paying for the widgets promptly. You will explain to them what happened when the widget supply stopped, explain how you tried to get other widgets, but to no avail and explain what losses you have sustained as a result.

Of course the other side will also make an opening statement and they will attempt to put a different spin on things, depending on their theory of defense.

After opening statements, the actual presentation of evidence to the jury will begin.

You will present your case primarily through the testimony of witnesses that of course, can include you. Witnesses are first questioned by the party calling them, and then the other side is allowed to cross examine them. In this manner what the witness has to say is presented to the judge or jury, tempered by cross examination where the credibility or recollection of the witness may be challenged. By questioning witnesses properly you will be able to establish the things your lawsuit is all about. If necessary, that there was a contract, that the defendant was supposed to be, and had been supplying you with widgets, that the deliveries stopped, that you tried but could not get the widgets elsewhere, that it caused your own business to shut down, etc.

Your testimony as a pro se litigant without an attorney to ask you questions will be a bit different. No, you do not as the slapstick image suggests, go from the witness stand to the counsel table, ask a question, then run back to the witness stand to answer it. Humor aside, your testimony will actually take on more of a narrative nature. Understand that the other side will object to the things you say if they are not proper. If for example you start to talk about what someone else told you, expect as hearsay objection. And for objections you do have to step out of the witness role and into the litigant role to address the objection and argue whether the objection should be sustained or overruled. And of course you will be subject to cross examination. Lest you feel that being allowed to testify in a narrative form is some sort of free hall pass to let you to go wherever you like, bear in mind that you can be called to task in cross examination regarding anything you say in your "direct".

In the course of presenting your case you will almost certainly be introducing documents of various kinds. These can include the contract documents, any correspondence related to the contract or performance under the contract, any emails, notices, invoices, bills and so forth. In short, any document that will help the judge or the jury understand what went on that resulted in the lawsuit. Some documents are more important than others. The contract of course is virtually indispensable in a breach of contract claim involving a written contract. Emails to or from the other side concerning the failure or inability to deliver widgets are likewise critical. In trying a case, especially this kind of case, documents are a very important element for still another reason. Juries (and to some extent judges as well) will focus more on a written document, something that they can hold and look at, than on the testimony of a witness that may have been given days before they actually get to review the evidence and consider it. Put another way, a jury is going to pay much more attention to an email that they can touch and hold and pass around the jury room, from the defendant that says "We will not be delivering any more widgets", than they will to the same facts given by testimony that they heard one time, three days ago when the defendant testified.

Of course each witness that you call in support of your case will be subject to cross examination. Everyone has seen movies and television shows featuring courtroom scenes. Less the drama (in the real world the witness never caves on the stand admitting that "it was all a lie!"), cross examination is a useful and universally used tool to promote truth and the integrity of the judicial process. It allows the opposing party to question the witness, raising possible doubts about the truthfulness or accuracy of the witness' testimony on direct examination.

This is not a time when you should be relaxing or staring out the window. The rules governing the scope of direct and cross examination14 provide a relatively broad scope for cross examination, but it is not unlimited. Simply attacking the character and integrity of a witness for example is not permitted. The questioning must relate to some aspect of the case, or be directly related to the witness' credibility. If the other side's cross examination questions meander away from these areas, you can and should object. Often an attorney on the other side, with nothing else available, will try to attack the witness with questions that might put their character into question, but have nothing to do with the matters they are testifying on.

---

[14] Rule 611 of the Federal Rules governs in Federal Court. Most states have similar rules and they are often found in separate sections or rule sets focusing on evidence.

In addition to keeping the scope of cross examination within the scope of the rules, the other reason you need to be paying attention is that during cross examination of your witnesses, you need to be preparing for re-direct. This is your opportunity to try to "fix" any damage done to your witness' testimony by the other side during cross examination. The rules again will limit the scope of examination at this stage. You cannot go into new matters, or simply repeat prior testimony. What you can, and should do, is to take this opportunity to repair any damage done to your witness' testimony during cross examination. Following your re-direct examination, the other side will have another opportunity to cross examine (re-cross examination) the witness.

To see how this might work, we'll take a specific bit of testimony from our widgets example. It was pointed out earlier that one of the things any aggrieved party is expected to do in our legal system is to mitigate its damages. That means when the defendant tells you that he is no longer able to supply the widgets under the contract, you are not entitled to simply "cash in" on this occurrence. You have to at least try to cut your losses, that is, mitigate your damages. One way of course would be to simply buy the widgets from a different source. So at issue in this breach of contract case might be the question of what you did to try to minimize the effect of the defendant's failure to perform by making an effort to locate another source. To do this you might put on the witness stand an employee to whom you had early on designated the task of finding widgets.

On direct examination you would call the witness, ask him to identify himself and ask him basic questions about his knowledge of your business and the process of using widgets in the manufacture of wagons. You would ask him what happened in your place of business when the defendant stopped delivering widgets. You would ask him about his efforts to locate widgets from another source. Let's assume that he called another supplier nearby but did not call suppliers in nearby towns. In contacting the other supplier he learned that they had no widgets available, their production already having been committed.

The other side will try to undermine this testimony by getting the witness to admit on cross examination that he contacted only one other widget manufacturer when in fact there were many more across the country that he could have called. Obviously this would be harmful testimony to your case. If the other side can show that there were other sources that were not explored, then your damages come into question and in turn, your entire breach of contract claim.

Either in the answers to the other side's attorney, or in re-direct examination is where this issue will be addressed. You would have anticipated this issue as part of your planning. Perhaps during the conversation with the other supplier availability from other sources was discussed.

Perhaps he had gotten quotes from other suppliers in the past that were too high to be feasible. Perhaps shipping costs from distant suppliers made in impractical. Regardless, the damage done with the admission on cross examination that only one supplier had been contacted must be addressed.

Your employee may be prepared and simply respond to the question of why he contacted only one other supplier with something like, "I already knew that there were no other widgets available". Here is where you just have to be a little flexible as the questioning unwinds. If your employee satisfactorily addresses the issue, then all is well. On the other hand, if he doesn't then you, on re-direct, will need to ask the questions necessary to show that a much more extensive effort was made but it was to no avail. There is no magic formula here, no set of questions that you can download, or no instant course in courtroom maneuvering that will help you. Everything will come down to preparation, organization and planning.

When you get to the conclusion of your evidence, it will be time to rest. Do not be in a hurry. In fact, it is perfectly acceptable to ask the judge, especially as a pro se litigant, for a brief recess to allow you to review your notes and outline versus what you have presented. This is critical.

Once you utter the words "plaintiff rests", that means you have presented your entire case. It is over. If you have neglected to establish every essential element of the case, this is the point at which you will lose. The other side will move for dismissal and if you have not met your burden, the motion will be granted. So this is the time to go back through your checklist, identify each and every essential element of your claim and be sure it has been established. Any issue that has not been resolved by agreement15, by admitting allegations in the answer, or by discovery responses must be established by evidence. Once you have satisfied yourself that you have addressed all the issues, you can rest, and the defendant will present its case.

Following presentation of the plaintiff's case, the defendant of course has the opportunity to present its case. The process is the same. Witnesses will be called for direct examination, cross examination and optionally, re-direct and re-cross examination. The difference of course is that you will be focusing on making sure the direct examination by the other side stays on track, and on cross-examining a witness.

Your focus here is different. When you were presenting testimony your objective was get your evidence before the jury (or the judge) and then to fix or minimize any damage to your evidence inflicted during cross examination. Now the other side is presenting evidence, and it is incumbent upon you to make sure that they present only that evidence (opposing you) that is competent and relevant,

---

[15] The parties early on often agree on portions of a case that are not in dispute. In this case, there might be an agreement early in the case that there was in fact a contract and that a particular written document is that contract.

and presented in accordance with the rules of evidence in your jurisdiction. When a witness has finished testifying you will want to cross examine them, but only to the extent necessary to attack or refute evidence they have presented that hurts you, or supports their position.

To do this, in preparation for the trial you should familiarize yourself with the rules of evidence in your jurisdiction. There just isn't time to be looking them up as the questions and answers are bouncing back and forth. You should be able to object to leading questions (those that suggest the answer), hearsay testimony (where the witness relates what someone else has told him) and irrelevant testimony. Do not believe for one second that an opposing attorney will not try to take advantage of the fact that you are appearing pro so to slide all sorts of things past you. Do not expect a judge to act as your "protector". Assume that any testimony that you do not timely object to will make it into the record.

If you don't think that this kind of testimony can hurt you, consider this example from our widget case and think again. Your opponent, the owner of the company selling you the widgets is on the witness stand. His attorney has asked him if widgets were available from some other company. He promptly answers: "sure there are plenty of widgets around town. I talked to the guy at Acme Widgets and he said they had plenty of them."

This testimony is absolutely devastating! "The guy" is not available to confirm or deny that he ever said such a thing.

This is exactly why there is an evidence rule against hearsay. A witness can say that anyone, not present to refute, said anything. Unless you know to object, the other side will run all over you.

In addition to limiting the testimony on direct to that which is admissible, when the direct examination is concluded, it will be up to you to cross examine the witnesses. The cardinal rule of cross examination in any case is that if it's not necessary, don't!

That's right. If the witness has not hurt you on direct examination, and if there is nothing that you need to elicit from him, just say "I have no questions for this witness". Despite what you may have seen in movies and on television shows, there is simply no requirement anywhere that a witness be cross examined. To the contrary, if there is nothing to be accomplished by it, cross examination can hurt you. You may inadvertently give the witness the opportunity to get something into evidence that might have been objectionable on direct examination. By cross-examining the opponent's witness you are creating his right to re-direct examination. He might be waiting for a second chance to get in something that he forgot on direct.

If you do have to cross examine a witness to attack some damaging testimony, be specific. Use leading questions. Don't ask any questions that you don't already know the answer to and limit the cross examination to what is needed. Remember that generally the re-direct examination will be limited to things that you covered on cross examination, so only go as far as you need to. The more areas you ask about on cross examination, the wider the scope of the other side's re-direct examination.

Following presentation of the defendant's case you will have an opportunity to reply. This is not to be considered a chance to present your case all over again, but instead, to address issues raised by the defendant in their case. If for example they have alleged an affirmative defense, such as the statute of limitations already discussed, or failure to mitigate damages, in your reply you would have the opportunity to present testimony or evidence on those issues.

Once all the evidence and testimony has been presented, and the phases of the trial have been concluded, it will be time for closing arguments. Just as with opening statements, these will always be part of the trial if there is a jury. A judge sitting without a jury may or may not allow closing arguments. Here is where you have the opportunity to summarize for the jury the evidence you have presented, to point out the strengths of your case and the weaknesses of the other side, and argue to them why they should return a verdict in your favor.

The only thing to do once the closing arguments are done is to wait and see what the decision or verdict is. In fairness, there are other, more technical issues that must be addressed, but for the most part, this is how you will present a case for breach of contract.

Breach of Contract – Defending the Lawsuit

If the roles are reversed, and you find yourself receiving a summons and complaint the same underlying principles apply, but of course there are some variations.

As with everything else discussed in this book, the best option of course is not to be in this situation. While this may sound like casual, almost flippant advice, it is stated seriously. The pieces of a lawsuit start falling into place long before the lawsuit is filed. They start to develop during the negotiations, preparation, drafting and execution of the contract. They develop as the parties work with each other in performance of the contract. Since we don't have the benefit of a crystal ball when entering into a deal, it is incumbent upon you to try to anticipate the potential problems, as well as solutions when entering into any contractual relationship. In the course of negotiating the contract, attention should be paid not only to the typical terms of the deal, but also to factors that will influence and govern what will take place should the deal go south. This is easier said than done. We're all human and at the inception of any relationship, business or otherwise we are optimistic and positive. But as you negotiate or consider a deal, just take a look at all the litigation going on over broken contracts, and remember that when each and every one of the deals giving rise to lawsuits was hatched, the last thing on anybody's mind was a lawsuit.

It is at the negotiating stage that you addressed (or should have) such issues as where a lawsuit would be filed if it became necessary, whether alternative dispute resolution would be involved, which party was responsible for attorney's fees and costs, etc. If you have done well at that stage you will find yourself in a good (or at least as good as can be expected in litigation) posture in the event you are sued. The litigation will take place in your jurisdiction, convenient to you and potentially inconvenient to your opponent. If you haven't done such a good job of negotiating, you may find yourself at a disadvantage, but in any event, you have a lawsuit that you must defend.

Review the Complaint

The first thing to do when you receive suit papers, is pretty much, nothing. That does not mean you should toss them in the corner and forget about them. It means that you should stop, pause, reflect and carefully review before doing anything on the spur of the moment. As you will see, the initial response to a lawsuit is critical not only because it is required, but there are potentially a lot of options which must be carefully selected before going forward. Here are some of the things that you need to be looking at before actually ever filing an answer or motion:

Jurisdiction

Are you in the right court? Do you want to be in the court that the lawsuit was filed in? If not, can you do anything about it? There are a lot of issues need to be addressed at this level.

Personal jurisdiction may or may not be an issue. Remember, this is the power of a court to exercise personal jurisdiction over a person. If both you and the plaintiff are located in the same place, then this is not an issue. The situation changes though if you live in one state and the plaintiff in another. The plaintiff makes widgets in state A, and then ships them to you in state B, where you live and conduct business. Not surprisingly you notice that the lawsuit is filed in the plaintiff's state, which presents difficulties for you. The first thing to do then is to determine whether there is really any basis for you to be sued in State A. Even if there is a basis of some sort for jurisdiction to be asserted over you, you may still want to consider filing a motion to dismiss for lack of jurisdiction. While the issue of jurisdiction can be raised in the answer as well as in a motion, it must be raised in the first thing you file, or it is waived. You cannot for example file a motion to dismiss for failure to state a cause of action then later, when you file an answer, include a defense based on lack of personal jurisdiction. It will have been waived. If you are going to file a motion to dismiss, make sure you include all the grounds. Also, if jurisdiction over you is an issue that you want to preserve, be careful even of what you file after you have raised it. Some jurisdictions hold that if you avail yourself of the court that you contend does not have jurisdiction over you, that issue could be waived. This can arise if you file a permissive counterclaim, or a complaint against another person or entity (third party complaint) that may be involved.

You can also raise subject matter jurisdiction if the lawsuit is filed in the wrong court. Recall that various courts have different amounts that they will deal with. Many small claims or first tier courts will only take cases involving limited amounts, sometimes as low as $5,000. What you will find is that many people doing business as corporations will often file in a lower court because those courts sometimes allow individuals to represent their corporations, which is not allowed in higher courts. The potential savings often justify the lower amount that can be sought in such a court. This gives you a potential edge if you are representing yourself. You can often get a case kicked out of a lower court by filing a counterclaim that exceeds the jurisdictional limits. This is helpful if your opponent is doing business as a corporation and has filed in the lower court avoid hiring an attorney.

Respond to the Complaint

Once you have taken the time to understand what the complaint is all about, that is, what you are being sued over and by who, it is time to prepare a response. You have three options here. You can file a motion to dismiss, you can answer, or you can answer and counterclaim16. The motion to dismiss option has already been explored. If

---

[16] Technically you could also bring in a third party with a third party complaint, but this option is omitted here for the sake of simplicity.

your motion to dismiss is denied, you will be allowed time to file an answer. In many cases this time period is shorter than the original time to respond, so it would be to your advantage to be working on an answer even before your motion to dismiss has been ruled upon.

Possible Motion to Dismiss

Before answering is also the time to consider filing a motion to dismiss for failure to state a claim. If the complaint on its face is defective, that is fails to set forth the elements of the cause of action, or is directed against the wrong party, or someone who is not a party, it may be to your advantage to file a motion to dismiss. The grounds for a motion to dismiss will always be found in the civil procedure rules for the jurisdiction you are in. In federal court they are found in the Federal Rules of Civil Procedure under rule 12(b). Many states have adopted the federal rules, either outright, or in some variation, so the same rule number will apply. Unfortunately, this is not universal and you may have to do some searching to find the relevant rule. Also, some states use different terminology. Some (California is an example) still use a demurrer which is a holdover from old common law, but is effectively the same kind of creature.

Dealing with the proper response to being served with suit papers can get tricky. The important thing to remember is to make sure that the issues that are listed in Rule 12(b) and comparable state rules, are raised in the first thing that you file, or they may be waived. Other factors to consider are if you should bother with a motion to dismiss. Remember that almost all jurisdictions allow a plaintiff to amend a complaint. If a motion to dismiss will simply result in an amended complaint that fixes the problems, it might be better to wait and raise those issues later.

Answer

In any lawsuit, the complaint must be answered. It is the pleadings in the case; that is the complaint, the answer, any counterclaim and a reply, that frame the issues that are to be decided. Since everything else in the lawsuit will follow and be patterned after these pleadings it is very important that they be done correctly. The advice to do nothing at first when you receive suit papers is predicated on this premise. The reason is to make sure that you take time to carefully analyze the complaint and the circumstances giving rise to the lawsuit, and to formulate your answer carefully and analytically.

The time to answer a complaint varies from state to state and generally ranges from twenty days to thirty days. Failure to answer a complaint has serious and potentially dire consequences in that you may be in default. In such a case the court will deem every allegation in the complaint to be true and award the plaintiff judgment against you.

In answering the complaint it is necessary to go through each allegation of the complaint and admit or deny it.

There will be allegations that you may not be able to answer. You can usually just say that you do not have sufficient information to admit or deny them and therefore they are denied. The key is to address every allegation in the complaint. One technique to help ensure that you do so is to follow the paragraph numbers in your answer with the paragraph numbers in the complaint. That way your paragraph number one for example, addresses paragraph number one in the complaint. The likelihood of missing an allegation is reduced.

Affirmative Defenses

Once you have addressed each and every allegation of the complaint you must be sure to raise any affirmative defenses that you may have. As with counterclaims, discussed below, affirmative defenses not raised are waived and the right to assert them lost.

Affirmative defenses are defenses those that will defeat a claim even if what the plaintiff alleges is true. Things like the statute of limitations, lack of capacity to enter into a contract, a contract being void as against public policy, etc., are affirmative defenses. For the sake of presenting a clean, well organized pleading, many people prefer to place these defenses in a separate section, labeled as "affirmative defenses", and usually toward the end of the answer after each allegation of the complaint has been specifically addressed.

The problem with affirmative defenses is that while they are generally waived if not raised in the first pleading, it is often difficult early in the case to know if a particular defense will apply. Consequently, a good practice is to set forth all possible affirmative defenses initially, and then worry about which specific defenses apply later. Some affirmative defenses such as expiration of the period during which a claim can be asserted are common to almost all lawsuits, others apply only to certain kinds of cases. Contributory or comparative negligence for example are relevant to personal injury cases, but rarely applicable to contract cases. The rule of thumb is when in doubt, add it.

Counterclaims

Counterclaiming to a complaint is required if you want to raise your own issues regarding what has happened. In the widget example, assume that your opponent, the widget seller, has sued you for non-payment of amounts due for widgets. If you want to raise the issue of their failure to deliver the widgets, you must do so by counterclaim.

The important thing to understand here is the difference between compulsory or permissive counterclaims. A compulsory counterclaim is one that arises from the same circumstances and relationships from which the original complaint arises. A permissive counterclaim arises between the same parties, but on an unrelated issue.

The counterclaim for failing to deliver the widgets is a compulsory counterclaim. It arises from the same circumstances and relationship (the contract to provide widgets) as the complaint. This counterclaim if not raised in the first responsive pleading is waived and cannot be raised again either in the same lawsuit or any subsequent lawsuit between the same parties. If the counterclaim is merely between the same parties, but not related to the events and facts raised in the complaint, it is permissive. It may be raised as a counterclaim, or later in a separate lawsuit.

In raising a counterclaim while it is not necessary to repeat the allegations of the complaint relating to jurisdiction, identification of the parties, venue, etc., it is necessary to set forth factual allegations that will support your claim. Some things can be taken from the complaint to keep the counterclaim simple and succinct. For example, if the complaint alleges a contract between the parties, and you agree with that, i.e. the parties entered into a written contract there is no need to re-allege all of elements of a contract. The other party's assertion that a contract has been entered into, with your admission to that effect, establishes a contract. It is not necessary to go into all the circumstances giving rise to the contract, that it was executed, etc.

Discovery

Just as in the case where you are the plaintiff, once any initial motions have been disposed of, and pleadings filed and served, the lawsuit will progress to the discovery stage. The same principles apply. You will use the discovery process not only to learn about the plaintiff's case, but also to attempt to force the plaintiff to commit to specific positions that will be difficult, if not impossible to change later. As will be discussed in more detail the part of this section on contract interpretation, getting your opponent, especially in the realm of contract law to admit certain things can be extremely effective in winning your case. Because written contracts are accorded deference in the eyes of the law there are significant limitations on what other evidence can be considered in determining the relationship between the parties. This can be extremely powerful and defining exactly what document governs the relationship between the parties can provide a significant advantage. Discovery often provides the way to accomplish this.

Of course you also want to use the discovery process to learn about the other side's case. What are the damages they are claiming? Who will they be calling as witnesses at the trial of the case? Are there any documents out that will help or hurt you? If the other side is a corporation, what did the board of directors or shareholders have to say about this situation? Interrogatories will identify witness and possibly documents. Requests to produce are used to actually review or get copies of the documents. Requests to admit will help you get the some issues resolved and possibly limit the things that the other side may be thinking of presenting at trial.

Because the legal profession has effectively taken the discovery process and turned it into a major area of contention in lawsuits, you may find yourself forced to file motions to compel discovery in which you can address insufficient or vague responses. Don't be afraid to file these motions. Judges in general do not like discovery disputes and have little patience for silly responses obviously intended to make the process more difficult than it has to be. Discovery is designed to allow parties to learn about their opponent's case, witnesses, documents, damages and so forth. Do not allow yourself to be deprived of this information simply because an attorney on the other side wants to be difficult or seeks the opportunity to bill additional hours.

Summary Judgment

Once discovery has been completed consider, if there is a defect in your opponent's case, consider bringing a motion for summary judgment. If in the course of discovery you have been able to establish an affirmative defense – such as expiration of the time in which to bring an action, or an absence of any evidence to support an essential element of the claim - don't be afraid to file a motion for summary judgment.

Review the section on summary judgment for the specifics of what summary judgment entails and the standard for summary judgment.

There is little downside risk of filing a motion for summary judgment. Denial of a motion for summary judgment does not "count against you" later in the trial of the case. It will take some time and effort, but unless it is completely frivolous will not cost you anything to file.

Even of your motion is denied, it will often force the other side to disclose their strategy and tactics well before the trial of the case, giving you still another advantage. For example, if you set forth in a motion for summary judgment that the plaintiff has failed to identify damages arising from the alleged breach of contract, you will force the other side to set forth those damages or risk losing the case at the summary judgment stage. Unlike discovery responses, where attorneys like to hedge and waffle on responses, here you will get full a full and complete breakdown of what the damages are, how they will be presented, and how they relate to the allegations of the complaint. The other side will not be doing this in an effort to share information. They will do it to avoid the risk of losing the case outright on a motion for summary judgment. Think of it as a free preview of what they plan to show at trial.

The Trial

In defending a contract lawsuit, the principles of the trial are the same as when you are the plaintiff, except that the order of presentation is reversed. The plaintiff will begin with the opening statements and will present their witnesses first. As before, this does not mean that it is a time for you to relax and be entertained by the proceedings. If you have used the discovery process to your advantage, you should have been able to narrow the issues and in turn the things that the other side will be able to introduce through testimony. It I up to you though to object if questions posed are irrelevant or if for example questions about what someone understood the contract to mean are asked. In any contract trial good preparation includes becoming familiar with things like the parole evidence rule and principles of contract interpretation.

If you have filed a counterclaim it is important to remember that unlike the plaintiff who will have an opportunity to reply, you have only one opportunity to establish the elements of your case, and that is when you respond to the plaintiff's case. You must both put up testimony or introduce evidence in opposition to what the plaintiff has presented, and, present your own evidence to support your counterclaim.

Just as when you are the plaintiff, you should have prepared ahead of time a checklist of the elements of both your counterclaim, as well as what the plaintiff must prove to prevail. Do not be afraid of standing up after the plaintiff as presented his case and moving for a dismissal if one or more elements of the case have been overlooked. If your opponent has established that a contract existed, and shown that there was a breach, but has not shown any damages, say so.

Finally, closing statements (after all the evidence has been presented) will, just as when you are the plaintiff, conclude the case.

Lawsuits to Interpret Contracts

No matter how carefully you prepare a contract, review it and revise it, there will always be some term or condition that is susceptible of being interpreted in more than one way. Different interpretations of contracts can result in an honest disagreement between parties who otherwise are trying to honor their obligations, or can constitute a convenient excuse for a party with less integrity, seeking some excuse to avoid its obligations.

Either way, if through discussion the parties cannot agree on the meaning of a term or condition in a contract there is a remedy in the form of a declaratory judgment. There is a separate section on declaratory judgments because such an action can be applicable to a multitude of situations and issues. It is though particularly well suited to resolving contract interpretation issues.

Declaratory judgment actions like these are unique in that unlike a breach of contract action, it is not necessary to establish any damages, or even that a contract has been breached. Either party is entitled to have a court interpret a contract so that it can know its rights and obligations.

In determining whether or not you should bring a lawsuit to interpret a contract, it is important that you understand the principles that will govern such a suit and in turn, determine the outcome.

In virtually all jurisdictions the decisions relating to contract interpretation state that the main objective of a court is to determine the intent of the parties. That much is relatively clear and undisputed.

Where the difficulty often arises is in how this principle is applied.

Written contracts are given deference in these cases as they should. After all, what is the point of having a written contract if it is going to be ignored? Consequently, the first rule of contract interpretation is that where the parties have reduced their agreement to writing, and that writing both addresses the issue in dispute and is unambiguous, not only will the written contract govern, other evidence cannot be considered to further interpret it.

It is only when the contract does not address the issue in dispute, or is vague or ambiguous, that other evidence can be considered to determine the intent of the parties. Other evidence can include statements made by the parties, conduct of the parties, custom and usage within an industry and if a particular interpretation of a disputed clause makes sense or is reasonable. Finally, if a term or language in a contract is ambiguous, the rule is that it will be construed against the party that drafted the contract.

To get an idea of how this would work, go back to our widget example. Assume that time of payment for the widgets is an issue. If the contract states that payment will be made within thirty days of delivery, the issue is simple. Payment within thirty days complies with the contract. Payment after that breaches the contract. The intent of the parties is clear from the face of the contract and it is neither necessary nor permissible to look further. If you are the purchaser of the widgets and think you ought to have forty-five days to make payment because other sellers allow that and your seller has allowed it in the past, you will lose. The court will not re-write the contract for you.

The situation changes dramatically though if the term in the contract is less clear. If the contract sets forth a price for the widgets but does not state when payment will be made, or if it states that payment will be made promptly following delivery, everything changes. What does "promptly" mean? The failure to specifically define the period in which payment must be made on the face of the contract opens the door to all kinds of other evidence. When was payment made in the past? When do other sellers demand and other purchaser in the industry make payment? What was said to the purchaser by the seller about payment? While none of this could be introduced with an unambiguous contract, it's all fair game when the terms are vague.

One important aspect of a declaratory judgment action is that it is somewhat of an exception to a well established tenet of our courts which is that in order to have jurisdiction of a case there must be an actual controversy between the parties. The underlying concept here is that courts do not exist to answer hypothetical questions. Declaratory judgment proceedings are a creature of statutes and deviate from that principle to some extent. While there is no outright controversy in that such an action can be brought before there is any actual dispute, the purpose is to define the rights of parties in some form of relationship, contractual or otherwise. Consequently, it is important that the complaint in these actions clearly state that a declaratory judgment is being sought and what is to be determined.

Other than that, a lawsuit for a declaratory judgment proceeds much as any other suit with pleadings, motions and discovery.

In Conclusion

In addition to a basic understanding of how a contract lawsuit would proceed, you should have a heightened appreciation of the importance of carefully negotiating and drafting a contract. The clearer and more concise a contract is, the more it encompasses and addresses the situations that are likely to arise, and the more it defines how issues will be addressed, the less likely you are to me standing in that courtroom hearing the judge tell you to begin.

Handling Your Personal Injury Claim

Ok, now that you're an expert on the law of negligence, premises liability and insurance, it's time to get a grasp on how to actually handle your claim when you end up inured, or have property damaged as a result of one of these accidents.

Attorneys

The first thing that many people do whenever they've been injured, or something happens is run out and hire any attorney. While there are some cases, due to complexity or other issues that require the expertise of an experienced attorneys, most of these cases do not, and can be handled very well without a lawyer.

A blaring word of warning at this point. If you do feel the need for an attorney to help you in a personal injury case, avoid like the plague the "TV Lawyers". You know who is being referred to.

These are the guys with all the TV commercials and billboards. The TV commercials are either gimmicky or are oriented to depict the wisdom, experience and prowess (as in insurance companies fear us) of the attorneys.

There is never, under any circumstances any justification for you to hire these clowns to represent you in a personal injury claim, for a lot of reasons.

First, the "TV Lawyer" is marketing and volume oriented. Some of these people have never tried a case, the focus being on settlement, as quickly as possible, usually to your detriment.

Second, all those ads cost a lot of money. They have to churn a tremendous volume of cases, and that means you are not going to get the attention you deserve from an attorney.

Third, for the very same reasons, these attorneys settle case rather than try them and the insurance adjusters and defense attorneys know this. They fully realize that the "TV Lawyer" may file a lawsuit, but he will never set foot in the courtroom. This trait has become so egregious that there have been reported instances of these personal injury "specialists" telling clients who would not accept a settlement and chose to go to trial to find another attorney.

Remember always that a good, competent attorney does not need to advertise to such an extreme extent. Certainly a dignified website or ad in the yellow pages to make people aware is normal and accepted. Any hype, glitz, repeated television, radio or billboard advertising though should be a red flag for you.

If you find yourself in a situation where an attorney is needed, shun the hype and set about, as is described elsewhere in this book to locate a competent, responsible attorney.

You've Had an Accident!

The cruel hand of fate has focused on you and what was up until now a plain, uneventful day has just gotten turned upside down.

You stopped at a light when bam! You're hit from behind. Or you are walking down the aisle of the clothing department and feel a sharp pain in your leg. You look down and see that you've been badly cut by a sharp bracket protruding from a display case. These and hundreds of mishaps like them affect people every day. The law is to the effect that if they are caused by someone else's negligence, or a defective condition, or any of a number of other causes, then you are entitled to recover.

Damages in these cases include medical bills, lost wages, pain and suffering, compensation for any disability, temporary or permanent, loss of enjoyment of life and emotional distress.

The challenge is to recover what you are entitled to.

Record and Gather Information

Obviously in any accident that results in injury, the first thing is to render reasonable care to anyone that is injured, and to make sure that you yourself receive any immediately needed care. But since this is a book about law, not first aid, we'll assume that you have done all those things, and as cold as it may seem, focus on what you need to do to protect yourself legally.

The first thing, assuming of course that you are not the cause of the whole disaster, is to record and document everything you possibly can about the accident, visible signs (or lack of signs) of any injury, and damage to vehicles, and defective conditions. Do this even if you really don't feel like it. If you're hurt, delegate it to a friend or someone else on the scene that you can contact later. Today it is hard to find a smart phone that cannot take video as well as still pictures. Now is the time to use it! It will almost certainly be important.

Take as an example the severe cut received from the sharp bracket. Care to make any wagers on the likelihood of that sharp bracket still protruding from the display case the day after the accident?

How about that car full of people who claimed they were not injured but three weeks later hit you with a lawsuit for personal injuries. Would it not be helpful to have a video of them walking around, talking and waiting after the accident, obviously not in any pain and without any apparent injuries? If you can't document or record these things, get someone to notice and take notes so that they will remember later. If you have a friend or someone you know, just point out to them the things that matter.

"Here is what cut my leg. See how it sticks out from the display case but can't be seen?"

"Wow, look at all those guys that were in the other car. They look fine. Sure is a good thing no one was hurt."

If no friend is available, get the name and address of another witness and point these things out, telling them candidly that they may be called later as a witness. Pointing these things out to people makes it more likely that they will remember. Bear in mind that the sharp bracket is very important to you, and you will clearly remember it because it sliced your leg open. To someone else, unless it is pointed out, it will probably fade from memory.

From a technical side, unless it comes from law enforcement, and even then there had better be a good reason, no one can stop you from taking pictures or videos of an accident scene in which you were involved. Should anyone object, just tell the politely but firmly that you are gathering potential evidence and are entitled to do so.

In addition to pictures, record any statements or anything anyone says. The closer in time to the actual accident, the better. There is an important exception in evidence law to the rule against hearsay, and that is the excited utterance rule. It holds that if a statement is made in a moment of upset or excitement, it is admissible as an exception to the rule against hearsay, because being made spontaneously and immediately, there is little likelihood of fabrication. When the time comes you can get into evidence all sorts of exclamations and sudden statements that if made even minutes later would be inadmissible.

Again, you don't need anyone's permission to record things that they say at an accident scene.

Get identifying information from everyone involved as well as any potential witnesses. If it is a premises issue, such as the sharp bracket, get the names of all employees present. Do this as quickly as you can. Also, if you can record any statements of these people do it quickly. Once management shows up the first thing they will tell the employees to do is to leave or be quiet. Statements from employees made immediately after an accident can be invaluable.

Document Medical Care

Recording actual medical information when you receive treatment is not the challenge. Thanks to an explosion of medical malpractice suits over the years, medical care providers have turned documenting medical diagnosis and treatment into a veritable science. The challenge to you as a potential personal injury claimant is to make sure it is documented in a way that is helpful to you. The best way to do that is to provide a good and detailed explanation of what happened, including specifically how different parts of your body were affected.

If it becomes an issue a doctor's report that reflects that you were involved in an automobile accident and had recollection of your arm striking the shift lever, will be far more helpful to you than a report that simply states you were involved in a motor vehicle accident. Which version gets recorded is up to you when you tell the doctor in detail what happened (give a history).

As mercenary as it may sound when you first receive treatment for an injury is not the time to be stoic. Medical reports will be an important factor in determining the nature and extent of your injuries, and you need to understand two principles related to them. First, doctors use various forms of shorthand to record observations, and they can have devastatingly different connotations depending on who is hearing them. One term often used is a good example. A doctor will often record "patient presents in no apparent distress". In medical terms this means that there was nothing wrong with you that required immediate medical intervention. An insurance adjuster or defense attorney though will suggest that this term means when they doctor saw you there was nothing wrong with you.

Second, unless you have sustained such devastating injuries so as to make an indelible impression on the doctors, when it comes time to evaluate your injuries, whether by an adjustor or a jury, the medical reports will govern. Stated another way, down the road, when it is time to resolve your claim, if it's not reflected in the medical reports, it simply is not a viable fact. To see this in context, imagine a doctor testifying six months after you received treatment about your condition when you appeared in the emergency room. Which do you suppose is going to be more impressive testimony for a jury?

The patient had been involved in motor vehicle accident. Patient was articulate, in no apparent distress, no fractures evidenced on x-rays, vital signs normal.

Or

Patient had been involved in a motor vehicle accident, and complains of pain adjacent to cervical spine radiating into shoulders, and on right arm. Patient stated that he had struck his head on the corner of the seat and that his arm had struck the shift lever resulting in immediate severe paid which has reportedly not subsided. Vital signs normal. X-rays are negative for fractures, suggesting soft tissue injury.

Bear in mind the number of patients this physician is likely to see in this six month period and you will understand that if asked, he will be unable to recall if you were in pain at the time or not, unless it is reflected in his notes as contained in the medical records. This is not to say that you need to be rolling on the floor in simulated anguish, but be sure to make your point so that it is later reflected in the medical records.

In addition to the medical records maintained by the providers, keep your own records. If your injuries are serious keep a daily diary in which you record levels of pain, physical limitations on your activities, and changes in your lifestyle related to the injuries. If someone else is required to assist you with day-to-day activities, make a record of that.

Keep a summary of all expenses you incur and all travel related to you injuries or treatment.

Don't Make Any Statements or Sign Anything.

Aside from forms presented by law enforcement (if it is an auto accident) or consent forms for medical treatment, you should not be signing anything until you've had a lot of time to review and reflect.

This is certainly true regarding any form presented by an insurance company associated with the other side. Just as with any profession there are insurance adjustors that are meticulously scrupulous. At the same time there are those who will do anything to minimize a claim, regardless of the harm their conduct causes. While certainly not common, there have been instances of insurance adjustors appearing at hospital bedsides with release forms and checks, trying to induce injured accident victims to settle quickly and cheaply.

With respect to any insurance company associated with a potential defendant there is without exception no document that you need to sign early on, or without having time to reflect and review. Not a single one – ever!

Later, again if it is an automobile accident, you may be presented with a settlement check and release from property damage. In auto accident cases the personal injury claims and property damage claims are often settled separately. While this is acceptable, review the forms carefully to be sure that any release is limited to property damage. Be sure that the settlement amount is appropriate for the cost to repair or replace your vehicle.

If there is any doubt in your mind, remember the trusty cell phone or voice recorder in your pocket when you specifically ask the adjuster: "this is just for the property damage right? It has nothing to do with my injuries, medical bills or anything else besides the damage to my car correct?"

Another thing that will inevitably come up is that the adjuster for the other side, be it the driver of the other car in an auto accident, or the insurer of the owner of the property in a premises liability case, will contact you and tell you that "he needs to get a recorded statement" from you.

This is absolute nonsense. He might like to get a recorded statement, but an adverse insurance company has no specific right to be provided with such a statement, nor are you under any obligation to provide one. You should never give the insurance company for the other side a recorded statement. It will never help you and can potentially harm you.

When you are contacted and asked (sometimes the language is more akin to a demand, intended to intimidate or suggest that this is your obligation in order to help resolve this case) your response is always that you are under no legal obligation to provide such a statement and have no intention of doing so.

This will be an exercise in wills early on and remember that in the person of an adjuster is someone who has years of training and experience in dealing with claims. Do not allow yourself to be either intimidated or beguiled. The typical response from the adjuster to a refusal to give a recorded statement will often be some combination of feigned offense, indignation, or a suggestion that you must have something to hide by refusing.

The truth is that you really are under no obligation to speak with an adjuster at all, at any time, and until you are ready to resolve your claim, it is seldom to your advantage to do so.

Still another issue to watch for is an attempt to gain access to your medical records or be allowed to discuss your injuries with your doctor, again, under the guise of "helping to resolve the case". Until you are ready to resolve your case or claim, you are under no obligation whatsoever to allow access to your medical records or to have anyone providing you with medical care to discuss your condition, diagnosis or treatment with any adjuster, attorney or anyone else associated with an actual or potential defendant. Regardless of how forcefully it is suggested to you otherwise, your right to privacy in this context is absolute.

Just as with giving a recorded statement, allowing an adjuster to see your medical records before you are ready to present your claim is not to your advantage.

Probably the most important thing to remember if you've been injured in an accident is that it is your claim and you can determine when and how to present it.

A final note on this topic, to be sure that you have not misunderstood, is that all of this applies to the insurance company or adjustor for the other side. There will be times when your own insurance company contacts you with requests. This is entirely different. Remember the relationship between insurance companies and the policyholders. When it is your insurance company, things are different, and you need to act accordingly. Your policy of insurance may for example have a provision that requires you to give a recorded statement as part of the required cooperation. Do not confuse cooperating with your own company with dealing with the insurance carrier for the other side.

Policy Limit Settlements

In this day and age there are some jurisdictions where statutory mandated insurance coverage amounts have not kept pace with rapidly rising medical costs. There are numerous cases involving serious injuries where the available insurance coverage will clearly be inadequate.

In these instances, a combination of statutes and common law decisions often put insurance companies in a position where they will very quickly tender their policy limits. Some statutes define failure to do so as prima facia bad faith insurance bad faith claims practice. There has been at least one jurisdiction that developed a common law doctrine in this regard to the effect that failure of an insurance company to tender policy limits in the case of an undisputed liability claim that clearly exceeded the policy limits had the effect of eliminating the limits of the policy.

Faced with these issues, in personal injury cases, most often in auto accident cases where liability is not an issue and damages obviously exceed the limits of the policy, an insurance company will often contact the potential claimant and offer to pay the maximum limit of its liability.

An example would be if you have been badly injured in an auto accident that was undisputedly caused by the other driver and had already incurred medical bills that far exceeded the limits of the other driver's liability insurance policy. At some point, relatively quickly, you would be contacted by the adjustor and informed that the company was tendering its policy limits.

The problem with this is that the insurance company has a contract (the insurance policy) with its insured and must protect them. The result of simply paying the policy limits is that the insured is left liable for anything above the policy amount. To address this, many insurance companies will try to secure a release for their insured in exchange for policy limit payment.

This is where you have to be careful.

First, if the insured has adequate assets from which a judgment could be satisfied, it would not make sense for you to accept a small portion of what you might be entitled to in exchange for a release.

Second, jurisdictions vary on how this is addressed, but there is the danger that you might be inadvertently releasing other potential defendants. The law in some jurisdictions provides that a settlement and release with respect to one liable party operates as a settlement and release as to all. You must carefully review the law in your jurisdiction on the effect of any such settlement. You must carefully determine how deep your potential opponent's pocket is before you sign a release.

Again, remember, this is your claim. You should take and keep control and never allow yourself to pressured or intimidated in any way.

Presenting Your Claim

Since you now know everything that you could possibly ever learn about personal injury law, the law of negligence and premises liability law, it time to talk about what you actually do with all of that. How do you get from having a terrible day and ending up injured, to taking a check to the bank?

Most personal injury claims are covered to some extent or another by insurance, and it is the insurance claims process that will be addressed here. If the claim cannot be settled then you will file suit and it will be handled the same as any other court case discussed throughout.

The first thing you should understand is that at least at first, until they realize that you know what you're doing, an insurance adjuster will be more than happy to deal with you when you represent yourself. They assume that anyone without an attorney will not know the process, their rights, or how to negotiate a settlement. Put another way, they will try to run over you. Also, it's a lot easier to settle a case when you don't have to worry about the attorney's one third (or higher) share of the settlement.

It is important that you understand several things about personal injury insurance settlements.

First, they are generally final. If you are injured and are receiving medical care or treatment that will continue over a period of time, with a few exceptions, you do not want to be settling the case until you have received all the treatment necessary.

The exceptions to this rule are if the injury is serious enough that an insurer offers policy limits. As long as you are sure that there are no other sources of funds, or other insurance, then you might as well take it, because that's all you're going to get. Just be absolutely sure that you have exhausted every possible other source of insurance, or liable parties with the ability to pay, because release agreement here may very well act to release everyone else, know or unknown.

The other exception to the rule against settling is if you just absolutely have to have funds now. While insurance companies vehemently deny it, they make a practice of using the "you need money now and don't have it" rule. Simply stated, if you have been badly injured and are disabled while being treated, you may be in desperate need of funds. Often there is a loss of employment income. If you have no health insurance, medical bills become staggering. Even with insurance the amounts that you may have to pay can be overwhelming if you're not able to work. The insurance companies are well aware of this and will often capitalize on desperation to offer an inadequate but absolutely needed settlement. If you are in this predicament there is little else that you can do, but you do need to be aware of what is happening to you.

Ideally, you will not be in total economic chaos. Most injuries are not so severe that they totally disable you for any length of time, health insurance pays the medical bills and if you're smart and prudent, you will have (in the case of a car accident) bought personal injury protection insurance from you own carrier and it will be kicking in you keep you afloat.

This puts you where you belong – in control – instead of at the mercy of an insurance company.

When to Settle

Being in control, you decide when to settle. You may not be able to command as large a settlement as you would like, after all the adjuster is there to make sure they pay as little as possible, but you are in absolute control of when the case will settle.

Absent a tender of policy limits, you do not want to settle the case until you are able to determine all the losses that you have sustained as a result of the accident. You know the obvious ones. You went to the emergency room, you have doctor's bills, you bought medicine, and you were out of work for a couple of weeks. But don't forget other, less tangible losses.

One that almost everyone is familiar with is: it hurt! Sure, injuries hurt. Pain is not good. You are entitled to be compensated for that pain. What about disability? Will that fractured arm heal with no residual effects whatsoever? Highly unlikely, especially as we get older. Bring this up to your doctor and ask him to assign an impairment rating.

Only when you are sure that you have a handle on everything related to the accident should you even begin discussing a settlement. This is not to say that you should ignore the adjuster. Take any opportunity to let them know that you are in no rush to settle the claim. If you have it, mention that your personal injury protection insurance paid your medical bills and lost wages, so you're not in any rush. Let him know that you are waiting to see about any personal disability. This accomplishes a couple of things and lays the groundwork for negotiations. First, it lets the adjustor know that you are not in any way desperate. That weapon is gone from his arsenal. Second, it lets him know that you understand what is involved in the claim, have done your homework, and know what you are doing.

How to Value Your Claim

One of the most challenging things facing you in settling with an insurance company is determining the value of your claim. It is of course the proverbial tug of war. You would like to be paid as much as possible for your injuries. The insurance company would like to pay you as little as possible. But to get a reasonable settlement, you have to understand how that is determined. Common sense tells us that if you were slightly injured in a rear-end accident, incurred medical bills of $500 and lost no time from work, the insurance company is not going to be waving a check for $100,000 in front of you to settle that case.

More realistically, at some point you're going to be talking to the adjuster and they will ask: "what will it take to settle this case"?

A far more serious question than first appears. Come back with the $100,000 in the example just discussed and they know they're dealing with an idiot. You will have no real credibility in terms of settlement negotiations. Come in with a low number, and you might have a settlement, but how much did you leave on the table.

The better response is "I really couldn't say. Let me put everything together and shoot you a settlement demand."

Wow! A lot of things are going on here.

First you've again let him know that you understand. "Settlement demand" is a term of art and it suggests that you not only "know the lingo" but understand that putting together and considering all the factors that determine the settlement value of a claim is too complicated to deal with in a simple question and answer session.

You've reiterated that you're not in a hurry and would rather take your time assessing all the factors.

Finally, you've reinforced your control. "This case will settle when I am able to assemble all the information and analyze it, not when you Mr. Adjuster decide to toss a number out."

So, Put Together the Demand

The good news is that approached methodically and logically, putting together a settlement demand is fairly straightforward.

First factor in and realistically assess the liability issue. Often there will not even be a question. Which driver ran the red light or the stop sign will be clear. The rear end accident takes little imagination. In other cases though, it may be less clear. In those, you will need to make a realistic assessment, should the case go to court, how the liability issue will be resolved, in terms of likelihood of a decision in your favor versus against you. You should be able to either eliminate liability as a factor to consider at all, or, be able to make an objective assessment of the likelihood, in terms of a percentage, that you will prevail.

Now put that aside to get back to later.

The next thing to do is to attach a dollar value for settlement purposes to your injuries, with no regard for the liability issue. To do that, you simply lay out on a piece of paper or a spreadsheet every loss caused by or related to the accident and assign it a dollar value.

Some things will be easy to value. You have receipts to the penny of your medical expenses. You know how much pay you lost by being out. You know how far it is to the doctor's office and to the pharmacy and the IRS publishes every year what a mile of car travel is worth.

Other things are more difficult. How do you put a value on that throbbing ache in your injured shoulder every morning? Or the fact that you can't play with your children in the yard? These are more difficult but there are some tools to help you.

In terms of long term issues, a tool often employed by personal injury attorneys in presenting to the jury is a mathematical approach, beginning with the question of "how much money would you take each day to experience this kind of pain? If I gave you ten dollars in the morning to hurt all day, would that be enough? Would you take $5? The key is to use a small enough number so that the average juror is thinking "heck keep your $10 – I don't want to hurt." Then apply the fact that there are a lot of days. Once you have them thinking of a number, the rest is just simple math. Insurance companies (ironically) have created actuarial tables that tell us how long we will live. Not you individually of course, but generically. They tell us that a 35-year-old Caucasian male will likely die when they reach a certain age, say 82.3. This is where the lawyer's math trick kicks in. If he's gotten a jury to agree in their own minds that $10 a day for that painful shoulder is reasonable, watch the math. 82.3-35=47.3 years, or

17,264.5 days which at $10 per day comes out to $172,645.00.

That's a far cry from taking a wild guess and saying, "gee, my shoulder hurts, how about $10,000 to cover that?"

Of course you can't get an insurance adjuster to go for this – they know what you're doing. But it will get the value out of the nominal range and again, will let them know that you understand how all this works.

As a practical matter, there is an even better way to approach valuing the intangibles, and that is to see what real juries have done with similar cases. There are companies that gather data on actual jury verdicts in courts all around the country. With the miracles of technology, these are sorted and indexed by type of injury, amount of medical bills, kinds of medical procedures required to treat the injury, extent of permanent disability and amount of lost wages. Notably absent from the factors are the intangibles such as pain and suffering, and loss of enjoyment of life. That is the purpose of the correlation of the data – to see what the juries have awarded over and above the "raw numbers" damages.

By plugging the known factors into the search these databases will provide the statistical results of all relevant jury awards – high and low, average and mean.

Moreover, this data is cross indexed so thoroughly that it even presents an index number by state and county.

Everyone is aware that juries in some locales are more generous than in others.

Armed with this data you can determine that statistically, for an injury similar to yours, with medical expenses in a given range, if the case were taken to trial you could expect a jury award somewhere between the high and the low amounts, using the average a god valuation point. By inserting your state and county you could those figures for your location.

This is a powerful tool in terms of discussing a settlement. It is hard for an adjuster to argue much with the numbers that tell with at least some predictability the outcome should the case not settle and go to trial.

The Settlement Demand

The settlement demand, presented to the adjuster when it is time to settle is an organized, logical presentation of this material.

Start with an introduction, describing the accident, the parties, and the available insurance amount.

If liability is not an issue, that should be stated immediately. "This was a rear end accident in which I was sitting stopped at a red traffic signal and struck from behind by your insured. Liability is not an issue in this case and will not be further discussed."

If liability is an issue, leave it until later.

Set forth in list form the special damages - that is those that you can attach a firm number to.

Then set forth the intangibles such as pain and suffering, permanent disability, and emotional distress. Add a number, but explain below it how you arrived at it, e.g. $4.00 per day for permanent pain, etc.

Add up all of these numbers and you will have your total damages.

Following that insert the results of jury verdict research with an explanation of this represents a probable outcome if we are not able to settle the case.

At the end state that under all the circumstances you would agree to settle the claim for "X" dollars. This amount should be at the high end of the jury verdict ranges but not be higher than the total damages you have calculated. After all if after adding up everything, including amounts you deemed appropriate for pain and suffering, you come up with $25,000, asking or $50,000 just makes you look ridiculous.

Finally, if liability is an issue, then you need to address it. If you have determined (and be honest with yourself) that a jury may assign some liability to you, now is where you factor it in, just before setting forth the actual demand. You would insert a section for adjustment for liability. You would acknowledge that all the figures presented assumed uncontested liability, but you acknowledge a possibility of some liability assigned to you. If you feel that you might be assigned 20% of the liability (perhaps someone made a left turn in front of you but your were speeding), you would simply reduce the final figure by 20%.

There is a difference of opinion as to how and when to present and address this. It becomes a judgment call for you. On the one hand some say that it is better to present the demand without adjustment for liability, making that a negotiating point. Others argue that presenting the issue upfront preserves your credibility and actually defuses the ability of the other side to demand concessions.

The inexorable rule is that you must, while still being logical and credible, present as high an initial demand as possible, because it can never go up, only down as the other side begins challenging your points and arguments.

Negotiating the Settlement

This is no different that arguing over the price of a used car. The trick is to have a logical and objective basis for your demands. Never forget, the adjuster does this for a living. Unless you are extremely accident prone, you only do it on occasion. The person that just starts throwing numbers around is doomed. The adjuster simply refuses and says "that's too much – we can't pay that". Without a firm basis you just end up lowering your demand until you get to a number that makes the adjuster happy, obviously substantially less than what you would have wanted and probably a lot less than you could have received.

Do not bid against yourself. Send in your demand, if it is done properly, a response by an adjuster that it is "too high" without more is not acceptable. Tell them that. "I've sent you a detailed settlement package based on verifiable factors. If you are serious about settling this case you need to give me a more meaningful response than it is too high."

If he just throws out a number, turn things back against him. "Aside from the fact that that is a number that your company would love to settle this claim for, will you tell me how you arrived at that?" After all, you went through the effort to submit an objective settlement demand. You are entitled to the same in return.

Insurance adjusters in response will always come back with something to the effect of, "our underwriters have done an in depth analysis of this claim and that's what they have determined is a fair settlement". Don't hesitate to respond by suggesting that perhaps it's what a jury is likely to come up with that is the more relevant measure of the value of the claim.

This back and forth negotiating is fairly common, and it is a process that will eventually end up at a number you both can live with, or it will be an impasse, with filing suit the next step.

Sometimes, it's just not possible to settle these claims. Insurance companies are notorious for delaying, knowing that people in an accident often need funds desperately.

They will often throw out a take it or leave it offer. Tactics used by insurance companies have grown so offensive over the years that many courts have recognized a separate cause of action against them, arising out of such bad faith claims practices.

When this happens, the only option is to file suit. Later, in another section, you'll learn how to do that.

Alternative Dispute Resolution – Arbitration and Mediation

As court dockets become more and more crowded, as the costs of litigation skyrocket, and as it becomes more and more difficult to resolves disputes in court across the board, there has been a growing trend to lean toward what is called alternative dispute resolution.

While the term Alternative Dispute Resolution refers to any mechanism or system that shifts a court case from the traditional path of lawsuit to trial, the courts have focused on arbitration and mediation. So, while there are an almost infinite number of variations and permutations, most alternative dispute resolution options generally in use today can be broken down into two main categories: Arbitration and Mediation.

The trend in this direction is well under way, and there appears to be every indication that the use of alternative dispute resolution will increase rather than decrease. Consequently, if you want to represent yourself in court, you need to be familiar with the concepts and basic procedures.

The extent to which alternative dispute resolution is used varies from jurisdiction to jurisdiction and the range of options is substantial. Some jurisdictions have no provision whatsoever for any alternative dispute resolution. In others you cannot get to trial without at least attempting either arbitration or mediation. The kind of alternative dispute resolution and at what point along the litigation process it must occur varies from jurisdiction to jurisdiction. In almost all jurisdictions it is not required until discovery has been completed, on the theory that it is not possible to have a meaningful mediation or arbitration until both sides are fully aware of and familiar with the case.

Depending on where you are and in what court your case is, you may not have a choice. You may find yourself confronting the prospect of alternative dispute resolution whether you like it or not. So here is what you need to know about it.

While people casually use the terms arbitration and mediation together, suggesting they are closely related, the only thing they really have in common is that they are both called forms of alternative dispute resolution. Beyond that they are substantially different.

A final note of introduction. Arbitration and Mediation are not the only forms of alternative dispute resolution. There are mini trials, trials with private judges, mediation advisory panels (where a panel of attorneys listens to and reviews the case and give an opinion as to how they think it will turn out) and within these categories, dozens of variations and options. However, since arbitration and mediation are the most common and popular, those will be the focus of this discussion.

Arbitration

Arbitration is a process in which the decision making and fact finding that are normally associated in the legal system with the judge and jury are shifted elsewhere.

In an arbitration the parties, or if they agree, a judge will select one or more arbitrators to hear the case, in the same way that a judge or a judge and jury would, and render a decision.

Arbitration is not new. Well before the trend toward alternative dispute resolution, disputes in specialized fields were subjected to arbitration by virtue of it being included in specific contracts and agreements.

There are several reasons why arbitration evolved as an effective form of dispute resolution even before being championed by the courts and legislatures.

While the American legal tradition is to have a dispute tried by a jury of one's peers, the reality is that in a technical society, that is not always the best, most efficient, or even the fairest way to resolve things. Especially when the dispute involves things of a complicated or technical, a jury, as a body of twelve people of various backgrounds and education often to not have the ability to grasp the important factors and aspects of the case. In a dispute for example over the contract rights to a complex chemical process, a scientist's testimony with diagrams about different molecular structures, is simply not going to be something that a jury is likely to understand or remember when it comes time to deliberate. A three person arbitration panel made up of scientists is far more likely to be able to evaluate those issues.

Arbitration is cheaper. The cost of a trial to the litigants is horrendous. The main reason that Be Your Own Lawyer was born, and why this book was written is that the cost of taking a civil case from inception to trial, with representation by an attorney is beyond reach of the average person. Though possibly not a serious an obstacle, cost is a factor for businesses too. Instead of months or years of legal skirmishing, extensive interrogatories and depositions costing thousands and thousands of dollars, litigants began turning to arbitration. Arbitration costs a fraction of what a civil case taken to trial costs.

Arbitration is quicker. The average court docket in many places in the United States is two years or more. An arbitration can be scheduled as soon as a dispute arises, and if it is not discovery intensive, the whole case resolved before in a civil case, the first depositions would be getting scheduled.

In that context, arbitration clauses found their way into many commercial contracts and into many consumer contracts in certain industries. For example, long before arbitration was embraced by the judicial system as a way to reduce case loads, it was impossible for someone to open a stock brokerage account virtually anywhere in the United States without agreeing that any disputes would be resolved by arbitration. Automobile dealers have a long history of having arbitration clauses in their purchase and service contracts.

Various federal and state laws have put teeth into these arbitration clauses in the form of the Federal Arbitration and act similar state legislation. These laws basically provide that where parties have agreed to arbitrate, they must do so in lieu of a trial in a civil court.

Arbitration comes in many styles and flavors.

There may be one arbitrator or a panel of three or more. The arbitration can be binding or non-binding. That is the parties after they go through arbitration may still elect to go to court. It can be done pursuant to rules of a court system, or under the rules of an independent organization specified in an agreement, such as the American Arbitration Association. It can address the entire case, or be limited to specific issues decided by the parties.

Because different rules can apply, the form of the arbitration can be as varied as different imaginations can devise. There can for example be no discovery whatsoever allowed, or a set of arbitration rules may provide for full or partial discovery prior to the actual arbitration.

The rules for admission of documents may track the rules of evidence for courts in the jurisdiction, or they may be completely different, with a much more relaxed framework for getting documents into evidence.

Typically an arbitration will be much more relaxed in terms of procedural rules than appearing in court. You generally for example do not have to concern yourself with notice versus fact pleading. There are few stringent pleading requirements at all. Normally a request for arbitration, usually on a form provided, sets forth the dispute the arbitrator(s) are to address, while a response sets forth the other party's position. There will be no motions to dismiss or for summary judgment. No motions to compel, or to amend pleadings. The thought processes behind all this is that the arbitrator, or the arbitration panel, has enough expertise and knowledge to understand the issues and the procedures so that all the formalities of a civil trial are not necessary.

The kind of arbitration environment that you might find yourself in will depend primarily on how you got there. The trend toward alternative dispute resolution notwithstanding, there are still guarantees in the form of federal and state constitutions as well as federal and state statutes, that limit the extent to which your right to trial by jury in certain matters can be curtailed by forcing you into arbitration.

That is why for example in many jurisdictions the arbitration is non-binding. The hope is that the parties after submitting the case to an arbitrator will accept the ruling, but in the end, they still have the right to pursue to case to trial.

It is far more likely if you find yourself in arbitration that it is pursuant to some clause in an agreement that you signed. Under these circumstances you may also have waived your rights to such things as trial by jury and agreed to resolve the matter in accordance with the rules and procedures of an independent organization.

Many people assume that because arbitration is less formal than a court proceeding, that preparation is not necessary. They often proceed to arbitration intending to just present their side and trust the arbitrator to make a fair decision. This is a mistake.

Even though arbitration rules are more relaxed and streamlined than those applicable in a civil trial, they must still be followed. The first thing to do when you find yourself looking at arbitrating your case is to obtain a complete copy of the rules and procedures of whatever arbitration process you're confronted with. If arbitration is required by the rules in your jurisdiction, the court rules will have a specific section for arbitration or mediation. You won't have far to look.

On the other hand, if you are in arbitration pursuant to an agreement before an independent organization, they are obligated to provide you with a complete set of rules and procedures. All you have to do is ask. But that works both ways. It is very difficult to justify appearing at an arbitration unprepared when all the information that you would have needed was there for the asking.

The actual arbitration process is actually much easier and "user friendly" than a civil trial. Of course it is. The parties are paying the arbitrators and there is only one arbitration to be scheduled rather than wrestling with a crowded court docket.

It should be pointed out that usually it is possible for the parties to "tailor make" the arbitration to suit the case by agreement. For example, one form of arbitration often used in personal injury cases is referred to as "high/low" arbitration. In many car accident case liability is not an issue. Usually the parties agree on which driver caused the accident, but disagree on the amount of damages to be paid. In such cases the matter can be submitted to an arbitration where the parties agree that the only task of the arbitrator is to determine an appropriate amount of damages to award.

How the logistics of an arbitration are handled differs somewhat between a court ordered arbitration and an arbitration pursuant to agreement.

In a court ordered arbitration the judge may appoint an arbitrator, or a panel of arbitrators, or, the parties may be allowed to select from a list. The arbitration will usually not be scheduled per se by the court, but the order providing for arbitration will usually contain a deadline by which it must be completed. Within that time frame the parties are free to contact the arbitrators (together, not separately) and arrange things like date, time and place.

If the arbitration is before an independent organization, as is more common when it is pursuant to agreement or contract, there is a quite a bit more flexibility. The parties are usually allowed to agree, (unless it is specifically addressed in the contract giving rise to the arbitration) whether to have one arbitrator or more. The arbitrators are generally selected by the parties from a list provided by the organization. Organizations that provide arbitration services typically have large lists of arbitrators available and as a result it is possible to select arbitrators that are not only generally experienced, but have knowledge and credentials in the area of the matter being arbitrated. The parties are free to set the date, time and place of the arbitration, and since the arbitrators are being paid by the parties, there is more flexibility.

Usually if logistically possible, an arbitration will take place in a conference room setting as opposed to a courtroom. You should not let the informal environment detract from the importance of the proceeding. Your case will be decided in the conference room of the Hotel Excelsior just as surely as it would be in the huge courthouse downtown! It is an adversary proceeding regardless of where it is held. Be prepared!

There is no need to go into great detail about how to actually participate in arbitration. Except for the location where it is held, and the applicability of different rules, probably somewhat less formal, it is not substantially different than presenting your case in court. The plaintiff begins its case with witnesses and evidence. The defendant responds. The plaintiff may have the opportunity to reply. Missing will be the motions and maneuvering since they have no place in an arbitration. Also probably at least curtailed, will be the opening and closing statements. Added to the mix will be the ability, depending on the rules in place for the arbitrator(s) to ask questions, of the parties and in some cases of the witnesses.

The entire demeanor of the arbitration process is more to get at the facts and decide the case than to worry about the formalities and ritual sometimes associated with court.

Mediation

The only thing that mediation has in common with arbitration is that they are both forms of alternative dispute resolution whose names often appear together.

Mediation is different than arbitration both in form and in process.

Mediation is a process in which the parties are encouraged to reach a settlement with the help of a trained mediator.

Mediation has become popular with the realization that the vast majority of court cases do not go to trial, but instead, settle before trial. The problem is that they often settle "on the courthouse steps". That is after all the discovery has been gone through, after all the motions have been filed and handled by the court, after the case has literally been prepared for trial by both side, often after a jury has been summoned and is waiting, the parties settle. The obvious question is would it not make more sense to settle earlier. After all, if there was a basis for settlement as the parties walk into the courtroom, that basis surely didn't materialize out of thin air on the day of the trial. It was always there.

That is the purpose of mediation. To try to get the parties to agree, either to a full settlement of the case, or at least as to some of the issues well before the trial. Mediation, along with arbitration has been so successful that almost all jurisdictions have some form of program, with varying degrees of voluntariness in terms of participation.

Unlike arbitration, mediation is a process of settlement. The mediator cannot force a settlement, or make a decision. A mediator will try to work with the parties to negotiate a settlement.

Logistically, just as with arbitration, a case may get to mediation either by virtue of a mandatory alternative dispute resolution program in your jurisdiction, or, though less frequently, by virtue of a contract or agreement that contains such a clause. If there are contract clauses regarding alternative dispute resolution, they usually provide for arbitration as opposed to mediation.

As with arbitration, either the court will appoint a mediator, or if an independent organization is used, the parties will select one from a list of qualified neutrals.

Since it is far less formal than a trial or an arbitration, the way a mediation is conducted will vary from case to case and from mediator to mediator. Mediations are almost always held at informal locations, such as a conference room or similar venue.

While there is no universally prescribed style or mechanism, because it is after all a concerted attempt to get the parties to agree to a settlement, it will often include a mechanism for the mediator to work with the parties together as well as individually.

In a typical mediation, the mediator will open the proceedings by introducing himself and laying out the ground rules and basics of the mediation. These will include such things as:

-         how he intends to conduct the mediation

-         stressing confidentiality. (Most jurisdictions shield mediators from future disclosure of anything that transpired in the mediation) He will point out that nothing said in the course of the mediation is discoverable and everything is absolutely confidential

-         stressing that this is not a hearing but an earnest effort to achieve a settlement

-       pointing out that he is not a judge or an arbitrator and will not be rendering a decision, but instead trying to help achieve a settlement

-       that he has formed no opinion regarding the case and in fact knows very little about it, relying on the parties to educate him as to the facts and issues

The foregoing will be in lieu of any set or rules or procedures that would be associated with an arbitration, so it is clearly a simpler, less cumbersome process.

Once the preliminaries are taken care of the usual format of the mediation is for the mediator and both parties to meet, if feasible around a conference table, and begin by each side setting forth their positions. Normally the plaintiff would begin, giving a general outline of the case, followed by the defendant doing the same. The mediator will of course note the differences in positions and will ask questions of the parties about the case. He will ask questions, while everyone is together about the posture of any prior settlement negotiations, the posture of the case: whether discovery is complete, and whether there are any specific areas upon which the parties can agree.

It should be remembered that while of course the goal of the mediation is to achieve a complete settlement, there is always the option of reaching settlement on specific issues. If the parties can agree and stipulate to some things, then those may not need to be re-litigated. The parties may even agree on certain things, and agree to submit the remaining issues, those on which they are unable to agree to arbitration.

Once the mediator has a good picture of the case and the positions of the parties, he will generally break the parties up and continue the next phase of the mediation by meeting with the parties privately.

In private meetings the mediator will again stress the confidentiality aspect of the process and in particular will often stress that whatever is said in a private session will not be disclosed to the other side, either in a private meeting with them, or in a subsequent joint meeting.

The purpose of the private sessions is to allow the parties to disclose aspects of the case that they do not want the other side to know for one reason or another. Here is where the parties can candidly discuss with the mediator the weaknesses and problems with their respective cases, and their situation regarding a settlement. For one reason or another a party may be anxious to settle a case, but not willing to let the other party know it because it would compromise their negotiating position. Take for example in a business dispute case where fraud may have been alleged. If the defendant is in the midst of refinancing its debt, it may have been informed by its potential lender that the fraud lawsuit would have to be resolved before the refinancing could proceed. Obviously the defendant does not want the plaintiff to know if the pressure it is under to get the lawsuit settled.

Another purpose of the private meeting is to allow the mediator to point out strengths or weaknesses in each party's case. Mediators are often selected for their experience either in the area of the dispute, or in having tried cases in the past arising out of the same area. Without drawing the attention of the other side, the mediator could point to areas that might be harmful to the case.

Finally the mediator in a private session can get a true feel of hat the party would be willing to settle for. The nature of negotiation between adversaries makes such disclosure impossible without a mediator. In discussing a settlement amount it is axiomatic that any initial offer or demand will not be reflective of the amount that would really be accepted or paid. No matter what language or terms are used to let the other party know that this offer is demand is the absolute final offer or demand and failure to meet it will result in trial, the other side will always take that offer or demand as a starting point. As a result settlement offers and demands will often be all over the place. By knowing a party's true position, the mediator will a have a fixed as opposed to a moving target toward which he can work to achieve a settlement.

The mediator may alternate between private meetings with each party, followed by another joint conference at which, any issues agreed upon can be discussed. As issues are narrowed the likelihood of settlement increases, so the psychology at a mediation will be to keep any momentum toward settlement going.

One result of this is that mediations, unlike arbitrations, are seldom broken into multi-day segments. There is a lot of psychology at work in mediation, including getting the parties to be thinking that a settlement is not only possible, but imminent. That all goes away if the process adjourns, to be begun again at some time in the future.

While mediation is a relatively uncomplicated process, and it appears to be no more than everybody sitting around the conference table to talk about the case, don't be lulled into complacency.

Expect the mediator to be a skillful negotiator. His job is to get a settlement. It does not have to be a fair settlement, and he will seek the most concessions from the side most likely to give them. He will use various techniques to try to get each side to make concessions. He is human he will follow the path of least resistance.

Bear in mind that as alternative dispute resolution becomes more and more common, attorneys spend more and more time learning effective techniques and strategies to apply to it. There are courses on mediation for attorneys to take as part of their continuing legal education requirements. Law schools now teach courses on how to participate in alternative dispute resolution. The techniques the mediator might use to elicit concessions and how to resist them are probably known to the other side's attorney. You are at a disadvantage.

Here's an example of what could happen to you....

Let's say the mediator has elicited from you your rock bottom number and gone to meet with the other side. He returns and tells you that they have given him theirs, and while he can't disclose it, you are still pretty far apart. His job is to close the gap. He will choose the easiest route. Let's say that the strength of your case depends on a legal issue – perhaps whether a kind of evidence will be admissible if the mediation fails and the case proceeds to trial. He asks you about it and how sure you are that the judge will rule in your favor. That is one technique that you will see often in a mediation that is, asking you to consider and acknowledge the ways in which certain outcomes could develop.

You have been complacent. You thought this was just going to be a friendly gab session.

You have not reviewed the law. And don't have the cases handy to show the mediator your position is strong. He asks you where your case will be if the judge rules against you. You have to admit that not allowing your evidence would be very harmful.

Now here's where he nails you! He suggests that if you aren't sure that you will win on getting the evidence in, perhaps you've set your bottom number a little high. Because if you're not sure about it and the judge rules against you, you could end up with nothing…. "Perhaps you should rethink it."

Then he throws all the tried and true mediators' darts at you. If you can settle the case you would not have to worry about a trial. You could get your money within a few days instead of waiting for the case to work its way up the docket. A smaller assured amount now has a lot more value as compared to uncertainty down the road.

Mediators are usually experienced and have a wide arsenal of techniques to try to get parties to settle. They don't get paid to just sit there and smile! And once he sees a weakness, he will focus on it and keep chipping away. In this scenario if there is a settlement, it won't be a good one for you.

On the other hand, if you come into the mediation well equipped, with full knowledge of the case law, your response to his question about the likely outcome of the ruling on the evidence will be entirely different. Instead of saying that you're not sure, or at least expressing uncertainty, you tell the mediator that you just can't see any way that you can lose on the issue, and show him the cases where the appellate courts have said that your kind of evidence is admissible. Remember, the mediation is an informal, relatively unstructured process, so when you're talking privately to the mediator, it's perfectly acceptable to stress your strong points. Now, you've given the mediator a very good reason why you are not going to further reduce your "bottom line" settlement figure.

Moreover, when he goes back to meet with the other side, he will convey to them that you have done your research and are confident of your position.

If you get nothing else out of this book it should be to do your homework and be prepared. It makes all the difference in every aspect of how you handle your case from deciding to file a lawsuit, to giving a deposition to the final conclusion.

Because the terms arbitration and mediation are often used together people mistakenly often the impression that they are similar. So to conclude, the following are distinctions between arbitration and mediation:

- In arbitration, one or more arbitrators make a decision concerning the case. In mediation, the mediator never renders a decision.

- Arbitration is an adversary proceeding, where evidence is presented and witnesses are heard. In mediation the parties work with a mediator to try to reach a settlement

- Arbitration has rules providing for a structured proceeding. Mediation usually does not.

- Arbitration proceedings are either recorded or summarized with the decision becoming part of the court record. Mediation proceedings are confidential and cannot be used for any purpose. The only report to the court is that the case did or did not settle.

The mediation will progress in the way discussed, and mediations have been known to take a full day or longer. Through a process of meeting with the parties, eliciting concessions on minor points that add up, then having everyone meet together again, to consider the progress, a skilled mediator can overcome the natural hostility and suspicion that the parties have for one another and reach a resolution. If no settlement results, then the mediator simply reports to the court that the mediation took place but that there was no settlement. If there is a full or partial settlement, then expect to execute an agreement, even if it is handwritten, before leaving the mediation. One thing that has been learned painfully over the years is that if an agreement is not reduced to writing, before the parties leave a mediation, it is highly unlikely that the agreement will survive. One or the other will find fault with the agreement, have second thoughts, want to reconsider or some combination of these. Obviously a full settlement of the case is the preferred outcome. Recognize though that in the spirit that something is better than nothing, often cases are partially settled. For example, in the personal injury case discussed, the case may at the beginning of the mediation been completely disputed. That is the plaintiff alleging that the defendant caused the accident and that he suffered horrific injuries; while the defendant denies being at fault and denies the extent of the injuries claimed by the plaintiff. A possible partial settlement of this case might be that the defendant admits liability, and the parties agree that the damages will not be less than "X" dollars or more than "Y" dollars. The parties also agree that the plaintiff will be evaluated by a doctor that both sides agree upon. While a full settlement would have been preferred, this mediation was eminently successful. All the issues have been disposed of except how much the plaintiff is entitled to recover and even that has been limited to an agreed upon range.

The reality is that alternative dispute resolution works. It is often a very good way to simplify the process of resolving these cases. Historically it is cheaper and faster than going to trial. And finally, as the trend continues, you are not going to have much choice.

Expect to be confronted with and have to become proficient at representing yourself in some form of alternative dispute forum. Ignorance is bliss and knowledge is strength, so once you realize that a mediation or arbitration is imminent, it's time to get to work!

INFORMATION ABOUT THE LAW

The first section of the book dealt with the actual questions surrounding representing yourself. The second section dealt with the process itself. It focused on giving you an idea of how the system works, and how to handle a civil case from beginning to end.

This section is oriented toward giving you more information about the law itself. It begins with a very general overview of American Law and outlines the different courts available in America to resolves disputes. Once you have been given an overall background, various legal topics, relevant to representing yourself in court are explored.

It is not necessary to read this section of the book. You can read the first and second section and come away with a good sense of how a court case progress. Likewise, you can read this third section and gain some insight into general legal topics.

Common sense though would tell you that you are better served by reading all sections in that they complement each other. For example, in the second section the issue of how to question a witness is raised. In this part of the book, the chapter on evidence will help you understand far better how the rules of evidence come into play during the questioning process.

It is also important that you understand that it is impossible in the confines of a single volume to educate you on any particular area of the law. This is an overview. If you choose to represent yourself, it is important that you used this information as it is intended. As a starting point to familiarize yourself with the law that applies to your particular case.

Enjoy!

American Legal History

Law! What is it? Where did it come from? Why do we need it?

Some form of legal system has existed among people as long as there have been people. As soon as people began living together, disputes arose. It quickly became obvious that there had to be a way to resolve those disputes without resorting to mortal combat.

Likewise, as people began to evolve from a nomadic hunter/gatherer existence to a more stable society, a system was needed to determine how people conducted themselves. Property rights needed to be defined. Rights and obligations with respect to others had to be set forth. Standards of acceptable conduct had to be set forth. In short a legal system of some kind is necessary for any functioning society.

Over the history of mankind, legal systems have taken many forms and have been presented in many ways. When single rulers prevailed, whether called kings, or chiefs, or emperors - they were essentially the law. Even in that context though, we see in history an effort to record and make known and define the law. After all, law is of no value unless the people know it. A law that provides for punishment for some transgression is of no value unless everyone knows what it is they are supposed to do or not do. So, throughout history we see various codifications of the law, the Code of Hammurabi being an early example. Law has also been inexorably interwoven with religion - the Ten Commandments being a good example. Often religions, such as Islam have an entire legal system incorporated into their dogma.

The result today is that every country has some sort of legal system in place by which its citizens are governed. While legal systems differ from one another income respects, they all have certain features in common.

They are all codified in one way or another. That means there is always some place one can go and find out what the law is. Without that, a legal system is of no value whatsoever.

They all set forth and specify conduct that is unacceptable and define punishments for those who violate the law.

They all define rights and obligations of people with respect to one another.

They all define property rights of people.

They all provide for resolution of disputes between people.

It does not matter whether the law regarding these matters is set forth in law books, or religious books, such as the Bible and Quran, is written on scrolls, or etched onto stone tablets. The effect is the same - a published legal system by which people in a society can conduct their lives in an orderly fashion.

In the United States, our legal system can be traced primarily to English Common law. The English common law dates back to the days of the crusades when the king designated judges to make decisions on legal issues. Scribes took down what was said in court proceedings and these records were maintained. When in the future, an issue addressed in these records arose; it was more efficient to refer to what a judge had already decided. The decisions of judges were collected and bound into volumes. These were referred to by later judges and used as the basis of later decisions. This referral to precedent is the basis of common law. The rationale is that by following previous decisions, there will be a consistency in decisions that will provide the necessary predictability of a legal system. The result is that the prior decisions actually became the law.

The other major legal system used in the western world is referred to as Code, or Napoleonic law. This system, derived from post revolutionary France takes a different approach. Under "Code Law" the emphasis is on detailed codification of the law by the legislative branch of a government. Under code law, while a judge may interpret a law, a previous decision does not effectively create or define the law.

American Law

In America, our legal system derives primarily from common law. The extent varies from State to State. The States that were the original thirteen colonies tend to have legal systems more akin to English common law, while western States depend more on statutes and laws enacted by legislatures. Louisiana follows to some extent the European code system. Given this historical background it's easy to see that from place to place in the United States there can be big differences.

All the law in the United States derives from the U.S. Constitution in one way or another. The U.S. Constitution established the parts of the federal government, defined the powers of the federal government versus the state governments and sets forth the rights of the people.

In the United States we are governed by a combination of statutory law (passed by congress or state legislatures) and common law (decisions of federal or state appellate courts). In addition to those there are local laws down to the county and municipal level. This interplay between federal and law is one of the things that makes the American legal system more complicated than most western countries. There simply is no single source where you can determine all the applicable law on any given issue.

Before you can successfully represent yourself, you have to have at least a basic understanding of the legal system.

So with a very general grasp of the origin of law in the United States, a more specific look at the court system will be helpful.

Every society has some form of legal system to resolve disputes. In the United States when you represent yourself you will find yourself in one of two separate courts systems – federal or state. Within each are a variety of specialized courts, agencies and divisions.

In the federal system there are courts of general jurisdiction, the Federal District Courts, there are appellate courts and specialized courts, such as Federal Tax Court, Bankruptcy Court, Federal Court of Military Appeals, and on and on. As a practical matter, in representing yourself, you will be dealing for the most part with only two of these – Federal District Court and Bankruptcy Court.

On the state level it gets a little more confusing. Each state has what is referred to as a court of general jurisdiction, but there are also innumerable permutations. Some states have courts broken down by the amount of money in dispute. Florida is an example. If your dispute is for less than $15,000 you will find yourself in County Court. More than that and you are in Circuit Court. In most states there are separate courts for family matters, but in others, domestic cases are resolved in the same courts as other cases. Most states have some kind of small claims court where cases involving lesser amounts can be addressed. Add to that the development of administrative law courts that deal with resolution of issues arising from regulatory matters and the operation of administrative agencies, and it is easy to see a potential complex and confusing system.

Just as important as understanding the court system is having a grasp of the system of laws that they work in and that you will have to deal with.

In the United States we are governed by a lot of laws from a lot of different sources, but here is a summary of law that may have an impact on any legal issues that you might have.

A. Federal Law

Our government is composed of both federal and state law, with the extent of each governed by the Constitution. There are areas reserved to the federal government, just as there are areas reserved to state governments, in regard to which the federal government has no authority or control. In broad terms, the sources of federal law are as follows:

1. Federal Statutory Law.

Statutory refers to statutes passed by a governing body. In this case it refers to acts of Congress, codified into the volumes and volumes of the United States Code. It is broken down into sections which address specific areas of the law. There are for example sections devoted to everything from criminal matters to securities laws, to agricultural matters. The United States Code, as one might expect is simply put, huge. Title 26 of the United States Code, dealing with the IRS and tax matters alone is about 75,000 pages long, and believed to be growing at the rate of 1% per year. The entire United States Code which includes 52 titles is believed to take up over twenty-five feet of shelf space (55 feet with annotations). A little imagination will give some idea of the sheer magnitude in terms of number of pages that represents.

2. Federal Judicial Decisions.

We have a comprehensive federal court system in the United States. The decisions of the District Courts, the Circuit Courts of Appeal (among others) and the Supreme Court are printed and published. These decisions can form the basis of future decisions and thus actually constitute law. This is the common law that was discussed earlier. Decisions can address statutes passed by Congress's, or can interpret provisions of the Constitution and in doing so, can have the result of actually creating law. An example that almost everyone is familiar with is the so-called Miranda decision. It gets its name from the plaintiff in a case who was seeking to be released from prison because his constitutional rights were violated. This decision, relying on the Fifth and Sixth Amendments to the U.S. Constitution, defined certain protections available to individuals arrested by police, or in the custody of law enforcement. Ironically, other than in the context of that decision, the so-called "Miranda Rights" do not appear anywhere. Nowhere in the hundreds of thousands of pages of laws enacted by Congress (the U.S. Code) is there anything discusses the right to counsel, or the fact that any voluntary statements made by an accused can be used against them. It just is not there. Congress never addressed those issues. Instead, the U.S. Supreme Court, interpreting the Constitution and the Bill of Rights, determined that the right of an accused to be represented by an attorney, in order to be meaningful, carried with it the Miranda Rights. The Supreme Court in interpreting the Constitution effectively created a law. The decisions of the Courts are just as important as what is found in the U.S. Code.

3. Federal Regulatory Law.

In addition to Congress, everyone knows that there are hundreds of federal agencies out there, comprising a veritable alphabet soup. Everything from the IRS to the FBI, to Energy Department, etc., etc. Many of these agencies and departments are empowered to create and issue regulations. Often when Congress passes a law it will include a directive to an agency to issue regulations. An example that everyone is familiar with is the IRS. The tax law in the United States is laid out first in the Internal Revenue Code, which is a separate section of U.S. Code. On top of that though there are the regulations issued by the Internal Revenue Service. These regulations are much larger than the Internal Revenue Code (enacted by Congress). Each section of the Internal Revenue Code has specific regulations associated with it. The difference between statutes and regulations is the source. Statutes are enacted by congress or a legislature, subject to the entire legislative process. Regulations are drafted by regulatory agencies and after being posted for comment on the Federal Register, go into effect. Collectively these regulations make up the Code of Federal Regulations. This material is broken down by agency and type of regulation, but within the 160,000 or so pages of regulations one can find anything from regulations governing what kinds of fertilizer can be applied, to how much fuel an airplane must have on board before it takes off, and everything in between.

B. State Law

1. State Statutory Law.

Just as Congress passes laws that affect us all, each State in the country has some form of legislature that passes laws that pertain to that State. Just as with federal laws, these laws are codified and are set forth in volumes similar the U.S. Code. They are also generally broken down by title. Some are more comprehensive than other, but all have effect throughout a particular state.

2. State Common (Judicial) Law.

Just as there is a system of federal courts, each State has its own court system. These always include some basic trial level court, some higher level court, and one or more levels of appeals court. While on the state level, the trial courts do not usually publish their opinions, the appellate courts do, and those decisions have the same effect with respect to state law, as the federal decisions have with respect to federal law. That is a State Appeals Court can render a decision published as an opinion that has the same effect of law as a statute passed by the legislature. More importantly, the decisions have precedential effect, so that once published, a trial court will look to those decisions in making rulings.

3. State Regulatory Law.

Again, just as with federal law, each state has its own host of departments and agencies. Each of these may have their own regulations that dictate how the agency does its job. Examples of these regulations are things such as regulations governing professional and occupational licenses, construction codes, health regulations and in fact regulations that address in some way virtually everything that we do. Regulations and the law associated with them is so extensive, and has become so complex that most states have an administrative law system, complete with courts that do nothing but hear cases involving regulations and issues surrounding them.

Any time you are considering any legal issue, your research must include possible regulations and administrative agencies. Just as in the federal system, most states have delegated considerable authority to agencies on the theory that they are better able to address specialized areas of the law. Whenever that is the case, you are expected to pursue to remedy or complaint within the administrative structure and only failing that, can you avail yourself of the court system.

C. Local Law.

In addition to federal and state legal systems, there is literally an entire third set of laws and regulations at the local level. Local law can be in the form of ordinances enacted at the municipal or county level as well in the form of regulations issued by local agencies. Do not let the fact that these ordinances and regulations are local and of limited geographic effect lull you into disregarding them. Building codes, zoning ordinances, noise and nuisance statutes are all examples of local law that can have considerable impact upon legal issues that you might confront.

Understand too that a local ordinance or regulation can have an impact even in a state or federal court proceeding. In any cases violation of ANY statute by a defendant is a prima facia presumption of wrong doing or liability. Do not fail to research local laws when you are planning and organizing your lawsuit or considering your options in any legal matter.

In some states there are courts at the county level that handle different levels of cases the state courts of general jurisdiction. These are often deemed county courts, municipal or city courts, magistrate's courts or justice courts. The name is not as important as the concept that these courts are intended to address minor issues (both criminal and civil) with very limited geographical jurisdiction.

In addition to court systems on a local level, there are also a myriad of local legal sources and entities. They scope of far too large to itemize in a single volume and the extent varies from state to state and from municipality to municipality. Regional "Authorities" created to govern and enforce the operation of specific facilities, such the New York Ports Authority, or a regional water and sewer authority are examples of such local legal entities.

Administrative Law

In addition to statutory and common law, we are surrounded in the United States by regulations and rules. The FCC has regulations and rules that dictate how the airwaves are used. The FAA has rules about flying and airplanes. The EPA has rules and regulations most people don't even know exists. Virtually every major federal agency has some relationship to rules and regulations. On top of the federal, we of course have rules and regulations at the state, county and even local level.

Because rules and regulations are intended to be enforced by and from within the associated agencies and governmental subdivisions, the intent is to make the enforcement and interpretation of the rules and regulations more straightforward and less complicated.

As often turns out in the case of governmental efforts, this has never worked, and the maize of government regulations can be as complicated as any court case. Things like interpreting building codes, zoning ordinances or similar types of regulation can be incredibly confusing because of the potential of different interpretations of the regulations and rules. There are people whose whole career is devoted to interpreting and analyzing the Internal Revenue Regulations.

Dealing with Administrative Agencies

The Agency Level

Everyone is familiar with how some sort of enforcement action begins in the realm of regulations or regulatory rules. The agency will send out some kind of communication, or you, needing some authorization will file some sort of application with an agency. Initial handling is routine, in accordance with printed and available procedural manuals and guidelines.

- Your application for a building permit is approved or rejected.

- The IRS would like some additional documentation regarding your tax return.

- You've received a notice from the city that the sign in front of your business violates the sign ordinance.

All of these and countless more like them are examples of dealing with administrative agencies at an early level.

What happens next depends on the agency, and you just have to do your homework and research as to how the agency is structured and how cases are handled at various levels. The good thing is that administrative agencies almost always have all the information on how to deal with the, what the procedures are, what must be done and what can be done, readily available.

396

A few things though are universal. Agencies are creatures of statute and function within a framework governed by regulations. There is absolutely no excuse for you to attempt to deal with any administrative agency without having done research on these regulations.

First, it is essential. The agency and the people you will deal with are governed by these very regulations. What happens with respect to your matter before the agency is dictated by these regulations. Wouldn't it be nice to know the rules?

Second the people you will deal with are human too. They deal every day with idiots and people too lazy to read the rules or familiarize themselves with the procedures. You will almost always find that letting the people who you will interact with know that you have taken the time and effort to learn and understand what is happening will be appreciated. That does not mean present it in a belligerent manner such as "I've read the rules and I know my rights". There are a lot of ways to let someone know that you've done your homework. You can ask a legitimate question that reflects knowledge of the procedures but perhaps a bit of confusion as to some aspect.

Third it is easy. The very thing that sets administrative agencies apart is that everything they do is spelled out. There is nothing, absolutely nothing for example that the IRS does or decides that is not spelled out in a regulation somewhere. Moreover, all of this information is readily available on the internet from a variety of perspectives.

Not only are the raw regulations and procedures available, but most government agencies have websites with useful, less formal guides and information sheets. There is simply no excuse to ever file an application, respond to an inquiry, or make any request of any government agency without having done basic research on the agency, its function and its procedures.

In terms of actually dealing with the agency, on a personal level, a couple of points should be observed.

To follow up on the people at agencies being human too, to put it simply, mind your manners. For one thing, threats and belligerence will get you nowhere. It is amazing how many people appear at government offices with a hostile attitude.

This is not only pointless, but stupid. Anyone that has followed the news understands for instance, that threatening an IRS employee with anything makes no sense. The threats are pointless and in the eyes of the employee, make you look like an idiot. They've heard it all before. They know that you won't "have their job". Threatening to "go over their head" has been heard so often it no longer has any real significance. This doesn't mean that you go to the other extreme and prostrate yourself before them. It means be courteous, let them know that you have done your homework and recognize that they are doing their job. At the same time, don't be afraid to let them know, again, politely, if it appears that no progress is being made, that perhaps this should move to the next level.

Recognize in that context too, that being human, you will also encounter agency employees that are hostile. Wouldn't you be if you spent eight hours a day, five days a week in the same cubicle reviewing tax returns? While most try to do their job, there are some that are bitter, frustrated, or simply incompetent. That is why every agency has levels at which decisions and procedures are reviewed, and from which people can request relief.

If you are in the middle of an IRS audit for example and the examiner is clearly hostile, challenging your explanation and documents to every query in a confrontational manner, there will come a time that to continue is pointless. Again, not being belligerent, but with knowledge (because you've done your research) of the procedures for an audit, you can simply say that it is clear that the audit at this level is not getting anywhere and that it may be time to request a supervisory conference with the examiner's manager. You would not know that you had that option if you had not read the procedures, just as you would not know that as long as you let them know it, you have the right to make an audio recording of the entire interview.

All of this can be handled in a professional and courteous manner. There is no need to become hostile, even if the agency employee is clearly incompetent or themselves hostile.

Another tactic that will often help, in several respects is when dealing with an agency employee, freely ask for information or assistance. Back to the underlying principles – these people are human too. Everyone likes to be appreciated and one way we are appreciated is by being able to give information. That's one of the main job gratifications cited by teachers – the ability to share knowledge. So ask the person the best way to accomplish something, or what happens next, or whether you've completed the application correctly. Of course there will be exceptions, but nine times out of ten, the response will be positive. Even better, you will often find that they will give you some information or some helpful tips that you were not even aware of.

Beyond the Initial Agency Level

Because of the nature of administrative agencies, there is always some form of hierarchal structure allowing for review, reconsideration or appeal of the actions and decisions of the people you initially have contact with. That process may be within the agency initially, but eventually, at some point or in some fashion the mechanism will provide for review of an agency decision by the courts.

To give you a couple of examples:

If it is an IRS dispute it is handled internally at several successive levels within the agency. If still in dispute the

400

IRS has an appeals office after which the matter will go to court. How it gets to court and what court it gets to depend on the nature of the dispute and elections that the taxpayer makes along the way.

If you are applying for Social Security Benefits there are initial claims to be filed, examiners that will make an initial decision, forms to request a review of that decision, and if the matter is not resolved, there are Social Security judges to take evidence and render a decision. Appeals though will eventually make their way out of the agency and into the court system.

On the state level, there are similar hierarchies. Requesting Workers' Compensation benefits begins in most states as an administrative process with the submission of claims forms, medical reports, accident reports, and so forth. If there is a dispute, most state workers' compensation agencies have internal hearing officers, examiners, or judges to consider all the evidence in various forms and make a decision. Once those have been exhausted, while it varies from state to state, there will be provision to have the matter reviewed by some court.

So generally, administrative actions are begun as a routine process within the agency, often form driven, and handled by agency personal.

Disputes, at least initially are handled internally by the agency.

If disputes cannot be addressed or resolved by the agency, there is always some form of judicial relief, but the form it takes, and the procedures to get there differ dramatically from federal to state, from state to state, and from agency to agency.

There are no easy, one size fits all, answers.

On the State level the two most common approaches have been to create a special court designated as an Administrative Law Court, or to have the state's court of general jurisdiction consider appeals from agency decisions. Separate agencies may still have their internal hearings process and officers since the difference in these two systems is where the case goes after it's exhausted all processes within the agency.

On a federal level, the federal administering agencies often have their own quasi-judicial sections where decisions of hearing officers are applied to disputes related to regulatory matters. A good example of such an arrangement is the Social Security Administration, something we can relate to. Decisions of the examiners and their supervisors are appealed to a Social Security Administrative Law Judge who presides over hearings pertaining to Social Security issues. Another example is the NTSB (National Transportation Safety Board), which hears appeals of decisions of the Federal Aviation Administration regarding certain matters.

Differences between Agencies and Court

Throughout the administrative process, from initial contact to judicial appeal, it is still an administrative matter and is substantially different than a civil trial or court case throughout.

In fact, they are two entirely different creatures.

While a court system is focused on the concept of an adversary procedure and covering a broad range of disputes, an administrative proceeding is geared toward a quick, efficient and inexpensive resolution of issues that are very narrow in scope. A circuit court will handle case that span a broad spectrum, from contract disputes to accident cases to business disputes. The IRS concerns itself ONLY with taxes. Your county zoning board focuses ONLY on zoning issues.

Jury trials are usually not available and that is true at any stage of the proceeding. Hearing officers or examiners usually initially consider the cases. Any proceedings after that are often appellate in nature and jury trials are not available in appeals.

Even if you end up, as part of the appellate process in a court, the manner in which the case is handled is completely different. Unlike filing a court case, which is generally available as a matter of right, an administrative law hearing is by and large an appeal from earlier decisions of the agency. This means that before a hearing can even be requested, one must have gone through all the preceding steps. The term that will often be heard is that it is necessary to "exhaust all administrative remedies" before proceeding.

It also means that there are limitations on what can and cannot be presented at an appeal hearing. This is one of the most critical aspects of any disputed administrative proceeding. You must determine at what point along the way, what is called de novo presentation of evidence introduction of new evidence) can no longer be made. There is always some such point.

Where that point occurs varies from agency to agency, from state to state, but it is absolutely critical that knowing where it occurs is included in your research.

Obviously at the first step in any proceeding, you are allowed to present all of your evidence and set forth your points. That will almost always hold true for some subsequent steps in the process. There comes a point though where the process becomes appellate in nature. At that point it is often no longer permissible to present evidence, in the form of testimony or documents, but instead the process is limited to correcting errors in the prior proceeding.

Errors in the prior proceeding are generally limited to errors of law or that the prior decision was not supported by substantial evidence.

This is an important concept in administrative proceedings, and basically stands for the principle that we are not going to keep arguing the same facts at every step of the way. The principle of substantial evidence addresses this issue. It basically says that if the prior decision is supported by a reasonable degree, or substantial evidence, it cannot be changed by anyone further up the chain. This is true even if the whoever is reviewing the decision feels that the preponderance of the evidence would have resulted in a different decision. As long as there is substantial evidence, which does not require it to be a preponderance of the evidence, then the prior decision cannot be changed at a subsequent step.

People often mistakenly assume that they can hurry through the preliminary steps in order to present their case to an administrative law judge. They believe that they just need to "get beyond the clerks and pencil pushers" and present their case. They are almost always extremely disappointed because often, the administrative law judge is such an appellate step. The administrative law judge may not be permitted to reconsider the evidence, but instead will be limited in considering only whether the prior decision was supported by substantial evidence and whether it is erroneous as a matter of law. Put another way, you only get one bite at the apple. Once the evidence has been presented and considered somewhere along the process, you don't get to "start over" and present everything from scratch again.

To get an understanding of how this process works, consider a couple of examples:

In a social security case, a claim is presented on the basis of documentary materials. Forms are completed, written statements submitted and medical reports filed. An examiner makes a determination based on these records. If the claim is denied a reconsideration is requested. If that is denied, the matter is set for hearing before a Social Security Administration judge. All three of these steps are referred to as de novo. That means at any point up to the hearing before the judge, any and all evidence can be considered and presented. If you have left something out at an earlier step, you can present it at the next step. Once though the process has gotten beyond the hearing before the judge, the issues are limited and the evidence is not re-presented. Subsequent steps look at the decision of the judge based on the evidence in the record, to see if there was substantial evidence supporting the ruling or there were any errors of law.

Another example is how workers compensation claims are handled in some states. Often there is a workers' compensation commission or board of some sort. If a claim is disputed it is heard in an administrative proceeding be a hearing officer who is often a member of the commission or board. This is where the evidence is taken, in the form of witness testimony or documentary evidence, including medical reports. If there is an issue with the decision of the hearing officer, a review or appeal to the full board or commission is the next step, but unless there is an extremely good reason, no evidence is presented to this panel. They review the decision of the hearing officer only to the extent of whether it is supported by substantial evidence or is based on legal errors.

Where this demarcation point occurs in any administrative proceeding is extremely important. Your research in preparing the case must include determining the point at which the proceeding becomes appellate; that is where no additional evidence can be introduced. Fortunately this information is readily available with a little digging. Either the statues governing the agency, or the regulations propounded by the agency itself will set forth the procedures at each step, to include what evidence can be presented and considered.

Another major difference between court and administrative proceedings concerns the manner in which evidence is presented. Rarely will administrative agencies adhere to the same rules of evidence as in court. In the context of why we have administrative agencies, this makes perfect sense. How long would it take to resolve an issue before the IRS if every bank statement, every canceled check, every receipt had to be entered into evidence based on the testimony of someone familiar with the record?

Administrative proceedings are oriented toward paperwork, forms, reports and documents, so it stands to reason that these should be admitted into the record freely. In a workers' compensation case for example, the hearing officer will routinely receive into evidence any medical reports pertaining to the injured worker. If it were a court case, it would require testimony from a physician to get those records into evidence.

The caveat of all of this though is that whatever you submit to the agency, in the early stages of any administrative action, goes into the record and stays in the record throughout the process, even if in appeals in ends up in court. If you submit it, you're stuck with it.

Administrative proceedings are usually well suited to representing yourself. Many of the rules and procedures are in fact not inclined toward appearances by attorneys. Many agencies allow representation by people other than attorneys. The IRS for example allows registration as representatives of accountants and others in addition to attorneys. Most administrative schemes are in fact devised to allow resolution of issues without an attorney, so you will almost always be able to represent yourself before these agencies without any problem. At the same time, it is just as important that you familiarize yourself with the rules and procedures, as well as the substantive law governing any agency before which you represent yourself.

Bankruptcy

Bankruptcy is a very specialized area of the law, administered by the United States Bankruptcy Court System. It is also an area that is ideally suited to avoiding costly attorney's fees and representing yourself in court. Everyone has heard of bankruptcy, yet very few people really understand what it is, how it works or what it entails.

Bankruptcy is a creature of statute – that means there is no constitutional right to file bankruptcy and it did not originate from common law. It is governed by the Title 11 of the United States Code, and the Federal Rules of Bankruptcy Procedure. Bankruptcy is intended as a means for people and companies that have encountered financial difficulties to get a new start, or to get relief from creditors and lawsuits while they try to regroup. We've all heard of major corporations going into Chapter 11 bankruptcies. These are complicated reorganizations that have nothing to do with what will be discussed in this section. Here, we will discuss bankruptcy as it applies to individuals.

Bankruptcy can provide relief if you are in financial straits. But before you file, or let someone file for you, please read this section completely. It is not long but may save you a lot of problems and expense. Especially please read the part on bankruptcy considerations and issues before you proceed, either on your own or with an attorney.

Before talking about things you need to be thinking about before if you are even considering a bankruptcy, some general information will give you a better picture.

There are basically two forms of bankruptcy that are available to individuals. They are referred to by the Chapters in the Bankruptcy Code that pertain to them: Chapter 7 and Chapter 13.

Chapter 7

In a Chapter 7 bankruptcy, often referred to as a liquidation, all the debtor's (the person filing bankruptcy) assets that are not exempt are sold by a Trustee, and in return, all the person's debts (with important exceptions) are essentially wiped out. That is a Chapter 7 bankruptcy reduced to its bare bones ultra simple form. In reality it is more complex. First let's look at some important concepts. We said that all of a debtor's assets that are not exempt are sold. It is important to understand what is exempt, and which therefore the debtor is allowed to keep.

Exemptions

Understanding that it does no good to take all of a person's assets, leaving them with nothing, the bankruptcy code provides for a list of exempt property. Exempt property is property that is kept by the debtor during and through the bankruptcy process. It becomes complicated because although bankruptcy is a creature of federal law, it allows state law to govern what is and is not exempt.

There is a set of federal exemptions, but they are available only if state law either does not provide exemptions, or if it allows selection of state or federal exemptions. States have the option of deferring to federal exemptions, or providing their own exemptions. States also have the right to determine whether a debtor must use federal exemptions, state exemptions, or can choose. These exemptions can and do vary to that point that people filing a bankruptcy in one state have a completely different outcome and process than those filing in another. For example some states, such as Florida, subject to certain conditions, have an unlimited homestead exemption. That means if you file a Chapter 7 bankruptcy in the State of Florida and own a million dollar house, free and clear of debt, you would be allowed to keep that house. If you reside on the other hand in a place like Alabama the situation is different. Like Florida, Alabama does not allow a debtor to use the federal exemptions, but allows only a $5,000 exemption in your homestead. The difference in the outcomes in the two states is obvious and dramatic. Take an average couple nearing retirement that have fallen on hard times. They happen to have a house worth $200,000. In Florida they keep the house. The same couple in Alabama lose their home.

So the first thing to know if you are contemplating bankruptcy is what the laws of your state say about exempt property. A general observation here is that the bankruptcy laws and exemptions do not favor or reward the conscientious and frugal among us. The individual who pays down their mortgage and tries hard to pay off things like car loans, generally loses most, if not all of their property in a Chapter 7 Bankruptcy proceeding, while the spendthrift, with credit cards maxed out, renting an apartment and upside down on his car loan loses little if anything, but walks away from thousands and thousands of dollars in debt.

Debts Not Discharged

In a Chapter7 Bankruptcy, your debts for the most part are discharged. As a practical matter, they just disappear. Creditors can no longer collect them so you simply do not owe them after the bankruptcy. It is important though to understand that not all debts are forgiven, or, to use the correct term, discharged. Nor does a Chapter 7 discharge operate to eliminate liens against property.

Between the bankruptcy code itself, along with amendments and other statutes, there is an ever growing list of obligations that are not affected by a discharge in bankruptcy.

-        Taxes, with some qualification owed to the IRS or to a state taxing authority are not affected by a discharge. So even if you file that Chapter 7 and get your discharge, the IRS will still be there.

- Alimony and child support obligations are unaffected by a bankruptcy, even to the extent of support arrearages that accumulated before the filing of the bankruptcy. If you have unpaid support obligations you normally cannot even get a discharge

- student loans with some exceptions are not discharged

- court fines and penalties including restitution

- debts to governmental agencies for fines and penalties

- debts owed for personal injury if due to driving while intoxicated

- debts incurred fraudulently may be not be discharged

Clearly, not every obligation that you have will disappear if you file a bankruptcy. To make matters worse, it is not always possible to predict if a specific obligation will be discharged. For example, the ability of a creditor to seek to avoid a discharge due to fraud is completely uncertain until the judge rules on the issue. A credit card company for example may argue that your obligation to them should not be discharged because you lied about your income on the application form. You will say that you did not lie and that even if you did, the credit card company did not rely on the misstated income. They would have issued the card regardless. Until the bankruptcy court judge rules on this issue you have no way of knowing whether this debt will be discharged, or will survive the bankruptcy to be collected later.

Limitations on Chapter 7.

Finally, not everyone can or should file a Chapter 7 bankruptcy. The bankruptcy code was substantially revised in 2005 with the passage of the BAPCPA (Bankruptcy Abuse Prevention and Consumer Protection Act). Prior to the passage of this legislation there was a widespread perception that bankruptcy abuse was rampant and needed to be curbed. Whether the extent of the perceived abuse was as represented, it was clear that the bankruptcy system was being abused. The scenario above referring to the spendthrift with no assets was actually far too common than it should have been. Literally an individual who owned no substantial assets could accumulate literally hundreds of thousands of dollars in unsecured debt, primarily credit card bills, and then, despite enjoying a substantial income and clearly having the ability if they so desired to repay at least some of the debt, were able to simply walk away from it by filing a Chapter 7 bankruptcy proceeding. What was perhaps most infuriating to observers at the time, critical of the lack of limitations in the bankruptcy code, was that these individuals, possessed of substantial earning capability suffered no apparent change in their lifestyle from the filing of the bankruptcy. Credit card companies and banks, knowing that they were not able to file bankruptcy again for seven years were happy to extend new credit. They kept their homes, cars and furnishings. The problem with the bankruptcy code before BAPCPA was that anyone could file bankruptcy whether insolvent or not.

BAPCPA addressed these issues and quite a bit more, probably going too far in response to real or perceived abuses. Bankruptcy is a much more difficult process post BAPCPA. Among other provisions, a means test applies which requires that if a debtor has the ability, measured against both statistical standards and the debtor's own financial situation to repay unsecured debt, a Chapter 7 will not be allowed, requiring the filing of a Chapter 13 repayment plan instead.

Another major change resulting from BAPCPA is that a Chapter 7 bankruptcy proceeding is no longer able to be dismissed solely by the debtor. The impact of this is that if you file a Chapter 7 proceeding and later find that you have issues, absent a showing of good cause you will not be able to get out of the bankruptcy.

File only after thoroughly analyzing your situation and exploring your options.

Chapter 13.

The other form of bankruptcy for individuals is filed under Chapter 13 and is often referred to as a wage earner plan. Available to individuals or couples with regular income, it basically requires the payment into a bankruptcy plan of a portion of income, to be applied toward payment of at least a portion of the debts. The plans can last from three to five years. Under the plan, if there is not enough income to pay all the debts over time, the unpaid portions, after successful completion of the plan, are forgiven, again with important exceptions.

A Chapter 13 bankruptcy is a powerful tool for several reasons.

First, following the restrictions and limitations applied to proceedings under Chapter 7 by BAPCPA, and due to the legislative intent of BAPCP, Chapter 13 proceedings are the preferred option within the bankruptcy system. When BAPCPA was passed, one of the concerns that motivated such a drastic change in the bankruptcy environment was that pre-BAPCPA with so many cases being filed as outright liquidations under Chapter 7, individuals, despite having the ability to at least partially pay, were simply walking away from unsecured obligations.

Everything in bankruptcy is traditionally oriented toward assets and liabilities as of a certain point in time: the filing date. Before BAPCPA no attention was focused on a debtor's future ability to pay at least part of the claims in a bankruptcy. The intent of BAPCPA was to change that mindset and to treat the future earnings of the debtor as a factor in discharging debts, with a bias toward Chapter 13 proceedings in which part of a debtor's income for a predetermined period would be used to pay a portion of the debt. Consequently, taking the various applicable provisions of the bankruptcy code as revised by BAPCPA in context, they clearly reward and encourage Chapter 13 cases, while discouraging Chapter 7 filings.

Many people shy away from Chapter 13 proceedings for a variety of reasons — some valid, some not. First, people perceive that a Chapter 7 is better because it "makes their debts go away" while with a Chapter 13, they have to pay on them for years. They also are put off by that very five year concept. In a Chapter 7 the whole proceeding, including a discharge is over within a few months, while yes, it is true that a Chapter 13 can run on for five years, during which time payments must be made, and approval of the court required to refinance property that is collateral for secured creditors.

But once the human foible of immediate gratification is set aside, and the provisions of Chapter 13 of the bankruptcy code examined in more detail, it becomes apparent that in the total scheme of things, these disadvantages though readily apparent, become minor and insignificant when compared to the versatility and range of options available. Put another way, the advantages you can gain, and the things you can do with a Chapter 13 plan make the fact that it drags on for a few years pretty insignificant.

Here are some of the things you can do with a Chapter 13, along with some comments comparing those options to a Chapter 7 proceeding.

Catch up arrearages

This one of the strongest features of a Chapter 13 proceeding and the reason people often file at all. While a Chapter 13 cannot adjust or modify a debt secured by a first lien on your residence (your first mortgage) it can require the lender to accept payment of any past due amounts over a longer period. The typical scenario (using simplistic assumptions) is that you have mortgage payments of $1000 per month and due to illness, or temporary unemployment or some other reason you were not able to make the mortgage payments. The loan is five months past due and the lender had demanded that you immediately pay the past due payments plus the next regular payment immediately to prevent foreclosure. You are back at work and you can make the payments, probably a little more, but you just don't have the $6,000. In a Chapter 13 plan, as long as you make your regular payments, you can force the lender to take the arrearage - $5000 in this case - over a five year period. Instead of having to come up with $5,000 immediately, you pay an extra $85 or $90 per month. You keep your house. In a Chapter 7 there is no such option. If you do not pay the arrearage in full and make the regular payments the lender secures relief from the automatic stay provided by the bankruptcy and proceeds with the foreclosure.

Modification of Secured Claims

Debts not secured by a first lien on real property can be modified. This is another very strong provision of Chapter 13. The bankruptcy code provides that a secured claim is secured only to the extent of the value of the collateral. Any amount in excess of the value of the collateral is unsecured. A debt obligation can be restructured as long as the creditor receives at least as much as would have been received in a Chapter 7 liquidation. This means that the amount of any secured claim (debt) other than your first mortgage is a secured claim only up to the value of the collateral as of the time the bankruptcy was filed. How does this help you?

Watch!

Assume you have a car loan and owe $10,000 on a two year old car. The original payments at 9% interest were about $310.00 for a five year loan. You have missed five months' payments. The lender wants the payments caught up and wants you to resume making payments. They want five monthly of payments at $310 or $1,550, plus the next $310 payment to keep from repossessing your car.

Now let's look at the magic you can conjure up in a Chapter 13 proceeding...

You go to Kelly Blue Book or NADA and learn that after two years the car is only worth about $6,000 as a trade-in. That's after all what the lender would get for it if they repossessed it. Now here's where the Chapter 13 provisions come into play. First, instead of being secured to the tune of $10,000, the debt owed, the lender is secured only to the value of the car - $6,000. The rest is unsecured and shortly you'll see how that basically means you pay virtually nothing on it.

Moreover, you can modify the loan interest rate to the rate published periodically by the bankruptcy court (now around 4%) and modify the payment term. So here's how your car payment obligation will look...

Loan amount, $6,000 @ 4% for 5 years (duration of the plan), with a payment amount of $110.50. More importantly, compare the amounts to be paid to the lender. Unadjusted loan terms would have required the three years of payments at $310 per month (36*310=11,160), plus the arrearage of $1,550, or $12,710 in order to keep the car. In the Chapter 13 proceeding you will pay $110.50 for sixty months or $6,630.00 – a little less than half – and keep the car.

In the extreme, this technique can even be used to eliminate liens and obligations. In the midst of the recent real estate recession it was and to some extent still is, not uncommon to find that a house has decreased in value to the extent that it is worth less than the first mortgage. To the extent that there then may be a second mortgage, that second mortgage would be entirely unsecured. Instead of paying the full amount to the second mortgage lender, you can characterize it as an unsecured creditor and it will receive the same proportionate amount as other unsecured creditors provided in your plan – often as low as 1% of the claim.

Greater Flexibility

In a Chapter 7 the only property that you can keep is property that is exempt. That means a second car, an investment property, a second home, all are lost. A Chapter 13, so long as creditors receive what they would receive in a Chapter 7, can be tailored to allow those assets to be retained.

Considerations

It sometimes appears, especially during tough economic times, that bankruptcy is the answer to everyone's prayers and the ultimate solution. It is certainly touted that way by all the attorneys who spend enough money to retire the debt of a small country on advertising… "Stop Foreclosure", "End Harassing Calls", "Get control of your finances", ad infinitum.

Bankruptcy has its advantages. It also has its pitfalls for the unwary. Careful considerations to all the advantages and disadvantages should be given before filing. Even more consideration should be given to the information from various sources that will bombard you on the one hand about how bankruptcy is the greatest thing since sliced bread, and on the other, warn you of the dire consequences of even conjuring up the word "bankruptcy".

You will have to carefully research the issues and considerations on your own. It is even very difficult to find an attorney that will really give you competent advice. The complexity of the bankruptcy system has spawned an environment where most small firms or solo practitioners avoid bankruptcy cases. There are a lot of reasons for this, but generally, because of the work and liability involved, combined with the competition from the "bankruptcy mills" in terms of fees, it just does not make sense for a small firm or solo practitioner to become involved in the occasional bankruptcy.

Nor should you trust any of the attorneys actively advertising bankruptcy services. These people run mills, pure and simple. They spend a lot of money on advertising and depend on volume. The attorney's involvement is usually minimal with work delegated to paralegals and assistants who do nothing more than assemble information to be fed into a computer that spits out completed bankruptcy petitions and schedules. These are the people you would deal with in such a law office and they are not competent to provide advice or meaningful information, aside from forms and procedure, about the bankruptcy process and its consequences.

If you have real questions (beyond how much does it cost) find an attorney that handles bankruptcies but is clearly not operating a high volume assembly like operation. The fees may be higher – after all he doesn't have the benefit of a dozen cases a week - but it will be worth it to have someone knowledgeable looking at your situation and giving you prudent advice.

With respect to a lot of the factors and considerations, a little research and homework on your own will work wonders. Here are some of the things you should be looking at and going over in your mind if you are even thinking of filing a bankruptcy:

Why are you considering a bankruptcy? Beyond the obvious that you can't afford to pay your bills, what is the real problem? Is it a single issue like a looming foreclosure or just being overwhelmed with a multitude of claims? How critical is time? There is a big difference in contemplating bankruptcy because lawsuits have been threatened and dunning letters received versus trying to deal with the sale of your house at foreclosure next Tuesday.

Do a careful inventory of your assets and liabilities. Do this objectively. What do you own? What will be exempt? What do you stand to lose if you file a bankruptcy? This means taking a long hard look at the kind of bankruptcy you are contemplating – a Chapter 7 or Chapter 13 - and the exemptions available to you. As has been discussed, the answer to this question will be substantially different for an individual residing in Florida than in Alabama.

Will bankruptcy help you? This is not as silly a question as it sounds. Of course the filing of a bankruptcy, with the imposition of the automatic stay will bring immediate relief, but it is temporary and extremely short-lived. The stay will be quickly lifted with respect to secured property, and you will have to be making arrangements to surrender to the trustee any property that is not exempt.

What is your realistic economic outlook? How did you get into the predicament that has you contemplating bankruptcy? Was it an accident or illness that kept you out of work for a while that is now resolved. Did you lose your job, but have now found another, or are you still unemployed with no good prospects in sight? Or is your predicament the result of a failed business transaction or arrangement that needs to be straightened out so that you can move on?

Obviously if you had a temporary problem that has left you with piled up bills and past due payments, a bankruptcy, particularly a Chapter 13 proceeding may be just what the doctor ordered. On the other hand, if your predicament is permanent, or not going to be resolved in the near future, a bankruptcy may do nothing but prolong the inevitable.

Do you have other issues that may surface as problems is a bankruptcy, such as have conveyed property within the past few years, or having embarked upon a plan to protect your assets? Generally these are easier to defend and protect in state litigation than in bankruptcy court with its bread sweeping federal jurisdiction.

Filing and Preparation.

Once you've decided to pursue the bankruptcy option, and have tentatively decided which Chapter to proceed under, you are ready to begin getting ready to file.

The time factor will dictate how much information you gather and organize ahead of time, as it will dictate the kind of initial filing. Bankruptcy, recognizing that there may be emergency situations where filing as soon as possible is essential, allows for a "hurry up" filing procedure. This involves filing nothing but the petition and a matrix of creditors along with a statement of your social security number. Of course everything else is due within a very short period, but this will get the case filed and stop any proceedings against you or your property.

Unless your bankruptcy presents some highly complex or unusual issues it is perfectly reasonable for you represent yourself. Virtually the entire bankruptcy process is forms driven, that is, pre-printed forms are completed and filed. Every bankruptcy court in the country has a website where you can download all the forms needed, refer to the local rules and avail yourself of all the information you could need to file pro se. Some districts even have pages on the website dedicated to individuals who are representing themselves. Just remember, you can represent yourself, and your spouse of course, if she too is filing, can represent herself, but you cannot represent any business entity that you might have, including one person corporations or limited liability companies. Those must be represented by an attorney admitted to the particular district where the bankruptcy is filed.

Both forms of bankruptcy require the debtor(s) to complete forms that are referred to as the petition, schedules, and statement of financial affairs. The petition is what constitutes the case filing, and it specifies whether the filing is for a Chapter 7 or Chapter 13 case. The schedules list all the debts of the debtor as well as all the assets, together with the income and expenses on a monthly basis. The statement of financial affairs is a lengthy series of questions, which, when properly completed, sets forth the financial picture of the debtor(s). In addition to the completion of these forms, it will be necessary to provide bank statements, cancelled checks and recent tax returns.

Finally, after the case is underway, in a Chapter 13 case, the debtor(s) must submit a proposed plan in which they specify an amount to be paid to the trustee from income each month, and how this amount is to be apportioned among different creditors. If approved, this will result in the plan payment amount being withdrawn from the debtor(s) wages each pay period, and paid to the trustee.

The filing of the petition itself acts as an automatic stay. That means that no action can be taken against you or continued by any creditor. All collection efforts must stop immediately. Any pending court actions are stopped. A trustee is appointed to take control of all the assets of the debtor(s) that are not exempt, and to marshal those for the benefit of the creditors. Once the petition is filed, the first thing that will happen is a first meeting of creditors. The debtor(s) must appear at this meeting, where creditors may ask questions, and the trustee appointed to the case will have questions. At this early stage, these will generally involve issues surrounding the schedules and statement of financial affairs, the location of property, how values of properties reflected in the schedules were arrived at, etc. If the case is more complex, or involves issues that need to be explored further, a subsequent examination of the debtor(s), under oath may be scheduled.

Following the first meeting of creditors, the trustee will determine in a Chapter 7 case if it is an asset or no asset case. An asset case is one in which the trustee believes there will be nonexempt assets available to sell and make a distribution to creditors. In a no asset case the trustee feels that all assets are either exempt, or are of no significant value.

Once the first meeting of creditors has been had, and assuming there are no problems or issues, there will be nothing left to do in a Chapter 7 case. If there are no non-exempt assets nothing more will happen until the Court, about ninety days later, issues an order discharging the debtor. This means that any debts that you had as of the time of the filing of the bankruptcy, with the exception of course of those debts and obligations that cannot be discharged, are gone. No one can take any action to collect against them or require you to make any payment.

In a Chapter 13 case, things are a bit more complicated. At the time the petition and schedules were filed, you should have filed a Chapter 13 plan. This is a document in which you set forth specifically how you want to address your debts and obligations. In this plan you specify how much money each month is to be paid to the trustee for apportionment to your creditors. This is where you state how you wish to handle any back mortgage payments, whether you want to modify the rights of any secured creditor, and how much money you want to pay to your unsecured creditors.

This part of the bankruptcy will be more involved because the plan will have to be modified at least once if not more. Why? Because the first plan will almost always be wrong. When you file the initial plan, with the rest of your schedules, it will be based on the information about claims and amounts due that is probably not current. Your estimate for example of how much is due you mortgage lender in arrearages will almost certainly not be the same as the number that the lender presents. Any creditor wanting to be included in the payment plan must submit a proof of claim. Any creditor affected by the plan may object. When the amount you insert into your plan for mortgage arrearage for example differs from the amount of the lender's claim they will object. The trustee can object.

None of this is fatal. It is common and expected. The remedy is to revise the plan to reflect the correct amounts due creditors. The problem exists at all only because at the time the original plan is filed, you do not have the benefit of having before you the proof of claims of the various creditors. Just think of the objection process as a means of reconciling differences in math and accounting.

Once an objection is filed, a plan confirmation hearing is set. It is unlikely that you will ever have to attend such a hearing in that the discrepancies are usually simply resolved with the filing of an amended plan.

When the plan is submitted you need to be sure to send the first month's plan payment to the trustee. Even if the amount is later adjusted, trustees expect you to demonstrate good faith by beginning payments, with the understanding that any discrepancies in amount will be resolved later. Once the plan has been approved, the trustee, if you are employed, will seek a pay order, requiring the plan payment amount to be deducted from your paycheck and sent directly to the trustee. If you are self-employed, it will be your responsibility to make the trustee payments every month.

Once the plan is approved, and payment arrangements are made, there is little more to do. You must of course in addition to the plan payments keep your mortgage payment, if any current, and pay the rest of your bills. You cannot dispose of any assets handled in the plan without the consent of the trustee. For example, if your plan includes payments for a car, and you wish to replace the car, the plan needs to be adjusted and an order issued allowing disposition of the collateral.

A Chapter 13 plan will run anywhere from 36 to 60 months. If the unsecured creditors are not paid in full through the plan, it will probably run to 60 months. At the end of that time, any unsecured debt is discharged, all property vests back to you if it already hasn't, and you can get on about your life.

A bankruptcy can be a valuable tool in getting you back on track. Both forms of bankruptcy available to consumers have their advantages and their disadvantages. No bankruptcy should even be considered until you have made a careful and objective assessment of your situation to include your obligations, your assets and the extent to which a bankruptcy can address help or hurt you.

Contract Law

Contract law is as old as the concept of law itself. We see references in old writings to agreements between men (yes the old law is sexist and not politically correct) and how to make them binding. Any time there is a promise of some future performance in exchange for something, there is a contract. If farmer A with a donkey and farmer B with a cow meet and decide to exchange the animals, it is a simple exchange and absent anything else to be done, or any promises made, not a really contract. If however farmer A gives farmer B the donkey, with the promise that farmer B will go to his barn, get the cow, and deliver it to farmer A, you have a contract. Farmer A gives up his donkey in exchange for a promise by B that the cow will be delivered.

As with so many things in the law, the underlying principals are incredibly simple but don't remain that way for long. If something was promised in exchange for something else, there had to be some assurance of getting what was bargained for. If you were promised some form of payment for constructing a building, there had to be some assurance that when finished, there would be payment. As a result we see references to contracts, promises and agreement as far back as the Code of Hammurabi. Recognizing the importance of promises and agreements, every culture and society has had some form of contract law.

Of course the complexities of modern contract law are a far cry from early contract law. While the underlying principals are the same there is an almost infinite array of factors and considerations that make contract law the subject of entire multi-volume treatises.

Contract law in the United States has its basis in English Common law. With roots firmly embedded in common law roots, a lot of the principles that will be discussed in this section are based on decisions in cases over the years stemming from both American and older English courts. More recently, due to the complexities of contract law, and a need to make things more consistent in the face of transactions that span state lines and international borders, a statutory framework for commercial contracts has evolved. It is found in the Uniform Commercial Code.

Contracts impact just about everything we do. Your insurance policies are contracts. When you buy a ticket to travel on a plane, train or bus, you are entering into a contract. Even when you buy software, the act of installing the software on your computer results in creation of a contract. A contract can be as short as a paragraph or even a few sentences, or it can run hundreds of pages of fine print.

This section is not intended to make you an expert in contract law. The law of contracts fills volumes. Commercial contracts, that is, contracts between businesses have their own entire section of the Uniform Commercial Code devoted to them. Because contract law has its roots in common law, there are hundreds and hundreds of decisions in various jurisdictions that address various aspects of contracts. This is stuff well, well, beyond the scope of this book, the interest and attention span of most people. The purpose here is to acquaint you with the general principles of contracts and how to deal with them on your own. Being your own lawyer is not just about going to court. If you find yourself in court, something has gone wrong. It is far better to know how not to be there at all. A good understanding of contracts, what they are, how they work, and what they will and will not accomplish will go a long way toward accomplishing that goal.

What is a Contract?

A contract in its simplest terms is an agreement between two or more competent parties (they can be people or companies) whereby each of them is to do something. The doing something can be making a payment, or performing a service or delivering something. It can be as simple as "I will pay you for this ticket and you will let me ride the roller coaster", to spelling out acts and things to be done over a span of years. Contracts can be oral or written, but there are some contracts that must be in writing.

Contracts generally have certain elements in common. The legal requirements are set forth in more court cases that could be listed here, but generally there must be an offer, an acceptance of that offer, and valid consideration.

First there must be the offer and acceptance, often referred to as a meeting of the minds. There must be an agreement. That means that if an offer is made, it must be accepted as made. An offer by itself is of no effect until accepted. The offer can be made to a specific person, or it can be a general offer, open for acceptance to anyone. If any part of the offer is changed, the response becomes a counteroffer, and no contract is formed until that has been accepted. For example, A offers to paint B's house for a certain amount of money. B responds "that's fine, but it must be finished in two weeks". There is no contract because B changed the offer which included no time limit. Unless A agrees to the time limit, there has been no agreement. This example is used because it makes it very easy to see how this principle presents itself every day in real life.

The agreement must be supported by consideration. Each party must give, or give up something in order for the contract to be binding.

In addition to the legal requirements, a contract must meet other conditions in order to be enforceable.

The contract must be between competent parties. You cannot bind a six year old to pay you money (even if they had it) since a minor is generally not deemed competent to enter into a contract.

A contract must be for a lawful purpose. A contract may be void as against public policy. Some contracts involve things that society does not allow. A contract between parties cannot overcome public law and policy, so when there is a conflict, the contract will not be enforced. Thus for example a contract to commit a criminal act is not enforceable.

On a more practical level, a contract is an agreement between two or more parties to accomplish some purpose or to do something. It can be to construct a house, or pay an obligation or any of the thousands of things that are the subject of agreements in our world. Obviously everyone knows intuitively what a contract is, but in reality, it's very hard to really get a grasp on it. Clearly if you have a carefully drafted fifteen page agreement that identifies the parties, what is to be done, when it is to be done and so forth, signed by everyone, you probably have a contract. No one will argue that. But what about more abstract situations? What about the farmer who promises to give his neighbor a cow sometime in the future in exchange for two pigs right now? What about the guy that says he'll fix your car for "x" dollars but when you pick it up, it's quite a bit more?

There are situations that arise every day where the underlying question is whether there is an enforceable contract and if so, what is the actual agreement? In the real world of contracts, the first thing you have to contend with is if you even have a contract. Then you need to go on and make sure the contract means what you think, or intended it to mean and finally if it is enforceable.

435

Sophisticated and esoteric legal theories aside, there are a some things that in one way shape or form every contract must have to be enforceable. The contract must identify the parties. Who is to be bound, who is to do what. The contract should define a time for performance. In the example of the farmer and the cow the obvious question is when. If the cow can be delivered anytime between now and forever, then there is no real agreement. The time does not have to be expressed in traditional terms relating to time such as date and hour. It can be on the happening of some event. For example, if the second farmer does not have but is building a barn, the agreement could be that the cow will be delivered as soon as the barn is completed. The point is that there must be some identifiable time or event upon which the obligation to deliver the cow comes into being.

The contract must contain an agreement between the parties. There must be the proverbial "meeting of the minds". It can be formal or informal, written or oral, but there must be something that both parties can agree to. This agreement can be express or implied. For example, when you take your car to be repaired, there is a contract. Forget about the pre-printed work order form – just the act itself constitutes a contract. What is the contract? It is simple. Mechanic will fix car. Customer will pay to have car fixed. Customer will pay money when car is finished. There has been an agreement. It might not be a complete agreement. It might not for example provide for specific price. Missing might be an agreement as to when the car will be fixed and so forth. That is an entirely different topic that will be addressed later, how the law will fill in the blanks.

Bear in mind that a contract can be either in writing or verbal. If proven, and if not otherwise barred, an oral contract is just a binding as a written contract. Notice the qualifiers in the last sentence: "if proven" and "not otherwise barred". That of course is the core of virtually every problem with verbal contracts and is why written contracts predominate. Who said what and meant what, to whom and when..... are just the beginning of the problems that have arisen with verbal contracts.

Because people, when pausing to prepare written contracts are far more likely to attempt to address at least all the details that occur to them, it is also more likely that a written contract will cover issues that would otherwise be the basis of a dispute. Because of the issues inherent in attempting to verify and prove not only what was said, but what the intent behind the words was, our legal system has of course embraced written contracts as the preferred form, and they are awarded a different status than oral contracts. In fact, some agreements in order to be enforceable must be in writing. The overwhelming deference to written contracts is embodied in two separate legal principles.

The first, evidenced by the Statute of Frauds, or equivalent law, either statutory or precedential, stands for the principle that some contracts must be in writing. Examples are contracts concerning an interest in real property, contracts dealing with payment of money above a certain amount, and contracts that call for performance over a period beyond a certain limit. You can't orally agree to sell your house. You can't enforce a contract to be paid huge amounts of money. You can't enforce an oral contract to buy or sell goods twenty years in the future.

The second principle, known as the parole evidence rule provides that written contracts are entitled to deference. Evidence that contradicts the clear terms and conditions of a written contract will not be allowed. There is of course a lot of logic and common sense there. What after all is the point of a written contract if the plain language appearing on its face can be challenged every time a dispute or question arises? The "I know what it says, but that is not what I meant" argument is thus usually not allowed.

In case you haven't grasped it by now, there are of course exceptions to both of these principles, and nothing is as simple as it first seems in the law. For example, an oral contract that would otherwise be barred by the Statute of Frauds (requiring a written contract to be enforceable) can often be resurrected and enforced based on performance by one of the parties. A good example might be if party "A" tells "B" that if he repairs the broken down barn on the farm, "A" will give him an acre of land. "B" diligently repairs the barn and asks for his land. "A" refuses. At first glance this contract would not be enforceable because it concerns land and is not in writing. But the performance by "B" changes things and in most jurisdictions there is an excellent probability that the contract would be enforced to some extent. Note that of course this assumes that the promise can be proven which gets us back to the problems with an oral contract.

The other very important point to remember is that in most arrangements or relationships where a contract might be appropriate or in dispute, there will almost always be other legal theories that can be pursued. Seldom will a contract be the only way that the issues can be addressed. Even though the existence of an oral contract may be precluded by the Statute of Frauds, there are theories such as Promissory Estoppel, Unjust Enrichment, Money Had and Received, to name a few that can be pursued. So for example, where someone has been promised something and acts based on that promise, the promisor may not later be allowed to escape the obligation merely because the contract was not in writing. Even though there may not be a contract that can be enforced, there are alternatives. The concept of contracts, requirements that they be in writing, and alternative means of recovery are very important to us all on a practical matter. Far too often people try to claim a right or entitlement only to be confronted with the question "did you get that in writing?" or some variation. It is important in understand that presence or absence of a written agreement, notwithstanding things like the statute of frauds, is not necessarily the end of the issues. While the existence of a properly prepared written agreement might make things simpler, there are other avenues to achieve the same objectives.

Important Contract Considerations

While you should not expect to be an expert in contract law after reading this section, you should at least be prepared to look at contracts, both before and after you enter into them, with a more critical eye. The first part of this section focuses on things to look at before you sign a contract in particular things that should be in the contract and things that should be deleted. Of course you are going to have more control over your fate in the realm of contract law if you can address issues ahead of time.

When either preparing or being presented with a contract to sign, the number of things that you can change will vary tremendously with the kind of contract and the relationship between the parties. If you go to your bank and want to open an account, you will be presented with an account-holder agreement. This one is sadly not negotiable. If you want the account, you sign the agreement as presented. If you don't want to sign it, you don't get the account. On the other hand, there are far more contracts that you might enter into that do provide for at least some degree of flexibility.

Nor should you be intimidated by pre-printed contract forms. This is a tactic used by businesses at all levels. At the business-to-business level it even has a name. It is referred to as the battle of the forms. The thought behind this practice is that if someone is presented with a pre-printed form, that does not on its face appear to have any room to make additions or changes, they are likely to sign the form as is. They have agreed to all the contract terms as presented (even the fine print on the back) when otherwise, these would be subject to negotiation. A great example of this can be found in the process of a business, especially a larger more structured business, acquiring goods or services. The company wanting to get something will send the vendor a purchaser order. The vendor in turn will send a proposal or order form. Both of these forms invariably have at least one full page, usually on the reverse of fine print setting forth terms and conditions. Each company is trying to impose on the other its terms and conditions. How that plays out has been the subject of countless court battles. While the obvious response to these "forms" is to settle ahead of time the terms and conditions that will apply, that is seldom done. Small companies or individuals will agree because they want the business. Large companies will allow the conflicting forms to prevail, secure in the knowledge that in the event of a dispute they can, with far more resources, prevail in, and even bully a small vendor or customer in a court battle. Of course how you deal with pre-printed forms depends on your relative bargaining position, but many more times than you would think, these pre-printed forms can be marked up, terms crossed out, and other terms added.

So whether you are presented with a pre-printed form, or are trying to put together a contract to deal with some issue, you need to understand the basics of what's in a contract, what it can and can't do for you, and things to be thinking about. While there are far too many kinds of contracts floating around to talk about all of them, in the context of things that you are most likely to encounter, here as some basic nuts and bolts ideas:

Parties.

Make sure that the parties are correctly identified. If you are doing business with a small company, make sure that the principals are included as parties or at the very least guarantee the company's performance under the contract. Don't be afraid to insist. They want your business, or they wouldn't be talking to you. Make it clear that you are not going to rely on a contract by a corporation that may be nothing more than a name. In other sections the example of a contract with ABC Roofing is used. In a case such as this just make it clear.

> "Mr. Jones I've been dealing with you. You're the one that has made me promises about the kind of roof you would install. You're the one that will either be doing the work or supervising it. So if I'm going to sign a contract for this roof, you will have to be included as a party or at least guarantee the performance of ABC Roofing."

Mr. Jones may refuse, and that's ok. If it's a deal breaker for him to be personally liable, then he probably did you a favor.

Likewise, if the shoe is on the other foot, if it is not appropriate for you to be on a contract and you have no incentive to guarantee a contract, don't. It again depends on the relative bargaining power of the parties and the merits or benefits of the parties. You can negotiate with ABC Roofing because it is a small company. You are not going to be able to get the CEO of Home Depot to personally guarantee a product sold in one of his stores. At the same time the need to be concerned about getting Mr. Jones to sign or guarantee the ABC Roofing contract is not an issue with a product purchased from Home Depot.

Look out in this regard for definitions. In some more modern contracts, where the emphasis is on plain language and simplicity, there are often definitions of terms in the agreement. Pay attention to these! A term often encountered is "we". The contract will often contain a definition of "us" and "we" that includes not only the people that you are doing business with, but other actual or potential parties, such as those to whom the contract may be assigned (transferred). These are not impermissible per se, but you need to be aware of the terms and their effect. Back to ABC Roofing. Especially if you selected this company because of the people involved, do you really want to sign a contract that allows ABC

Roofing to assign the work to some party that you know nothing about?

Terms and Conditions.

Make sure the contract says what you discussed and agreed. Make sure the contract says what you think it does. Remember the parole evidence rule. You cannot come back later and say that your agreement with the other party was something other than what is set forth on the written contract. Arguing that you really meant something different or that "this is not what the salesman said", to alter a written contract is seldom an option.

Read the contract, especially if it has a lot of fine print. Don't be intimidated by statements such as "it's a standard contract", or "it's all just 'legalize' for what we talked about".

If you are in a bargaining position (and sometimes of course you are not) don't be afraid to insist on changes to pre-printed forms. They're NOT etched in stone!

Here are some things to make sure are in your contract:

Subject of the Contract.

This seems so basic that it should not be an issue, but it is. One need only look at the multitude of lawsuits in the courts that arise from disagreement over what was actually agreed to. A couple of examples might be helpful.

You sign a contract to have a swimming pool installed in your backyard. Sounds simple right?

Maybe.

What about the part that says the price includes standard decking? What's that? To the pool company, it's three feet of concrete around the pool. In your mind it was concrete at least large enough to put a recliner on so that you could enjoy the sun. You didn't agree on an important term.

Or, you contract with a tree company to come to your home to cut down a large tree. When they leave, while they have taken the bulk of the tree, they leave behind all the debris, including leaves, small branches, etc., and the huge stump is still in the ground. You assumed that your agreement with the company included removal of all debris and tree parts. When you ask they point out that it included only removal of the large parts of the tree - trunk, large branches, etc. - and that the other clean-up was your responsibility. You clearly never agreed on the specifics of the contract.

Time.

So many people take for granted that things will happen as they assume they will. Remember the contract for the pool? It's signed, and you've already got a mental image of you and your family enjoying the pool this summer. But a question now pops up. How long do they have? You assumed that the pool company would come out, begin work and continue until the pool was done. They understand the contract to mean within a reasonable time (a pretty elusive term). A common practice among some companies is to sign the contract, get started, then, when another contract is signed, get started on that job leaving the first for sometimes several weeks. This allows them to begin more jobs. Of course it leaves you with an empty hole in your backyard for a good part of the summer. Make sure that your agreement specifies when the pool will be finished, what delays are acceptable, and what happens if it's not finished in time. Do not rely on the courts to imply a reasonable time because such things are elusive concepts at best. This is especially true if time is critical to performance of the contract.

Even if a time is specified, if it is in fact critical, make sure the contract says so. This is why you will see in many contracts words like "time is of the essence" or similar language. As you will see from the section on litigating contract disputes, this language is at the very least important and could be essential to bringing or defending a breach of contract action. Why? Because as you will learn, one of the elements (along with a valid contact and a breach) of a breach of contract cause of action is damages that arise from the breach. Expressed another way, every violation of the terms and conditions of a contract will not in and of itself give rise to a breach of contract claim. Late performance, absent damages or a provision expressing that time is a critical element, will often not be the basis of a successful breach of contract action. So if you have a contract for something to be done within a defined time frame, it is essential that you express that in the contract.

Damages.

Be sure that your contract addresses what you are entitled to receive and how you will be compensated if the other side breaches the contract. Some may say that this is easy. It's the value of whatever you contracted for. Even when it appears simple it can get tricky. Look at a seemingly simple situation. You contract to purchase $5,000 worth of widgets. They never arrive and the contract is breached. Damages? The obvious answer is $5,000 right? Maybe, but probably not.

What if the widgets are used in your manufacturing business and without them you can't produce your product? What if you had a deal to sell your some of your product at a good price but couldn't perform because you had no widgets? What if the price of widgets goes up since your seller breached and it will now cost you $6,000 to buy the widgets he had promised to sell you?

What about the swimming pool? You sign a contract to install a swimming pool and even provide in it that the pool must be finishing within four weeks. The pool company does not complete the pool on time. A month after you thought you and your family would be having the neighbors over for a cookout by the pool, it's nothing but a giant mud pond in the back yard. The only guests appearing have been the mosquitoes happily breeding in the stagnant water collecting at the bottom.

Obviously agreeing specifically what the consequences of a default are is important. It is even more important when the "damages" that is what you suffer as a consequence of the breach are more difficult to measure. What are your damages? There has clearly been a breach of contract, but what can you recover? The pool contractor will argue that you have been at worst inconvenienced but have not suffered any measurable damages. You will argue that getting the pool finished so that you could enjoy it for the summer was the only reason you signed the contract at all.

It is in these cases, where damages are hard to quantify, that it is essential that the issue be addressed in the contract. One way to do that is to provide for what is often referred to as liquidated damages. The term itself acknowledges that there is difficulty in measuring the damage that would result from a breach, so the parties are agreeing up front what that will be. In the case of the swimming pool a possible term might be that for every day past a stated deadline that he pool is not complete, a specific amount would be deducted from the contract price. But these have to be negotiated ahead of time. First, you can't change the contract later unless both sides agree which is not likely once there is a dispute. Second, from a practical perspective, up front is the best time to make your best deal.

So in this example, when you're negotiating with the pool company, make it clear to them that you are only entering this contract because you want a pool this summer, so if you are going to sign a contract, they will have to guarantee that. They will counter that there are a lot of things that they cannot control, such as weather. Through a give and take you can arrive at an agreement that allows them a certain fixed time to complete the pool, excluding days on which they are not able to work due to weather, and that upon failure to meet the deadline a certain amount, perhaps $100 a day will be deducted from the contract price. You are far more likely to be able to negotiate an arrangement along these lines before you sign the contract, when they are anxiously anticipating your deposit check, than later, when they haven't shown up to work for two or three weeks.

People are often reluctant to address the issue of damages because no one wants to begin a deal anticipating that it will go south. That does not though make it any less important. Just remember that every lawsuit involving a contract started out with everybody happy. Without being sure that damages can be quantified or otherwise determined, and carefully defining what will transpire in the event of default or breach, there is the possibility of having basically a worthless contract.

Disclaimers.

Virtually any pre-printed contract that you will see, and most contracts that are drafted, will contain some form of disclaimers, which will limit warranties or liability. Just because these are commonplace does not mean that you should ignore them, or, where you are in a negotiating position, accept them. These terms essentially seek to limit a party's liability in the event of breach.

One of the most common disclaimers in contracts as well as in warranties (which really are a form of contract) is for consequential damages. Consequential damages are those which are incurred as a consequence, that is, because of a breach or failure but usually not directly. Direct damages are the actual, immediate result of the breach. Consequential damages are the subsequent effects. How far along a chain of events "damages" can be linked to a breach or an event is of course the crux of many lawsuits. To illustrate, go back to the case of the undelivered widgets. The direct damages are the cost of the widgets. The consequential damages are the loss of profits incurred because there were no widgets to produce the buyer's product. Many contracts will have a blanket disclaimer that upon breach there will be no liability for consequential damages whatsoever. Others qualify the disclaimer. These clauses are not per se objectionable as long as you appreciate their effect and they are drafted in accordance with the intent of the parties. If the seller of the widgets knows full well that they are going to be used in the buyer's manufacturing process and that the absence of widgets will cause losses far greater than the value of the widgets, he should not be allowed to disclaim liability for consequential damages. On the other hand, if the widgets are sold at a discounted price, and everyone understands that they may or may not be available, then such a disclaimer may be appropriate.

Other disclaimers go to the promises, express or implied that are made or could arise. Everyone has seen the huge bold print on contract forms that disclaim liability or state there are no warranties, express or implied. Read these disclaimers in the context of what you are contracting for. If you are signing a contract with ABC Roofing for the installation of a roof which you expect to be of reasonably good quality and workmanship, why in the world would you allow them to disclaim "any and all warranties of any kind, express or implied" as the term often appears in bold print? Is this really what you want to agree to? That you agree they are not warranting their product? Just because it's printed on the form in big bold type does not mean it's etched in stone. You can get it clarified, modified, or even eliminated.

Pay Attention to the Boilerplate.

Or as they sometimes say, "the devil is in the details". The dangers here lurk in the parts of a contract that people tend to gloss over as being a bunch of meaningless "legalese". It is here where you will find those clauses and provisions that will haunt you if you ever need to think about enforcing the contract. Often the section will be given an innocuous heading such as "miscellaneous provisions", "general terms and conditions", or something similar. The first paragraphs will often indeed be innocuous, stating things like "paragraph headings are for identification only". But be careful and read on, because in addition to what has already been discussed, here are some of the things you will find buried in these "innocuous" sections:

- provisions as to jurisdiction and venue. You live in Idaho and signed an extended warranty to provide repairs to your car. Did you really mean to agree that any disputes arising under the contract would be resolved in the Circuit Court for Dade County Florida?

- attorney's fees and costs. Did you really want to agree that if there was any litigation arising out of the contract you signed, regardless of why, that you would be responsible for the other side's attorney's fees but they would not be responsible for yours?

- arbitration. Most commercial contracts today have some form of arbitration clause. These are fine as long as you understand what is going on. These clauses provide that in the event of a dispute arising from the contract, the matter will be resolved not by a lawsuit, but by arbitration. This in and of itself is not ominous, but it is important that you carefully read the clause and understand what it provides. Look for what kind of

452

arbitration, where it will be held, before what organization and pursuant to what rules and procedures. There are some real potential traps here. For example in the past, many automobile purchase agreements included an arbitration clause that provided for arbitration before the NADA (National Association of Automobile Dealers). Think about it. Do you really want a panel of automobile dealers resolving the dispute you have with an automobile dealer? Some of these are not subject to change, but surprisingly, a lot are. In this example you might find that the dealer really wants to make the sale and will not mind scratching through NADA and inserting "American Arbitration Association", for example.

- indemnification. Almost all form contracts contain some clause or language in which one party agrees to indemnify or hold harmless the other from various events or occurrences. Since most people don't know what indemnification means, then often gloss over these clauses. These need to be paid close attention to because they can be incredibly dangerous. A blanket obligation to indemnify means that you will be responsible for any loss, cost or expense the other party experiences related in any way to the contract. Some clauses are reasonable and relevant to a contract. Others are overreaching, requiring one party to effectively insure that the other will sustain no losses regardless of fault. Did you really mean to take on this obligation when you signed pool contract?

- jurisdiction and choice of law. Another common provision, especially in pre-printed contracts relates to where and under what law any disputes arising under the contract will be resolved. While the choice of law is usually not critical, since most contract law is either based on common law or the uniform commercial code, the location is often critical. It is not uncommon to see contracts that specify that any dispute arising under them will be resolved in the courts of some state other than where the contract is to be performed. Usually this is a state convenient to the party preparing the contract. In some cases, with less scrupulous parties, it is simply a state chosen to be as inconvenient as possible to the other party. This is not a small matter and the term of art "inconvenient" in this context is a gross understatement. Imagine that you live in California and have signed a contract with a solar panel vendor that provides that if there is a dispute it will be litigated in the seller's home state, which is Florida. Unless the amount in controversy is huge, you would never be able to justify the cost of litigating three thousand miles away. The consequences of such a clause can literally mean that you are unable as a practical matter to ever enforce, or protect your rights under the contract.

These are just a few of the gems often found in those "boring and mundane" sections of contracts. They appear in both pre-printed and drafted contracts.

General Observations About Contracts.

While every contract is entered into with presumably good intentions, the abundance of lawsuits relating to contracts is an attestation to the reality that disputes and understandings can and will arise. If you have to go do battle over a contract, be sure that the contract is in your favor and that there are no "dangerous" or one-sided clauses. Remember that the bulk of winning a contract lawsuit or dispute is accomplished with the drafting of the contract – not in the trial of the dispute.

One way to prepare deal with the negotiation and execution of a contract is to put it in proper perspective. Contracts exist for two reasons. One reason is to be sure that there is a true understanding between the parties. Usually, once people have undertaken the task of reducing an agreement to writing, they will be more likely to recognize missing elements, things that are vague or ambiguities and make an effort to address them. Recall the farmers and the pigs for the cow. The farmer to receive the cow could be assuming that he would get the brown cow that he had looked at. The farmer to contribute the cow could have assumed he would give the black cow. No devious intent here. No intent not to honor the commitment. A genuine misunderstanding that a written agreement would have prevented. "If you give me two pigs today, by the end of the month I will give you my brown cow."

The other reason for a contract is to provide a basis for the parties to enforce their rights. When the farmer shows up with the black cow, the other brings forth the contract and points out that it specifies the brown cow. This addresses any claim of confusion or misunderstanding. The farmer, having given his pigs also is in a position to go to the local judge and demand not the black cow, but the brown cow, as set forth in the contract.

Colloquialisms aside, your purpose in signing a contract is to make sure that if the other side does not perform, you have the contract to rely on with which you can go to court and demand your brown cow.

Every contract should be signed with the idea in mind that you may be in court relying on it to express and say what you intended, so be sure that it does. Keep these thoughts in mind when you negotiate or review a contract. If all goes well, the contract will never be looked at again. The farmer will receive the cow for the pigs. The new roof will be both attractive and functional. The pool will be promptly finished and gleefully enjoyed. It's when these things don't work out that the contract and what's in it comes into play. Every contract should be prepared and negotiated as if it was going to be the subject of a lawsuit!

Addressing Contract Issues

Ok, for one reason or another, you're in a dispute involving a contract. Here's where all the stuff you've read about should help you. Or at least give you a better idea on how to move things along in your favor. As you're probably tired of hearing, since contract law fills volumes and millions of pages, this is not going to make you an expert at resolving contract cases. It should though, give you a good idea of what's going on and what you can do to protect yourself.

To keep things organized this is presented from throughout from two perspectives. On the one hand, you're trying to enforce a contract. On the other someone is trying to enforce a contract against you. In each case three issues are dealt with. There are two kinds of contracts, oral and written. The major differences arise from establishing the existence of the contract an interpreting it. Once that has been done, except for isolated issues, such as a shorter or longer statute of limitation, enforcing either contract is substantially the same. So this discussion is will start with the issues surrounding oral contracts in terms of proving them and defining their terms and conditions. There are a few issues surrounding written contracts in the same regard, so those will be addressed. Then, on the assumption that the contract has been established, and the terms defined, the issue of enforcement or proceeding to recover on a contract will be covered. Finally, because there are some concepts and things to know that are closely related to contracts, things like promissory estoppels, parole evidence and so forth will be touched on as additional tools to be used when the contract actions are discussed.

A.   Oral Contracts

Remember, unless for some reason that is discussed below an oral contract is barred, if you can prove it, and prove what was agreed to, an oral contract is just as enforceable as a complex written contract measured by weight instead of pages. The trick is proving it and proving what it consists of. A written contract is easy in comparison. Here it is. It says contract at the top. It's got lots of fancy legalize. It's signed at the bottom. Yep, it's a contract! Oral contracts are more difficult to get a handle on. There's nothing to touch or see.

In discussing oral contracts it would behoove one to bear in mind the old stand-up comedian line:

"I'm not sure that you understand that what you think you heard me say is not what I meant!"

When it comes to oral contracts the wisdom (or lack thereof) of that adage comes home in spades. Aside from the fact that oral contracts present additional issues to be proven, you need to understand that all is not lost. They can be dealt with and they can constitute the basis of a cause of action.

Proving and Interpreting an Oral Contract

There are two hurdles to overcome in trying to enforce an oral contract. First, you have to prove that the contract

458

exists at all. Next, because oral contracts are usually somewhat simplistic, you have to prove the terms and conditions that you are trying to enforce. Though it presents difficulties, it is far from impossible.

There are a multitude of different ways to prove the existence of an oral agreement. Proving that there is some form of oral agreement is actually not that difficult. If you will look at some of the common situations in life where the existence of an oral contract may be questioned, it becomes quickly obvious that both parties will have at some point to acknowledge that there was some form of agreement.

Example: You have provided repair work on someone's house and they refuse to pay you, stating that there was no agreement because "you don't have that in writing". The absurdity of that posture becomes quickly apparent when you visualize a court hearing with the homeowner on the witnesses stand.

> Mr. Homeowner was the plaintiff on your property on "x" date?
> What was he doing there?
> You knew he was there...
> You knew he was working on your house.
> Did you call the police because he was trespassing?
> So he was there because you and he had agreed that he would work on your house.

The same sort of reasoning applies to doing work on a car, working for someone on an hourly basis, delivering materials or products, etc. It is clear that the parties are doing something resulting from a mutual understanding, i.e. an agreement. The trickier part is to establish what was agreed upon. There are a number of ways to do that.

Define the issues that need attention and approach them logically. For example, to go back to our home improvement example. You've established that work was done for the homeowner that benefited him. You will easily be able to get him to admit that there was to be payment. Really, is he going to get up in front of a judge when you go to trial on the issue and suggest that because he is such a great guy and you're in such a charitable mood that you were working on the house for free? Of course not. The issue is no longer whether there as an agreement, or if you should be compensated. It is down to how much.

As you can narrow the issues, the easier they become to tackle. Here's how to establish that:

The most obvious of course are witnesses. And don't forget yourself and the other party. Clearly if you have someone that was present when you agreed to do the work that can testify that you told the homeowner that you would work for "X" dollars per hour, then the issue is probably almost resolved. But if it's just your word against the homeowner, your testimony counts for something, though of course it can't tip the scales all by itself. Never underestimate what you can get the other guy to say if you think it through. Again, imagine a trial in front of a judge and you are questioning your opponent:

> Mr. Homeowner you agreed to have the plaintiff do the work correct?
> And you knew that you would have to pay for the work correct?
> Since you say that you and the plaintiff did not agree on an amount would it be fair to say that you both assumed that he would be paid a fair amount for the work that he did?
> Wouldn't a fair amount be what other contractors charge and other homeowners pay for this kind of work?

That's just one of many ways to approach it. By starting with the givens, either in questioning or in negotiating (yes, I agreed for him to do the work, yes I knew I would have to pay him) you can easily get the other side off the simplistic position of relying on the absence of a written contract as an escape from obligations

The law allows missing elements of a contract to be determined from the conduct of the parties. If the homeowner repair work had been going on for several months and you had been submitting invoices for hourly work, and the homeowner had been paying them, the law will infer that there had been an agreement as to the hourly rate.

Sometimes, the custom and practice in the industry can provide the basis for missing elements of an agreement. The oral contract here probably did not include who would bear the expense of cleaning up the construction debris. The homeowner will obviously contend that that was included in the price while the contractor will argue that that is an extra expense not included in the quoted price. Evidence of how other people in the same business deal with the issue in contracts with similar pricing may help solve the issue.

Often there is no single best way to establish all the elements of an oral contract. The idea is to be very logical. Start with the known issues. Determine what is unknown and which of those are essential elements to establish your claim. Those elements are the ones to work on, using any or all of the available ways to establish them. Once you've done that, you will have established the oral contract.

Even if you can't establish an oral contract don't forget there are other ways to get the same relief. After the ins and outs of contracts and how to interpret them are explored, there will be a discussion on other ways to get from "a" to "b".

So when you let someone know that you intend to enforce an agreement that they made, and they respond with "do you have that in writing?," all is not necessarily lost. They could be in for some rude surprises.

Challenging an Oral Contract

When the shoe is on the other foot, a different approach is in order, but at the same time bear in mind the things just discussed so that you don't try to do something totally stupid, such as try to deny that any agreement existed, when in fact it did.

Here you have someone trying to impose an obligation upon you by virtue of a contract that is admitted not to be in writing, but to be verbal.

First, take a logical approach, just as in trying to enforce an oral contract. What was agreed to and what was not. What are you trying to accomplish? Are you trying to negate the whole alleged oral contract, or are you just seeing things differently than the other guy?

Clearly if there is some sort of relationship or interaction between the parties, trying to argue that there was no agreement of any kind, whatsoever, is seldom the best approach. This is especially true when there are other, less drastic approaches that will accomplish the same thing. However, it is not enough for the other side to prove that there was some agreement. They must prove all of the essential elements of a contract. If even one cannot be proven, there is no contract, oral or otherwise. Of course as pointed out, that doesn't preclude some other legal theory that you may need to deal with, but it will take the contract claim out of the mix.

So let's review. A contract requires an offer, an acceptance and valid consideration. A contract requires competent parties and a lawful purpose. If any of those elements are missing then no contract has been formed.

The realm that is most bountiful in terms of whether a contract was formed concerns the offer and acceptance. Even the offer is not often difficult to find but because the acceptance must match the offer, and respond exactly to the offer, it is where problems are most likely to be encountered. If you are trying to establish a contract, this will be the most problematic for you. If you are trying to show that there was no contract, this is where you are most likely to be able to show that an essential element is missing.

As usual, an example can be helpful. "A" says to "B", I need my house painted and I'll pay you "X" dollars if you will do it. We have an offer. "B" responds yes I will paint your house for "X". We have an acceptance. However, as soon as "B" diverges in any meaningful way from the terms of the offer in his response, the offer has been rejected. The proverbial "meeting of the minds" is missing and there is no acceptance. No acceptance means no contract. So if "B" says to "A" I'll be happy to paint your house, but "X" is not acceptable, there is no acceptance at all, the offer is rejected and that is the end of the process unless a new offer is extended. If "B" says to "A", I'll be happy to paint your house, but "X" dollars is not acceptable. I'll be happy to paint your house for "Y" dollars, the offer is rejected, there is no contract, but, there is a counter-offer. "A" must now, if there is to be a contract, accept the counter-offer or there is no contract. Whether the process ends or not depends on whether "A" rejects the counter-offer outright, or responds with still another counter-offer at a different price.

Bear in mind that so far only one element of the contract has been discussed – price. Begin to add additional terms, such as, time when the job should be started, time for completion, what kind of paint should be used, whether the price includes minor repairs such as caulking cracks, and the water gets a little murkier. It does not take a great deal of imagination to see that even with a written contract there is a virtual minefield of possible issues that could be raised to challenge the existence of a contract. Obviously that potential is multiplied many times over in the case of an oral contract where the agreement as to all of these terms must be proven in the absence of a writing.

To challenge an alleged oral contract on this basis it is simply a matter of logically setting forth the essential terms of the contract as alleged and showing that the plaintiff cannot establish that there was an offer and acceptance of those terms.

But that is only the first item in a veritable bottomless toolbox with which to challenge an oral contract. Here are some more things that you should be thinking of.

Is the contract one which must be in writing? For reasons already discussed, every state has some form of Statute of Frauds, usually in several different areas, that provides that a contract, to be enforceable must be in writing. You cannot have an oral contract to buy or sell real estate. You cannot have an oral contract to buy or sell goods over a certain amount in value. You cannot have an oral contract to do something later than a limited time, usually a year.

Consider also the statute of limitations to an action to enforce a contract. Most states have various limitation periods in which a suit must be brought. Very often the time to enforce an oral contract is much shorter than the time to enforce a written contract.

Also consider and explore contracts that are void as against public policy. This may be a little trickier because there is no single statute in any code of laws that says, "none of these contracts are enforceable because they are against public policy". Instead, you will often find them in various licensing statutes and regulations. So for example a contract that obligates you to pay a real estate commission, a finder's or similar fee to someone that does not hold a valid real estate license is in most states not enforceable. In fact, if you paid any of those, you can probably get them back. Similarly, an amount due to someone for repairs on your home may not be collectible under a contract entered into with someone that does not hold a valid contractor's license. The owner of a truck cannot contract with you to move your furniture unless he holds the proper licenses and permits allowing him to engage in that business.

Oral contracts are simple and often convenient. It is clear however that they should not be your first choice (unless you are challenging one) because the weaknesses and problems far outweigh any advantages.

B.   Written Contract Issues

Though to a lesser extent than with oral contracts, when it comes to establishing a valid written agreement, some of the same issues actually surface from time to time.

Missing or Ambiguous Terms

Often even a written contract will omit necessary terms and conditions. The house painting example might have been dutifully reduced to writing signed by both parties, specifying the price, the date to finish, whether there would be extra charges for minor repairs, but it may have failed to specify the kind of paint to be used. Obviously in a job like that cost of materials will be a significant factor. The painter is motivated to use the least expensive paint that will suffice. The homeowner of course wants the best quality of paint to insure longevity. The failure to address an issue such as this could, if raised before the work began, be grounds to find that no contract existed. Again this is a failure to achieve the proverbial meeting of the minds. If it arose after work had started, or even been completed, it would result in having to address potentially complex issues in terms of contract interpretation, and trying to discern the intent of the parties. So while a written contract may reduce confusion and ambiguity, it does not guarantee that those things will be completely eliminated.

In addition to an outright missing term, such as the kind of paint, issues arise when terms are vague or can be susceptible to being interpreted in different way. What about the foregoing example where the contract is worded to provide that "a good quality paint will be used"?

The obvious question is what does "good quality paint" mean? To the painter in means one thing. To the homeowner, expecting paint that will last twenty years or so, it means something entirely different. In this case, because the issue has been addressed, albeit not as clearly as it should have been, while it is still possible that it would be found that no contract existed, that is less likely. In the event of a dispute on that issue, it is more likely that a court would find a contract, and embark upon the task of discerning the reasonable meaning of "a good quality paint".

How these issues arise and how to deal with them in the event of a contract dispute will be dealt with a little later.

Void or Voidable Contracts.

As with any contract, reducing a contract to writing will not overcome such issues as it being void as against public policy, or unenforceable because of some specific statutory provision. So for example even a written contract providing for the payment of a finder's fee in a real estate transaction will not (depending on how a statute is worded) be enforceable by someone that does not hold a valid real estate license. Even reducing a contract to writing, no matter how intricate and detailed will not form the basis for an unlicensed contractor to collect for work done in most states. These contracts are either completely void, or are deemed voidable by a party as being in violation of public policy.

Form Contracts

In cases involving business transactions there is often the possibility of multiple agreements, or even what is sometimes called the "battle of the forms". The latter, occurring when businesses use pre-printed forms such as invoices or purchase orders that purport to incorporate terms and conditions, usually on the reverse side of a form, do not apply to most cases in which you will be representing yourself.

On the other hands, instances of multiple forms or agreements will impact you. Consider when purchasing a car or other large ticket item. You may be presented with several forms. These are all writings, but what really constitutes the contract? What if there is a conflict. You purchase a car and specify that the price will include a special kind of alloy wheel, which the salesman hand writes on an order form. But the invoice or other forms do not contain that language, and worse, the invoice contains language that says that this document represents the entire agreement between the parties. It gets confusing very quickly.

The fix is to stop.

Organize the writings if there are more than one, get an agreement, in writing that sets forth all the terms that you feel are important. Do not accept a seller's assurance to the contrary of what is set forth in writing, because that will, rarely be enforceable. If the seller won't organize everything and put everything in writing in a case such as this, take your business elsewhere. That will often not even be necessary. Businesses generate these forms, rarely at the same time and for a variety of reasons. Usually when the contradictions or inconsistencies are pointed out, some accommodation will be made to clarify. But be careful. Once you have signed a contract, especially one that contains language to the effect that "this document contains the entire agreement of the parties, and customer acknowledges that there have been no other statements, oral or written made in conjunction with this transaction", you are stuck with it.

As promised, the foregoing has no made you an expert on contract law. Such of course was not the intent. Hopefully though, it has given you some insight into how contracts work in general and what to look for and be aware of when you enter into any contract.

Court Rules

Before you get all excited and go charging off to represent yourself in court, you need to be sure that you have a good grasp and understanding of how the courts, wherever you might be, are organized and how they operated.

Courts are first provided for in the federal and state constitutions as branches of the respective governments. There are laws passed by congress and state legislatures that further define the courts, set forth the kinds of cases that they will take and general govern things like jurisdiction of the courts. These laws and statutes do not for the most part get into the day-to-day operation of the courts, that is, how the court functions, how it handles cases and how cases work their way through a particular court system. These things are governed by Rules of Court and these rules are critically important to how a case is handled, from start to finish.

A good way to gain perspective on this issue is to look at how things are handled in the federal courts, then to compare that to different approaches taken in a few states.

Federal Statutes and Rules for Courts

From a statute perspective you can find most of what you need in federal courts in Title 28 of the United States

Code. The statutes found here range from establishment of the courts, to where a particular lawsuit should be brought, depending on what kind of suit it is and where the parties are located.

Although there is some overlap such as with respect to evidence issues, the statutes on a federal level by and large do not get into the day-to-day operation of the courts.

For that the federal system relies on extensive and detailed rules, broken down into major logical categories. There are the Federal Rules of Civil Procedure, the Federal Rules of Criminal Procedure, the Federal Rules of Evidence, the Federal Rules of Appellate Procedure and so forth.

So with a few exceptions where there is some overlap, the division in the federal system is fairly straightforward. If you want to know what court you can file something in, or what kind of case you can file, go to Title 28. The logic behind this is that the jurisdiction of the federal courts is governed by statute and the constitution. On the other hand, if you want to know how long a defendant has to answer a complaint, or what kind of discovery is available, you go the Federal Rules of Civil Procedure. These are procedural issues that fall within the rule making authority of the courts themselves.

Even if you don't end up in federal court, the federal structure is important because so many states have adopted it either outright, or in some limited fashion.

The last part is extremely important!

You will find in many states rules of civil procedure that copy or borrow from the Federal Rules of Civil Procedure. They may even emulate them down to the same rule numbers.

But be careful. The rules are often different. And they may be different in very subtle ways. So merely because a state rule bears the same rule number as a federal rule you should never assume that they are the same.

A perfect example is Utah. Utah has Civil Rules of Procedure that track the federal rules. But if you look at the rules, say Rule 26 for example, you will see the problem. Rule 26 in both the federal system as well as in Utah governs discovery in a civil suit. And that is where the similarity stops. The Utah Rule is substantially different than the federal rule and if you waltzed into a Utah Court assuming that Utah Rule 26 was the same as FRCP 26, you would be in big trouble! This is not an area in which you should be taking shortcuts.

State Statutes and Rules

Many states track the federal system which basically has the major structural aspects of the courts governed by statutes while the day-to-day operation of the courts and handling of cases is governed by rules.

There are though numerous exceptions, in that in several states the rules, though drafted in the form of rules, are actually adopted by the legislature and codified. Thus you will find them in the statutes or code of laws of a particular state.

They serve the same purpose, and once you get into the particulars codes, they are organized and read just as if they were rules, but, for research purposes you need to be aware that they are often indexed and found with a state's statutes or code of laws.

Examples of states that use this system are California and Pennsylvania. So what you have in California is not Rules of Civil Procedure, but instead the California Code of Civil Procedure. It is part of the California Code of Laws and that is where you would look for the provisions that would in a federal court be found in the Federal Rules of Civil Procedure. In terms of application, there is no real difference. The distinction lies mostly in the manner in which you would go about researching these rules.

In order for you to know how to do things in court when you represent yourself, you have to research and review both statutes and rules and you have to know how each state divides them up so that you know where to look for them.

Court Rules Examined

Court rules are beyond important. They are critical. For the purpose of this section to avoid confusion, reference to Court Rules, also refers to, where they are organized that way, Code sections or statutes that serve the same purpose as Court Rules.

What They Are

Rules are of course what determine how courts operate, but they go much, much farther than that. They actually can and do determine the outcome of a case.

Rules come on several levels. All are important. An analogy might be competitive sports. You might have the greatest football team in the world, and have wonderful strategies for moving the ball, but unless you know, understand, and follow the game rules, it will be impossible to win.

In most state courts, and all federal courts there are universal rules. In the federal courts there are the Federal Rules of Civil Procedure, Federal Rules of Evidence and so forth. Every state likewise has rules that apply in every court of general jurisdiction. In addition, many courts, governed by the federal rules, or a statewide rule system, also have local rules. A Federal District Court is a good example. It is governed by the Federal Rules of Civil Procedure, but it also has the authority to impose its own rules. Depending on the way that the universal rules are structured, the local rules may even override the statewide or system-wide rules. What is common is a statewide rule on a topic directing each county or district to formulate and implement a rule. When this occurs, you would be required to follow the local rule even if it was different than the general rule. It is extremely important to review all of these, because the result may be different legal procedures within a state, from county to county.

What They Do

The rules govern how a case is conducted in the court.

The rules govern how evidence is presented, how things are presented to the court,

The rules govern how the case is presented.

The rules govern how papers are filed and how they must be presented to the other side.

They define the time in which an answer must be filed. They even define the contents of the papers.

For example, the court rules specify what kinds of things must be mentioned and in what order. Failure to comply with such rules can result in loss of the case. In this regard rules are often as important and sometimes more so, than the laws that define the claims or defenses in a case.

Kinds of Rules

The scope of court rules is broad and they come in all sorts of variations. Some rules are so detailed that they even specify the size of paper, the size of margins, and the type size that must be used.

Obviously, rules are as important as other sources of law. Failure to follow the rules can have disastrous results. Your case can be dismissed, or default judgment can be taken against a defendant if an answer is not timely or properly filed and served. Because court rules are so important, and because there are so many kinds and sources of rules, researching ALL the rules that apply in your case is one of the most important things that you must do.

All rules whether federal or state, are broken down into logical topics that deal with various aspects of the case. However, because all states are different, even to the extent to which they embrace the federal rules, only a general description can be given here. It cannot be stressed enough that being familiar with the rules in your jurisdiction is absolutely critical.

The first section of civil rules will usually deal with the kinds of cases and how they are brought or commenced. Here are a few examples.

Federal Rule (FRCP2): There is one form of action—the civil action.

California §307 CCCP: There is in this State but one form of civil actions for the
        enforcement or protection of private rights and the

redress or   prevention of
private wrongs.

TN Rules Civil Procedure: All actions in law or equity
shall be known as "civil actions."

This section of the rules (or section of the code) is also
devoted to such things as how to commence a lawsuit,
how to issue, or have issued a summons, how those
papers need to be delivered to (served upon) the
defendant and so forth. While all the rules are important,
this first set governs exactly what you must do to get a civil
lawsuit underway. Failing to comply with the rules on
issuing a summons and effecting service upon a defendant
can have an impact later as the case progresses that could
include having the whole case thrown out.

Think of the first section as "getting started".

The second section usually goes into what happens after
the action is commenced and the papers have been served
upon the defendant.

This section includes things like:

- How long a defendant has to answer or
  respond to the complaint
- What happens if there is no response
- If, and if so what issues must be raised in the
  first response or be waived
- How and when papers can be amended or
  supplemented
- How papers are signed, the effect of signing
  and how they are exchanged

Think of this section as the pleading or "papers" section of the various sets of rules. It governs how the lawsuit will be structured and how the various court papers are handled. It is of course far more wide reaching than just how to sign or serve a paper. It encompasses and governs the initial actual and potential challenges to the lawsuit itself as a legal matter. It is this set of rules that will dictate how and when to file a motion to dismiss, and how and when other pleadings (court papers) are to be filed.

The third section often refers to parties and contains rules that are unique to certain kinds of lawsuits, such as class action suits, shareholder actions and so forth. It also addresses issues like adding parties, who can add parties and what parties must be added.

This can be referred to as the section pertaining to parties. Here you will find the rules that tell you how to file a cross claim or a third party complaint[17].

The next section that we usually encounter is a significant one - it deals with discovery. Since there is an entire section devoted to discovery, we won't go into detail on the mechanics, but in this section you will find rules that tell you about the process of exchanging information with the other side before he case actually goes to a trial. These rules address things like:

- What kinds of discovery are available
- The scope of discovery
- Provision for initial automatic exchanges of information

---

[17] A third party complaint refers to a complaint directed against a party not originally a party to a suit, but who the defendant believes is liable in whole or in part for the claims against it.

- Limits on discovery
- Remedies for failure to answer, or for abusive discovery
- What the court can do if a party fails to participate in discovery

As you will read in the discovery section, this has become an important phase of a civil case, and therefore, these rules are very important. Here you will find rules about what you can ask the other side, what they can ask you, what to do if the other side does not respond, what you should do if the other side asks you, or requests things beyond the allowable scope of discovery. This is also an area where you will see a lot of local rules, especially in the federal court system, where each judge may have their own set of rules and procedures for discovery issues.

Once you get past the discovery stage of a lawsuit, it's time to start thinking it terms of actually having a trial. The next grouping of rules address issues related to actually getting into a courtroom and telling your story – the Trial.

This section of the rules deals with things like:

- Right to a jury trial
- How cases are scheduled for trial
- How witnesses are examined
- How various legal issues may arise and be handled
- Jury issues
- When claims may be tried separately or consolidated
- How instructions are given to the jury

481

Appropriately enough this is the trial section of the rules. It is here that you must be very careful, because in federal courts and in most state courts, there are a completely separate set of rules that come onto play here – The Evidence Rules.

The rules in the trial section of the Federal Rules of Civil Procedure, or their equivalent touch on things like how testimony is taken, but it is the Rules of Evidence that really get into the details.

It will be in the Rules of Evidence, or possibly called Evidence Code that you find the critical rules that govern how information gets to the judge or the jury. The issues pertaining to evidence are so extensive that a separate section has been devoted to it. For now, it is important that you be aware of how evidence matters are handled in your state.

After the trial section, there will often be a section on judgment and various motions, such as summary judgment, or setting aside a judgment or order of the court. While these are not likely to be encountered early on, it is important to be aware of them, because once a trial begins, you need to have these at your fingertips.

It cannot be stressed enough that if you are going to represent yourself in court and are going to trial, you HAVE to have a working knowledge of these rules. If you don't, you will be stymied and frustrated at every point.

If you don't familiarize yourself with the rules pertaining to court papers, you may end up making critical mistakes early on. If you don't familiarize yourself with the rules on evidence, your evidence will not get in because the other side will constantly object and you will not know how to respond. Likewise, the other side will get into evidence things that should be excluded, because you do not know to object.

The good news is that it is not that hard! You're not launching the space shuttle here. These rules are logically laid out and with a little studying, while you may not be ready to teach a class on the topic, you will know enough to try your case.

You should note that there are other sets of rules. In addition to evidence rules just discussed, there are other sets of rules that you will encounter. There separate rules that apply to appeals. Many courts now stress and promote forms of alternative dispute resolution, and there are rules that pertain to settlement conferences, arbitration and mediation.

The important thing you should understand from this section is not what all the rules say – that would take several books. It is to understand what the rules are, what issues they generally address, how important they are and how to find them as part of your preparation to represent yourself.

Declaratory Judgment

In most lawsuits, both as a practical matter and because of legal requirements there must be some element of damages – something at stake. From a practical matter, most people (there are exceptions) don't go to the trouble and expense of filing a lawsuit just for the fun of it. They are seeking something, usually a money judgment to compensate them for some injury or loss that has been caused by someone else. There are also legal issues that preclude filing a lawsuit in the absence of an actual controversy. Generally federal and state constitutions that enable the various courts that you may find yourself in, dictate that the jurisdiction of courts is limited to adjudicating actual controversies between real parties in interest. This is a long way of saying that courts are not supposed to, and will not hear esoteric "what if" cases if there is no recognizable dispute between real parties in interest.

To see what this means in a practical sense, consider a lawsuit for breach of contract. At common law, the elements of a claim for breach of contract, what you must both allege and prove, are the existence of a contract, that the party bringing the suit performed, that the other party failed to perform, and that the party bringing the suit was damaged.

Unless all of these elements are present, the lawsuit is subject to being dismissed. And note the requirement that there be damages. You can't bring a breach of contract lawsuit merely because the other side may do something that might cause you damage. You must be able to allege and prove that you actually were damaged.

Another example that is encountered quite often is what is referred to in the law as a nuisance. The legal and practical definitions are actually quite similar.

The law provides a remedy for annoyances, disruptions and similar problems created by the activities of others. Nuisances may be created by noise, odors, fumes etc. and the law basically provides that when such activities go beyond a certain point, those bothered by them have a cause of action. But wait. Just as in the case of contracts, the law requires, as an essential element of a nuisance cause of action, that there be damages.

It does not take much imagination to see that the requirement of damages in these two examples result in some very unreasonable and potentially expensive results.

Consider a contract situation where you know that the other side is likely to do something that in the end will violate the contract, but since there have been no damages yet, your hands are tied. An example of such a situation may be where you are a building contractor and have entered into a contract with a supplier. The contract specifies the materials to be supplied, but gives the supplier the option to substitute comparable materials. You learn that he intends to deliver materials that he deems comparable, but will in fact not be satisfactory for the building you are constructing.

Consider the nuisance situation. You live in a quiet area and learn that someone has purchased property adjoining yours and intends to open a roller-discotheque next door. You have seen another, similar business across town and the noise, going on until three in the morning is horrendous, to say nothing of the traffic and congestion.

Both breach of contract and nuisance causes of action require as an essential element, damages. As long as the supplier is merely contemplating providing unacceptable materials, you have not been damaged. Until the discotheque opens and actually makes noise, you have not suffered any actual damages. You have no legal recourse under either example until the damage is already done. That means you have to wait until something bad results from the other side's conduct, even though the results were predictable and obvious all along. Common sense tells us that there must be some way to address these controversies before things progress to that point.

Enter the declaratory judgment action.

Every state, as well as the federal courts, has provisions for commencing an action in which you request what is called a declaratory judgment. This remedy is almost always statutory in nature and therefore can usually be found in the various state codes of law. In the federal system there is a specific Federal Declaratory Judgment Act, along with a provision in the Federal Rules of Civil Procedure that establishes the framework for seeking a declaratory judgment. State provisions for declaratory judgments are similar. Most states have adopted some form of the Uniform Declaratory Judgment Act. Like the federal structure, you will often find guidelines for such actions as well in the Rules of Civil Procedure for that state.

The purpose of a declaratory judgment action is to settle important questions of law before the controversy has reached a more critical stage. It is a recognition that courts should operate as preventive clinics as well as hospitals for the injured.

A declaratory judgment action is literally what it says. It is asking the court to make a declaration which is legally binding, of an issue presented to it. A declaratory judgment can be combined with other causes of action, but the important thing to note is that in a pure declaratory judgment action, there is no money judgment issued, nor are there any injunctions or orders requiring someone to do or refrain from doing something issued. The court merely issues an order answering the issue put before it. That does not mean that the judgment is of no value. It at the very least establishes the law on the controversy between the two parties and can be used to form the basis of a cause of action for a money judgment, or an injunction.

The value of a declaratory judgment is immediately obvious in the two examples set forth.

In the case of the supplier intending to supply materials which you feel will not be in accord with the terms of the contract, it is not necessary to wait until the materials are delivered and possibly the whole project delayed when they indeed turn out not to comply with the contract terms. While you may not be able to file a breach of contract action until you have been damaged, you can file a declaratory judgment action. You can ask the court to take evidence as to the nature of the materials that the supplier intends to provide and which it contends fall under the "comparable materials" language of the contract and make a determination as to whether or not they do. You would have an opportunity for the court to review the contract, to hear witnesses testify about the materials, perhaps even consider technical reports, and then, issue a ruling. The advantage of this is of course it is a remedy available when a breach of contract action may not be, and it is a remedy that can be pursued early on. If damages are going to be incurred, they can be minimized if the parties can know ahead of time where they stand, and more significantly, what the likely outcome of litigation will be.

The same principles are present in the nuisance case. It is not necessary for you to wait until the discotheque is open and cranking out noise at obscene decibel levels. You can seek a determination by a court, in the form of a declaratory judgment, that the activities contemplated by the developers of the discotheque would constitute a nuisance.

There are of course limitations.

There must be an actual and justiciable controversy. To establish a justiciable controversy, a litigant must generally establish there is a present, substantial controversy between adverse parties with "legal interests susceptible to immediate resolution and capable of present judicial enforcement."

Put another way, declaratory judgment legislation does not give a court the authority to render advisory opinions, answer hypothetical questions, or determine issues not essential to the decision of the actual controversy. There must be a recognizable issue between real parties.

On the other hand, as long as those requirements can be met, virtually any real controversy can be addressed in a declaratory judgment action.

Bringing a Declaratory Judgment Action

Bringing a declaratory judgment action is much like brining any other kind of lawsuit. It is normally commenced with the filing of a complaint or petition, and the issuance of a summons.

A critical difference in a declaratory judgment action is that you should clearly denote it as such. Make it very clear on the face of the complaint that what you are seeking is a declaratory judgment, not money damages or an injunction. Many states have docket information sheets that must be completed when a case is filed. Be sure on this sheet to select declaratory judgment and not the underlying issue such as breach of contract. Finally, when you complete the section of the complaint that addresses the court's jurisdiction, state the court has jurisdiction pursuant to its declaratory judgments act, citing the section of the code or statutes that contain that act.

Other than the requirement it state clearly that you are seeking a declaratory judgment, the complaint is prepared just as in any other case. Establish the jurisdiction of the court over the parties and over the subject matter, set forth facts and allegations giving rise to the issue, and set forth the necessary elements of the cause of action.

For a declaratory judgment action you will need to identify the issue and be sure that it meets the requirements of a justiciable controversy. That may require that the underlying issue be pled. That is, if you are seeking a declaratory judgment to interpret the terms and conditions of a contract, you will need to set forth allegations that show the existence of a contract.

In general the allegations that you must plead in order to state a cause of action for a declaratory judgment are:

- A bona fide justiciable and substantial controversy exists;

- Between parties with adverse legal interests as to either present or prospective obligations
- A judgment would serve a useful purpose in clarifying or settling the legal issues; and
- A judgment would finalize the controversy and offer relief from uncertainty.

In terms of prosecuting a declaratory judgment action, the process is no different than any other lawsuit. The matter is commenced with a summons and complaint being filed and served. The defendant can respond by answering or filing a motion to dismiss (or equivalent pleading such as demurrer in some jurisdictions). The parties may engage in discovery, and may file motions for summary judgment.

While only a declaratory judgment is available as a remedy in such an action, there is nothing to prevent a party from combining a cause of action for declaratory judgment with other causes of action, so that different remedies are available at the conclusion of the case. So for example, while in a pure declaratory judgment action a court would not issue an injunction or restraining order, a plaintiff can easily add to the declaratory judgment claim a second cause of action where an injunction is sought.

Finally, it is important to understand that a declaratory judgment action affects only the parties to the proceeding. A party that has not been included, over which the court has not obtained jurisdiction and that has not participated in the proceeding is not in any way affected by the determination of the court.

Conclusion

While the topic of declaratory judgments obviously could merit an entire book devoted to it, this summary should have given you a basic understanding of what they are and how they can be used.

It is important that you are at least aware of them and have a general idea of what they can do for you. Many people are confronted with a legal controversy where they know intuitively that they have some recourse, but because they don't understand the concept of declaratory judgments, get bogged down. They either file no lawsuit at all, letting their losses pile up and the situation worsen, or they file a lawsuit before they have cognizable damages and become angry, confused and frustrated when the lawsuit gets thrown out. Knowing that you can address some of these controversies without having to wait to be damaged, gives you a meaningful advantage in representing yourself.

Evidence

Everyone has seen a TV show or movie depicting a courtroom scene where in the middle of one lawyer questioning a witness the other jumps up and objects. After some back and forth, the judge rules, either sustaining or overruling the objection. Sometimes the depiction is real in terms of whether a question should be answered, often it is just for the drama of the show or movie. These scenes do though underscore the need to have a basic understanding of evidence law of you are going to represent yourself in court.

Evidence law is the law that governs what will be allowed to be presented to the court and how it will be presented. Remember from the section on the trial of the case that each side must present evidence to prove their allegations, or disprove the allegations of the other side. It is critical that you be able to get this evidence before the jury or the judge. A court cannot consider what is not in the record. Since evidence not properly presented is not in the record, in the eyes of the court, it simply does not exist. Obviously it is critical that you know how to properly present your evidence so that it is in the record. If you don't, you are doomed.

Many people, even law students and many lawyers are mystified and overwhelmed with the concept of evidence law. There is no need for that. Evidence law, if viewed in the context of what it is designed to accomplish, is really fairly straightforward, and often, just common sense. Evidence law defines the kind of information that a court can consider and governs how the court can receive it. The intent of evidence law is to make sure that a court receives only evidence that is relevant to the proceeding before it, and that the evidence is reliable.

The very first thing that you need to be considering is just exactly what is evidence?

Evidence is the information that a judge or jury will consider when making a decision. It is what establishes the facts of the case. The court papers do not do this. All they do is establish a framework, outlining the case. By themselves they are nothing but unproven allegations.

It is the evidence that establishes whether the allegations are true. Evidence includes testimony of witnesses, documents, records, correspondence, and objects that may be relevant. Basically it includes everything that once properly admitted can be seen, touched or heard.

In the section on The Trial of The Case an example case involving a car accident is used. In presenting evidence regarding that case it is critical to remember that no one on the jury witnessed the car accident, or even talked to any eyewitnesses. There is no video. To understand what happened, and make a decision, the jury will have to rely on what they hear from witnesses, and from what they may be able to deduce from documents, photographs or diagrams after the fact. Given that this is all the jury will ever have to go on, it's obviously pretty important to make sure they get the facts that support your side. It's just as important to make sure that they don't hear any improper evidence from the other side.

The first thing that many people ask, especially in moments of frustration over rules of evidence, is: "if that's all it is, what's the big deal? Why can't I just tell the judge about my case and show him my papers?"

The answer is that there has to be a framework to make sure that only acceptable evidence is presented, and unacceptable or improper evidence is kept out.

The rules of evidence are there to set up an orderly process by which the jury or judge is able to receive and consider all proper, relevant and competent evidence, but are not swayed or influenced by evidence that is not proper.

Like so many things in the law, a little thought and reason goes a long way toward understanding. To appreciate the need for rules on how evidence is presented it might be helpful to look at two principles as examples. The issues of hearsay and document authentication provide good way to understand the basis of evidence law.

We've all heard about hearsay. There's not a courtroom drama ever, anywhere, from Perry Mason to L.A. Law and beyond, that hasn't included a scene where there is an objection about hearsay. So what's the big deal?

Hearsay occurs when a witness testifies about what someone else, not in the courtroom, has said, as evidence of the truth of whatever was said. A clear example comes from the auto accident case from several sections ago...

> Question: Do you know how the accident occurred Mr. Doe?
>
> Answer: Yes I do. The blue car plowed into the back of the green car.
>
> Question: Did you observe the accident (probably should have been the first question...)?
>
> Answer: No, but Mrs. Roe did, and she told me what happened.

This is objectionable hearsay. The witness is testifying as to the cause of the accident based on what someone else told him, and that someone else is not available to be questioned about it.

Even the slightest bit of scrutiny should reveal why this is objectionable. Mr. Doe, without Mrs. Roe in the courtroom can testify to anything. Moreover, even if Mr. Doe accurately and truthfully testified as to what Mrs. Roe told him, since Mrs. Roe is not in the courtroom it is not possible to cross examine her to determine the truth or validity of what she told Mr. Doe. There are always a lot of questions to be asked in determining if an eyewitness correctly observed something, or properly recalls it. None of those questions can be asked with Mrs. Roe not available to question.

The same concepts underlie why the rules of evidence require authentication of a document. To have a document entered into evidence, that is to be considered by the judge or jury, it is necessary to authenticate it. That means it must be established that the document is what it purports to be. If it is an agreement or contract it must be shown that it was executed by the people appearing on its face. If it is a photograph or diagram that it is in fact representative of the subject matter and the time it is representative of.

Using our ever familiar car accident scenario, if a picture of the intersection is offered into evidence, it must be authenticated. It must be established not only that the picture depicts the intersection in question, but depending on why it is being offered that it shows the intersection at or near the time of the accident.

The need for authenticating a contract is similar. If a written document is being entered into evidence to establish an agreement between parties, the judge or jury reviewing it has to have some basis for believing it to be real and genuine.

If it is a picture it can be done by whoever took the picture, someone who appears in the picture, or someone who can testify that the picture accurately depicts the subject matter on a specific date and time.

If what is sought to be admitted is a written document, such as a contract, or a letter, someone familiar with the document must be able to testify as to its authenticity. Any document can be forged, created or modified. This is especially true with modern technology where a photograph can be digitally altered and reprinted to show just about anything.

Even documents that consist of regularly maintained records must be authenticated. This is usually accomplished with the testimony of someone familiar with the documents, how they are stored and kept, why they are kept and what they are used for. You will often hear the person providing such testimony referred to as the custodian of the records. When the other side is attempting to use this technique you must be very careful of what records are being admitted and why. The purpose of allowing testimony of a records custodian to serve as the basis for admitting records into evidence is to deal with those records that are routinely kept and are often voluminous. It is not intended to allow opinion testimony to come into evidence without proper foundation, merely because it appears in routinely maintained records.

If this sounds confusing, it is because it indeed can be confusing. An example might be medical records pertaining to a plaintiff in an auto accident case. The office manager of the doctor's office may be called as custodian of the patient medical records to give testimony about those records, in support of an attempt to have them admitted into evidence. This is fine, within limitations. If the records show that the plaintiff was seen in the office on certain days, that he was given certain prescriptions and so forth, the testimony of the custodian would suffice to get them into evidence. On the other hand, parts of those records might be objectionable. To the extent that the record contains the opinion and findings of the doctor in the form of his diagnosis, treatment recommendations and prognosis, it would be objectionable. It is not proper to try to piggy back and slip in the opinions of an expert that should be introduced by testimony as part of regularly maintained business records. Having a good working knowledge of the rules of evidence will make the difference between allowing harmful but objectionable evidence in and keeping it out.

The Evolution of Evidence Law

As long as there has been some sort of legal system among people, there has been the challenge of determining and judging the truth of what is presented.

People lie. People are mistaken. Recollection is not perfect.

So in turn, every tribunal, court, forum or other institution for resolving disputes between people throughout history, has developed some system for filtering and screening what was presented to it. The methods cover a wide spectrum. While today we rely on the oath of witnesses to be truthful, and rely on rules of evidence, it was not always so.

In early courts the truth of what people had to say was tested by ordeal. The theory was that if one was honest and telling the truth a deity would intervene and spare injury that would normally result from what can only be described today as incredibly stupid endeavors. Thus we read about things such as the 6th century practice of ordeal by fire or boiling water. In the latter case a suspect had to reach into a kettle of boiling water to retrieve a stone. The absence of wounds or the complete healing of the wounds in three days signaled innocence while the converse resulted in a guilty verdict.

Though it took a very long time by modern standards, the flaws and shortcomings of such methods eventually were appreciated and evidence law began to work its way down different less drastic paths. The test by ordeal was replaced with being vouched for as being truthful by other members of the community followed by the giving of a solemn oath to speak only the truth. Later came the concept of imposition of a penalty for not being truthful.

Our system today is predicated on such a combination. A witness is sworn, or gives an oath that their testimony will be truthful, and hanging over their head is the potential of separate punishment for perjury. It's not perfect, but it beats keeping a kettle of boiling water in the courtroom.

In terms of historical development it also helps to understand the difference between those countries where cases were primarily heard by judges versus those, notably England at the time that depended on juries as finders of fact. The difference persists today. The United States, United Kingdom and closely related countries where trial by jury is the tradition have much more elaborate and detailed rules of evidence than do countries, such as most of Europe and Latin America where a case is heard by one or more judges. The rationale is that potentially improper evidence presented to a trained and experienced judge will be recognized for what it is, while juries, consisting of lay people with no training and varying degrees of education are more susceptible to confusion and improper influence. Consequently, if you ever have an opportunity to observe a trial in Europe or Latin America, you will notice immediately the lack of emphasis on the manner in which evidence is presented. There are very few objections, and certainly none in terms of "irrelevant" or "immaterial". The proceeding is in front of a trained judge who is trusted to have the knowledge and expertise to figure out, without input from the parties or their attorneys, what is and what is not proper evidence.

Evidence law in days past was based for the most part on common law, or court decisions regarding what and what was not proper. Today, while there is still some reference to court decisions, evidence law is for the most part defined in court rules and statutes. In the federal court system and in many state court systems as well there is a separate set of rules that apply to evidence issues. The trend appears to be toward states adopting to different degrees the federal rule framework. This framework, and what you are most likely to encounter, is a structure that defines concepts such as relevance, competence and admissibility, and then addresses some of the specific evidentiary areas in separate sections. You can get a feel for this structure just by reviewing the table of contents of the Federal Rules of Evidence.

Where to Find Evidence Law

Because of the way that evidence law evolved over the years, the rules and requirements are often found in different places, depending on the jurisdiction or kind of court that you are in.

Not every court and not every forum that you may find yourself in utilizes the same rules of evidence. The first thing to do regardless of where you are, if you are in anything other than the court of general jurisdiction, is to start from the bottom up so to speak.

Find the rules of procedure for whatever forum your case is in. If you are before an administrative agency, there will be separate rules for contested proceedings. Those rules may be agency specific or they can sometimes be found to be applicable to proceedings before all administrative agencies of a state. If you are in a small claims court there are likely to be rules applicable to that court. What you are seeking in this first step is to know if the rules of evidence applicable to the courts of general jurisdiction apply in your case. Often in administrative matters, or simplified courts, they do not.

It varies from state to state and from forum to forum. Some administrative rules for example specifically state that the Rules of Civil Procedure and the Rules of Evidence do not apply. In others, they apply. In still others, you will find that some apply, while some do not.

The same is true in some small claims courts. These courts are specifically designed and intended to expedite and simplify the handling of routine cases where the amount in controversy is not large. To accomplish this, the procedural rules and the manner in which evidence is presented are often relaxed or less formal.

Some examples of how you might find more relaxed rules of evidence:

-       documents, as long as they are signed might be admitted without the need for further authentication.

-       especially in things like workers' compensation cases, medical reports may be admitted without the need for authenticating testimony.

- witness statements may be allowed in the form of an affidavit, without the witness being required to be there.

Once you have determined to what extent the general rules of evidence apply, you can go research them, knowing exactly what is important and what is not.

Obviously if you are in the court of general jurisdiction, that is the primary court of a state, this consideration is irrelevant. You know that the rules of evidence will apply, and you can skip this step and go directly to researching and learning the evidence rules.

Unfortunately, the location, and difficulty associated with researching the rules of evidence differs from jurisdiction to jurisdiction. This is the result of several factors, but primarily of the process by which evidence law has evolved from basic common law principles to more structured frameworks.

In the federal courts it is fairly easy. Evidence issues are set forth in the Federal Rules of Evidence. All you really need beyond that is to make sure that the forum or agency you are in uses those rules, and to what extent.

In state courts it can get a bit more complicated. Some states have detailed evidence rules, emulating the federal system. California for example has its rules of evidence and evidentiary procedures neatly arranged in the California Evidence Code. Pennsylvania has rules of evidence presented in a separate title of its code of laws. Other states have their evidence law similarly organized.

Unfortunately, some states are not quite as organized or progressive. Often evidence rules are intermingled with rules of civil procedure. In some states in addition to some stated rules of evidence, portions of the applicable evidence law comes from common law. This is especially true in the more traditional aspects of evidence law, such as the rule against hearsay.

The good news is that evidence rules and the manner in which they are organized are constantly evolving and the trend, as with rules of civil procedure in general, is to track the federal system. The more states begin utilizing this kind of standardized approach to issues, the less difficult it will be to understand legal issues from state to state.

Regardless of where or how organized, you must identify and locate the evidence law.

In representing yourself, as the case moves forward, you need to be spending more and more time reading and studying these rules. By the time you get to the trial of the case, you should have a good grasp of the more general rules as well as those rules that might be specific to the kind of evidence that you are planning on presenting, or which you think your opponent may try to present. To understand, consider that no matter what kind of case you are involved in, you will need to know the rules pertaining to examination of witnesses, how questions can be asked on direct versus cross, and how, if a witness appears to forget something, you can ask questions to refresh their memory. On the other hand, if your case is about a car accident, you probably will not need to pay all that much attention to understanding the rules surrounding the extent to which testimony can be used to interpret the terms and conditions of a written contract.

Basic Principles of Evidence

Evidence law is extensive and covers a lot of different issues. There are volumes and volumes in law libraries on evidence. The good news is that a lot of this is theory and history. Getting a handle on the evidence you need to present your case is not all that difficult if you're willing to hit the books.

Since not all evidentiary issues will apply to every case, what will be presented here is a general outline and introduction of the concepts that you need to understand before you get into specific rules. These are concepts that will help you to understand the concept of evidence.

First, a very brief recap for perspective.

Evidence includes the facts and opinions that pertains to a case. It can be what a witness has to say about what they saw, or heard, or did. It may be a document: a letter, an email, or a contract. It might be a photograph or drawing. It can even be an object. Has anyone not seen on TV the "murder weapon" on the prosecutor's table? It also includes opinions of witnesses, both lay and expert.

Admissible evidence is evidence that the court allows to be admitted or placed into evidence because it is within the scope of, and is presented in accordance with, the rules of evidence. This is the ONLY evidence that the jury, or judge, or hearing officer or any other trier of fact, should see or be allowed to consider. It is because the last point is so critical that it appears repeatedly. There may be all the evidence in the world supporting your position, but if you can't get it in front of the jury, it's useless.

So to ensure that you are able to get the facts and materials that support your case admitted and before the jury, here are some ideas that you need to understand.

Relevance

The first requirement for evidence to be admissible is that it must be relevant. It must be related to the case being tried or the issues being presented.

The underlying logic is obvious. Evidence that has something to do with case or the people or things involved in the case should be considered. Evidence which has nothing whatsoever to do with the case and is completely unrelated, serves no useful purpose and should not be considered. The term relevance in legal terminology means the same as in lay terminology but within the context of a specific case. The evidence must not only have something to do with some aspect of the case, it must be evidence that has some tendency to prove or disprove a material fact or aspect of the case. The scope is broad. It can relate to facts surrounding the case, as well as a host of other things such as the people involved, the kind activities in issue and so forth. But even though broad, there are limits and lack of relevance is an objection that is often heard during witness questioning.

For example, if the matter involves a car accident, testimony from a witness as to whether the light was red or green would clearly be relevant. On the other hand, testimony from the same witness as to where he spent his vacation last year would have nothing whatsoever to do with the accident and would therefore be irrelevant.

But be careful. The scope is broad and most judges, if they are shown any relationship between the case and the evidence sought to be introduced, will err on the side of allowing it. Don't rely to any serious extent on testimony necessarily being kept out on grounds of relevance.

Competence

Evidence must be competent. That is there must be a basis for the judge to believe that the evidence is what it purports to be and that it first must come from a reliable source, with reliability having a lot of different considerations.

Competence has a little different meaning in this context than as when the word is commonly used.

With respect to a witness for example it means that what the witness is testifying to must be something that the witness is in fact able to testify to. It does not have anything per se to do with mental competence.

Clearly an observation as to the color of a traffic light is something anyone with normal powers of observation could testify to. But only if the witness were in a position to observe the traffic light. If the witness at the time in question had been for example inside a store, or had his back to the light, then he would be deemed incompetent to testify as to the color of the light.

Competence in terms of witness testimony can also be based on the witness's education, experience or knowledge. Continuing with the accident example, a lay witness would clearly be competent to testify as to observations – the color of the light, whether it was raining, time of day, etc. But without special training or expertise, the witness would not be able – that is would not be competent – to testify as the speed of an accident vehicle based on the length of its skid marks. Where a matter is more complex, it is necessary to show that the witness is able based on personal knowledge, education or experience to testify as to those matters. Competence is also dependent on what the witness actually was able to observe.

Evidence Must Be Admissible

The third hurdle to overcome in getting your evidence before the jury is admissibility. In addition to being relevant and competent, evidence must be admissible. That is not excludable under one or more evidentiary principles. It is in this area – determining if otherwise relevant and competent evidence is admissible - that so much confusion arises. The issue of admissibility really revolves around some basic principles of evidence law that you can expect to encounter from time to time when you embark upon the adventure of representing yourself. It might be helpful to address some of them.

Hearsay

We've all seen, in the same TV shows or movies we've mentioned, the attorney jump up and say "Objection – Hearsay!" The drama of the show aside, this refers to a reason why evidence otherwise relevant may not be admissible. Evidence, to be considered by a court, must be relevant and there must be a way to test its credibility. Hearsay, which is basically testimony about what someone else said to, or which was heard by the testifying witness, is objectionable because the person that really made the statement is not there to be cross examined. It doesn't take a great deal of imagination to see that if hearsay testimony was allowed, anyone could get on the witness stand and testify that someone else said virtually anything, with no way to prove or disprove it. Here the evidence may clearly be relevant, but because of the danger that it cannot be verified for truth, it is not allowed.

It is not allowed into evidence pursuant to what is called the Rule Against Hearsay. Originating in old English common law, the Rule is alive and well. The problem is that while the underlying principle is fairly simple and straightforward, the broad scope of the rule combined with exceptions to the rule, make for a fairly complicated little minefield for the unwary.

First consider that the hearsay rule extends not only to witness testimony but to written documents as well. So if someone tries to introduce a letter from a person not present in court, for the purpose of proving the contents of the letter that would be hearsay. The "something said" by a third party does not have to be verbal.

But, and here is where people really get confused, it must be offered to establish the truth of the statement made. For some reason that trips up a lot of people; even trained attorneys. Just because the testimony is about something someone else said, does not necessarily make it hearsay. Consider an example to show that the identical testimony can be hearsay, or not be hearsay, depending on what it is offered for.

A witness is testifying about a statement made by someone else to the effect that it was hot outside on a particular day.

If the statement is offered to prove that it was hot outside, then it would be offered in an attempt to prove the truth of the matter asserted (it was hot outside) and would be inadmissible hearsay. On the other hand, if the issue was if the witness knew if other people had been complaining of the heat, then the statement about it being hot would be admissible to show that indeed, there had been complaints about it being hot. Here the statement is not offered to prove the truth of the matter – if it was hot. It is being offered to prove that the witness heard others commenting on the heat. That is not hearsay and is admissible.

The distinction to be noted here is the way to analyze the evidence. First determine if the evidence is even hearsay. If it is not, then you need go no further. If it appears to be hearsay, then more analysis is required because there are exceptions to the hearsay rule.

Yes, of course there are exceptions. It's a rule. There must be exceptions.

To understand and appreciate the exceptions, think of the issue in terms of the reason for the hearsay rule to begin with. It is based on reliability and credibility. The courts do not want evidence considered that is not reliable.

The exceptions to the hearsay rule, and they are many, primarily address those cases where even though something might be hearsay, other factors overcome the reliability aspect and thus consideration of the evidence is appropriate. Examples of such exceptions are:

-        excited utterance. The theory is that what someone said at a moment of excitement, where there is unlikely to be time for reflection, is trustworthy.

-        admissions against interest. This is one of the most important exceptions to the hearsay rule. If someone says something detrimental to, or potentially harmful to themselves it is admissible on the theory that no one would fabricate testimony that was detrimental to them.

-        business records. Documents kept in the normal course of business are deemed trustworthy in that they are the same kinds of records always kept regardless of litigation, so it is less likely that they would be fabricated.

-        persons unavailable. This is a broad category with lots of sub-rules, exceptions and conditions. The basic idea is that where the original speaker is not available for one reason or another, the need to consider the evidence often outweighs the possible harm of the hearsay. It is important because in estate cases, will contest cases and so forth it often allows the admissibility of statements purported to be made by a deceased person.

It is beyond the scope of this book to explore in detail the hearsay rule and all of its exceptions. If the topic intrigues you, you need simply refer to Article VIII of the Federal Rules of Evidence. That Article expounds at length on the hearsay rule as well as numerous exceptions. You will find similar sections of evidentiary rules in must state rules.

The important thing to be aware of when representing yourself is not to get too hung up on trivia. For the most part if you are confronted with a hearsay statement in testimony, you will recognize it and if it is not subject to an obvious exception, object to it. Likewise, if you are questioning a witness and hear an objection on grounds of hearsay, be aware of how to respond. First, it may not even be hearsay if you can explain to the judge that you are seeking it for some other purpose that for the truth of the matter said. If you can't do that, be aware of the exceptions, generally at least, so you can get your evidence in.

Parole Evidence

Another broad realm of evidence law concerns what is referred to as parole evidence. Essentially this rule stands for the principle that you cannot introduce evidence to prove or modify the terms of a written agreement. The underlying premise is that the whole purpose of having an agreement or instrument in writing is to resolve the disputes regarding what the agreement of the parties actually was. That benefit goes by the wayside if in a dispute, the parties can effectively re-write the document on the basis of witness testimony.

In the context of a civil case where the issue is a written document which is or purports to be an agreement, neither party can offer evidence that varies the agreement, or usually, that concerns representations or statements made before the agreement was signed.

What this means is that if you are in a case where there is a written contract, you would not be allowed to testify, or have another witness testify about the terms of that contract. You would hear the language "the document speaks for itself" as part of the objection. Likewise, in such a case, you would need to object if the other side began testifying, or questioning witnesses about the terms of the contract.

Of course that does not mean that everything about a written contract is off limits. There are exceptions. There are always exceptions!

Once again, learned legal scholars have written volumes about the parole evidence rule. The objective here is not to make you an expert, but to give you enough of an idea of what it is and how it works to be aware that it may crop up as an issue and to set you in motion to get the help you need to deal with it.

Best Evidence Rule

Dealing with the same legal concepts as the parole evidence rule, the Best Evidence Rule provides that the best evidence of the contents of a written document is the original of the written document itself, and that other evidence may be admissible but only if it can be shown that the original document has been lost or destroyed.

For you as a practical matter this would only come into play if there was testimony about the contents of a written agreement or document that was not available. If the document is available, testimony about its contents would be objectionable in that the document, not testimony about it is the best evidence.

You will find this rule appearing in different ways in different jurisdictions. As is often the case, it is fairly well set forth in the Federal Rules of Evidence, as Rules 1001 through 1008. The important thing is that you are aware of the rule so that if the issue comes up it is not a complete surprise that you are unprepared to deal with.

This rule, as well as the parole evidence rule, are examples of how easy it is to deal with these issues by simple but thorough preparation and some time spent reading the rules.

If you are outlining your case at all, and planning as you should be, you will be well aware, long before anyone raises an objection, or moves to exclude some testimony that you are dealing with one of these rules. You will know that part of your case, or part of your opponent's case deals with the terms of a written agreement that will raise parole evidence issues. You will know early on if you have issues concerning the availability of an original document or writing.

A little time spent researching the law and rules in your jurisdiction will turn rules like this form a panic attack in the middle of a witness' testimony to something that is easily taken in stride.

Settlement

Still another area of evidence that is important to be aware of and to understand is anything to do with settlement discussion is usually inadmissible. This principle is set forth in Rule 408 of the Federal Rules of Evidence and is seriously misunderstood, especially by many attorneys.

The underlying principle is that settlement of disputes should be encouraged, not stifled. Negotiation is a much better way to resolve a case than by going to trial. To continue that logic, open and honest negotiation tends to be more productive than circumspect and cautious negotiation. The result of this logic flow is that people should not be inhibited during the negotiation process with the concern that offers or statements made will later be used against them. Thus the basis for the rule that compromise offers and negotiations cannot be offered into evidence. The rule actually derives from common law and that is the basis for the widespread misconception among attorneys that the rule means that anything said in the course of settlement negotiations is protected.

The rule does not say that, and it is important, when you get to the point of discussing a possible settlement that you understand this rule 408.

The fact that a broad common law principle has been specifically defined into a rule certainly helps. The rule itself in part "b" though makes it clear that there are in fact certain reasons why things said in the course of settlement could in fact be admissible. A recent federal appellate decision has made it clear that the exclusion from introduction into evidence provided by the rule does not go beyond that and does not constitute a privilege of any kind. Settlement negotiations may be discoverable for a variety of reasons.

Conclusion

There are numerous other rules that pertain to evidence that may otherwise be relevant and admissible. Some are grounded in public policy considerations.

For example, if a defendant in a case involving a construction defect goes out and repairs the faulty condition, the fact that he repaired it can usually not be considered to support the fact that it was faulty to begin with. Public policy dictates that owners not be discouraged from making unsafe conditions safe.

Another issue that may come up is self-incrimination. If you are involved in a case where a party, or a witness may be subject to criminal prosecution, you need to be aware that this protection may be raised to avoid giving testimony even in a civil case that could later be incriminating. Seldom will this hit you as a complete surprise though, and you should have ample time to deal with it.

You are not, now that you have read this section, an expert on, or even competent to deal with evidentiary issues. What you should have gleaned from these pages is a basic understanding of what the issues are and how prepare for them.

The important thing is to have a good grasp of how the rules of evidence are organized and set forth in your jurisdiction and as you work your way through the case, to continuously study these rules so that you have a good feel for what you can and cannot do it terms of presenting your case.

Jurisdiction

Everyone has heard the term jurisdiction, but few people really understand it. If you want to be your own lawyer and represent yourself in court, this is an important concept to understand.

For our purposes, we will be talking about the jurisdiction of courts as opposed, for example to jurisdiction of law enforcement agencies.

There are two types of jurisdiction that we have to consider: subject matter jurisdiction and personal jurisdiction.

Subject matter jurisdiction refers to what kinds of cases, including, where they arise, that a court can hear. A probate court (dealing with estate matters) does not have the authority to hear a case that revolves around who ran a stop sign and caused an accident.

Subject matter jurisdiction is conferred upon a court either by constitutional authority, or by statute. An example of the former would be the federal courts under the United States Constitution, and state courts of general jurisdiction which are generally provided for in the constitutions of the states. An example of a court created by statute would be family courts. These courts did not exist and had not been contemplated when the United States Constitution and the constitutions of the states were drafted. The need for

520

them arose later, and state legislatures passed laws creating them.

Subject matter jurisdiction also involves the question of where an issue arose. A California court for example would not have subject matter jurisdiction (even if both sides waived any personal jurisdictional questions) to hear a dispute that arose in Kansas, involving two citizens of Kansas, and had nothing to do with California.

Subject matter jurisdiction is also often defined by the amount in controversy. If a small claims court has authority to decide matters that involve up to $10,000, it has no jurisdiction to hear a case where the amount in dispute is, say $25,000.

Personal jurisdiction refers to the authority of a court to exercise power of a party, and is governed by various statutes, the constitutions of individual states, and the United States Constitution. The underlying principles at work are the need for courts to be able to exercise their authority, balanced against fundamental fairness and due process.

Personal jurisdiction addresses two issues. First, as discussed in the section on the summons, it requires that a person being sued has received proper and legal notice so that he can appear and defend himself. Second, is the question of whether a defendant is subject to the jurisdiction of a particular court at all?

Acquiring personal jurisdiction.

Fundamental fairness and due process as provided by the Constitution require that in order for a person to be subject to a decision or judgment of a court, regardless of where located, they must have had an opportunity to appear and be heard. They must have notice of the case or claim, and of any proceedings related to that claim. They must have a chance to appear and defend themselves.

The acquisition of jurisdiction by a court is generally accomplished with a summons. While this is normal a very short document, it is extremely important. Without a summons or comparable document having been issued, and properly delivered (served) to the defendant, the court is without jurisdiction to adjudicate the issues in that case with respect to the defendant. The court may make a ruling or a decision, but it will not affect a defendant that has not been served.

The court rules govern how a summons is to be served, that is, delivered to the defendant. Failure to serve the summons as required by the rules, especially if the defendant does not appear, may cause everything that takes place in a case or proceeding to be of no force or effect whatsoever.

The Rules generally require that a defendant be personally served, that is physically handed the summons and any related documents, but over the years exceptions and alternative methods of effecting service have evolved. The method of serving the summons is one of the most important things that needs to be researched. If you are the plaintiff, you need to be aware of what is required to accomplish service of the summons on the other side. If you are the defendant, you need to be able to know if how you received the summons was proper, and explore possible defects in service that could later be to your advantage.

The Jurisdiction of the Court

The next issue regarding personal jurisdiction is if a court, even if the summons is properly delivered, can even exercise personal jurisdiction over someone. You will often hear this referred to as in personam jurisdiction.

Clearly a resident of a particular state should be able to sue and be sued in that state. Nothing in that concept disturbs any sense of fairness. Nothing about a person in Pennsylvania for example suing someone else in Pennsylvania creates any sense of unfairness.

On the other hand, what about a person who lives in New Jersey, has never been to California, has never talked to or had contact with a person in California, is not involved in any business in California but is sued in California. That's a different issue and the basic sense of what is fair that we all have, is disturbed by that notion.

Obviously the simplistic approach would be to simply say that courts can resolve issues within their borders, but cannot reach beyond, and cannot exercise jurisdiction over anyone not within those borders.

That is unfortunately a bit too simplistic. Americans move freely from state to state. People from other states get into car accidents in states that they visit. They conduct business across state lines. Contracts are entered into between citizens of different states. All of these activities potentially create disputes between citizens of different states that have to be resolved somewhere. The "somewhere" is a subject of extensive debates on the question of jurisdiction.

The courts of all states have jurisdiction within their within their borders, but they also have the power to reach beyond those borders to citizens of other states. This is based on so-called long arm statutes, enacted in every state, which give the courts of each state the authority to exercise jurisdiction over residents of other states under certain circumstances.

We can all think of examples where it would be appropriate for a state to reach beyond its borders. Someone who enters a state and causes an accident, then leaves. Or who does business there, or who ships products there that cause harm. Making people in these circumstances subject to jurisdiction in a state other than where they reside seems more fair and equitable. In other cases though the concept of what is fair and equitable becomes somewhat less clear.

States invariably try to extend their power to the greatest extent possible, and therefore the long arm statutes are very broadly worded. Doing anything in a state that causes injury there, doing business in the state, entering into contracts to be performed in a state, even owning property in a state, can all subject one to personal jurisdiction. It is not necessary that the defendant ever actually be physically present. Actually long arm statutes are so all encompassing in most states that the issue of jurisdiction is usually resolved in the context of federal constitutional constraints, and therefore if jurisdiction is an issue, it is never enough to simply look at the long arm statute of the state.

The federal courts have handed down a long series of decisions, arising not only in the various federal courts of appeal, but in the U.S. Supreme Court as well, that limit the operation of these long arm statutes. The premise is basically that regardless of what a state may dictate by way of its statutes, it is limited by the due process provision of the fifth amendment to exercise personal jurisdiction over a non resident defendant only when there have been sufficient contacts with the forum state and the exercise of jurisdiction does not violate principles of fundamental fairness.

The critical thing to be aware of is the universally, the issue of personal jurisdiction must be raised in the first thing that is filed or served, be it a motion or responsive pleading. Anything else potentially waives the issue, and depending on where you are and what state is involved, that could be disastrous.

If a defendant has not been properly served, or if a defendant, as a resident of a another state would not even be subject to the jurisdiction of a particular court, the defendant may intentionally or unintentionally waive the issue.

Obviously, it is clear that if he decides to proceed with the case even though he knows of the jurisdictional problem, that he has knowingly waived it. What many people do not understand, and thus make a potentially sometimes serious error is that if there is a question of personal jurisdiction and the defendant makes ANY appearance other than to contest jurisdiction, the defect is waived and the court has jurisdiction.

This is so critical that we will repeat it!

If in responding to a law suit the defendant does ANYTHING other than contest jurisdiction, he has often waived any personal jurisdictional issues.

The way to address the issue of jurisdiction if you believe that you should not be subject to suit in a different state is to file a motion to dismiss for lack of jurisdiction. It must be filed before any other pleading or paper.

Subject Matter Jurisdiction

In addition to personal jurisdiction, you have to make sure that you bring your lawsuit in the right court. The authority, whether it be a constitution or a statute that established as court, both federal and state, defines the kinds of cases that the court is allowed and empowered to handle.

In the United States, compared to most other western countries, we have a complex and some would say convoluted court system. We have federal courts, state courts, county courts, municipal courts, and on top of that, we have courts dedicated to a single legal arena.

Obviously it does you no good to file a lawsuit in the wrong court.

Here are some examples of subject matter consideration:

Federal Courts: Unless there is a federal question involved, or the case is one specifically designated as being properly brought there, jurisdiction in a federal court is not proper unless the parties are residents of different states and the amount in controversy exceeds $75,000. So you cannot sue your neighbor who failed to repay a loan in federal court.

State Courts – amounts in controversy: Many states have court systems that are presented as form of hierarchy, with things like small claims courts at the bottom and increasing levels of amounts in controversy. The different levels often have differing rules so that the lower level courts may have simpler procedures.

State Courts – type of controversy: Many states have created courts for specific type of cases. For example, most states have separate courts that deal with probate and estate matters, family law issues, juvenile issues and so forth. There may be separate courts for civil versus criminal matters, but not always. Finally, many states have specialized civil courts, for example, business courts.

Pick the Right Court

While this plethora of available forums might seem daunting and confusing, it also provides a lot of potential advantages if you want to represent yourself in court.

The ability to select a court in which to bring a lawsuit can sometimes be a way to level the playing field between yourself and an opponent that might be represented by a large law firm with intimidating resources.

Here's an example. In the section on discovery we talked about how attorneys love discovery because it is a great way to rack up billable hours. Guess what? Some lower jurisdictional level courts don't allow any discovery. Simply by filing your case in such a court, you cut the big boys off at the knees. This can be such an advantage for you that you might even consider modifying what you are seeking to make your case fit the lower level court. For example, if you are seeking to recover $12,000 in a case for breach of contract, and the small claims court that does not allow discovery tops out at $10,000, it may be to your advantage to lower your demand to $9,999.99.

There are other considerations in picking courts. Some small claims courts don't allow jury trials. This can speed things up and keep the case simpler.

Another consideration is whether your case is business oriented, and whether you are doing business as a corporation, partnership or limited liability company. In most state courts of general jurisdiction, and in federal courts, you can represent yourself, but you cannot represent a company, even your own, without a license to practice law. In many states, the small claims courts have exceptions to this requirement and allow you to represent a company with written authorization. This can be a major issue for a small business owner who either elects not to, or does not have the resources to retain an attorney.

It can be used offensively. By bringing a case individually against a company, by filing in a court of general jurisdiction you can ensure that they have to retain an attorney. Legal and court costs are an essential and legitimate consideration in resolving cases by settlement.

You can also use the ability to select a court when you are on the other side. If your are being sued for example, and using the services of Be Your Own Lawyer would like to see the other side have to incur the expense of retaining an attorney, it is often possible to force a case out of a small claims court into a court of general jurisdiction by filing a counterclaim that exceeds the jurisdictional limit of the small claims court.

In short, there are lots of things to consider when deciding where to bring a lawsuit, or if you've been sued, whether to try to move it.

Personal Injury

If there is an area of the law where you can best represent yourself at and save yourself a substantial amount of money, it is in the realm of personal injury law.

This is the area of law for which we see all the billboards, all the TV ads and all the hype. Think about it for a minute. Would all these lawyers be paying all this money for all this advertising if there wasn't a ton of money in it? There is, and it's YOUR money! This is an area of the law that except for the most complex cases, you can always do better by representing yourself, even if it means going to court!

Personal Injury Law governs how any case where an injury results as a result of the fault of someone else.

Just as with every other topic that has been addressed, to win a case involving personal injury it is critical that you have a good grasp of the underlying principles. It's not quite as simple as the billboards and TV ads make it sound.

While cases that involve a personal injury are lumped together into one broad category, there are actually several legal theories and areas included. Even though for this section they have a common thread, that is someone sustained an injury, they have some substantial differences. Understanding these principles will greatly improve your prospects in pursuing a personal injury claim.

As is the case with most of this book, the intent here is not to make you an expert, or even proficient with regard to topics presented. The point is to make you aware of them so you know what to look for and give you enough of a foundation to be able to research the specific topics or areas that actually pertain to your case.

Negligence

Basic negligence is a common law principle, but, like so many other legal principles it has in different forms been reflected in various statutes across the country.

Basic negligence law derives from old English common law. As can be expected from any legal principle that derives from a history of court decisions, there is some confusion, but basically to establish a claim of negligence it is necessary to show a legal duty, a breach of that duty, an injury or damage caused by that breach. Negligence is the legal principle that we encounter most often in cases involving personal injury. At first glance that may seem confusing. "What does a 'duty' have to do with the guy that ran the red light and hit me?"

Hang in there. We're getting to that. This is another one of those times when you really do have to understand what the underlying law is and means. Why? Because if you remember the section about Pleadings and Papers, where alleging causes of action was discussed you will remember that if you are suing someone, you must allege in your complaint the elements of your cause of action. It's just not enough to say "that jerk was negligent and I should win!" So you come to the question of what must be alleged in a personal injury case, which in turn leads to the answer to your question of "what does 'duty' have to do with....?"

The key is to appreciate that in legal stuff the meaning of terms while technically correct, is often different than our day-to-day understanding of the meaning and use of those terms. The term "duty" in the context of negligence encompasses a huge range of things that people are supposed to do or not do.

There is in the law a recognized duty on the part of everyone in things that they undertake and do, to exercise reasonable care. There is a duty to obey the law. There are duties to maintain your property in a safe condition. There is a duty to warn of dangers. There are also duties not to do things. There are duties for example not to drive in a reckless manner, or to create a dangerous condition.

All of these duties arise from common law or statutes or from decisions interpreting the statutes. The first thing that you have to research then is the circumstances that gave rise to your injury or damage in terms of the duty to act or refrain from doing something that the law imposes on the potential defendant.

The next element to address is whether there was a breach of that duty. In many cases, such as where the

533

breach of the duty is relatively easy to define, such a violating a statute or law, it is fairly easy. In other cases it gets little murkier and you have to evaluate whether the duty was breached under all the circumstances and apply what is often called the "reasonable man" test. No, once again the people that penned the old court decisions were not politically correct, and it is therefore at least in the older cases dealing with negligence referred to as a reasonable man test as opposed to a reasonable person test.

In order understand how to do that, and how to first determine if you have a claim and if so how to pursue it, it will help to look at some different kinds of negligence and see how these tests are applied.

Generic Negligence

This term appears nowhere in any law book. It's used here for convenience to categorize the general negligence that is most often encountered in cases every day where something bad happens as a result of conduct that deviates from a standard of care. Basically, somebody messed up. This is the brand of negligence that pops up in auto accidents and in virtually every case where someone gets hurt in day-to-day life because of something someone else did, or failed to do.

There is a general duty imposed by the law on all of us as a consequence of living in a society that we will exercise reasonable care to not cause injury to others. It is a recognition that accidents occur, but that we have a duty to be careful to avoid it. The most familiar arena for these issues to arise is in automobile accidents, simply because those claims are so numerous, but it they apply everywhere.

There is first a duty to act in a reasonable manner. What does that mean? To a large extent common sense, because remember, the standard is what would a reasonable person do under the circumstances. The answers are not always clear cut and almost always depend on consideration of all of the circumstances. For example, is driving seventy miles per hour negligent? Your obvious answer is that it depends, and that brings us back to the circumstances. On a clear day on a dry interstate highway with virtually no traffic, it would be difficult to find someone that would deem it negligent, or a breach of the duty to operate your vehicle in a safe and reasonable manner to cruise along at seventy. Change the circumstances to heavy traffic at night with freezing rain making the road slippery, and obviously the analysis changes and the assessment becomes only a moron would drive that fast.

In context then if you are making a claim for injuries sustained in a car accident it is incumbent upon you to establish negligence on the part of the driver that caused the accident. How? By going right down the elements of the cause of action and making sure that each one is established.

A typical example might be helpful. You are involved in an accident caused by another driver pulling out of a driveway into your path.

The first element of negligence is to establish a duty. In traffic accident cases that is often easy to do in that all states have some form of vehicle code that spells out in intricate detail of how vehicles are to be operated upon the roadways. Remember that violation of a statute or law is almost always a breach of duty in and of itself. Searching your vehicle code you will inevitably find provisions that deal with right of way issues and require vehicles entering a roadway to yield the right of way. In addition, there is a general duty to keep a proper lookout and to operate a motor vehicle in a safe and prudent manner.

Here is this accident laid out in the context of negligence law, and in fact how it should be pled in your complaint:

-       driver "A" had a duty to yield the right of way upon entering the roadway. In addition, driver "A" had a duty to keep a proper lookout and to operate his vehicle in a safe and prudent manner.

-       driver "A" breached those duties in failing to keep a proper lookout and in entering the roadway from a driveway without ascertaining the way was clear and failing to yield the right of way to vehicles approaching on the roadway.

-        as a direct and proximate cause of the failure of driver "A" to conform to the duties imposed upon him, an accident ensued in which automobile "B" impacted the vehicle operated by driver "A".

-        plaintiff as an occupant of automobile "B" sustained injuries as a direct and proximate result of the failure of driver "A" to yield the right of way

Go back through the elements of negligence and you will see that each of them has been addressed. A duty. A breach of the duty. Injury caused by breach.

Note that in this example there was no mention of the "reasonable man". That is because violation of a statute is in and of itself a breach of a duty and therefore no need to address the issue of whether the actions were reasonable under any particular circumstances. The law specifies that the right of way must be yielded upon entering a roadway from a driveway. The inquiry does not have to go any further than that.

Of course not all questions of negligence are that simple or straightforward and many times it does become necessary to address the issue of whether the defendant acted reasonably.

To appreciate this, look at a different example, one that does not involve a detailed motor vehicle code a violation of which is an automatic breach of a duty.

Assume that while you are relaxing in your hammock on a fine summer day with a good book and a cold beer, your neighbor decides to cut down a tree in his yard. You heard the chain saw, but assumed, on the other side of the fence that he was cutting up firewood. Needless to say the tree does not fall in the desired direction and instead the top of it comes crashing across your fence, destroying your hammock interlude and sending you to the emergency room.

This is different. No vehicle code applies and while stupidity should be illegal, there are very few statutes that address the issue.

Now breaking down the elements of negligence is a little more challenging. Here's one way that it might look.

-    defendant had a duty plaintiff and other persons to exercise reasonable care in the felling of the tree.

-    a reasonably prudent person in the place of the defendant would have applied reasonable care, which would include not having undertaken to cut down a tree without proper training experience and assistance.

-    a reasonably prudent person in the place of defendant, utilizing reasonable care would have used safety ropes or tackle to ensure that the tree fell only where it was intended.

-    a reasonably prudent person in the place of defendant utilizing reasonable care would have warned plaintiff and any other persons in the vicinity that he was in the process of cutting down a tree.

- defendant breach his duty by undertaking to cut down a tree, an activity that he was neither trained for nor had experience in; in failing to take reasonable steps to ensure that the tree could only fall where intended, and in failing to warn plaintiff of the activity he was undertaking and the associated danger.

- as a direct and proximate result of defendant's breach of his duty, plaintiff sustained injuries.

Once again, all the elements of negligence have been covered in the allegations, but of course this time there was no vehicle code to rely on. Instead, it became necessary to rely on the common law principle that everyone had a duty to exercise reasonable care.

There are several categories of negligence and each will be discussed in turn. First though a couple of concepts common to all forms of negligence should be addressed. These are the idea of contributory or comparative negligence and negligence that is so serious, so beyond reason that it is treated differently, that is gross negligence and recklessness.

Contributory or Comparative Negligence

Contributory negligence is not a different kind of negligence per se, it is a term used to address the negligence of the plaintiff. It is the legal expression of the common sense realty that seldom is one person all to blame and the other blameless. If you are contemplating bringing any kind of claim for personal injury arising from someone else's negligence, you must have an understanding of the concepts surrounding contributory and comparative negligence, because you will with absolute certainty have to deal with them. Both of these legal concepts arise from the premise that one should not be able to recover for injuries received in an accident if they actually caused, in whole or in part, the accident to occur. From that basis, the two concepts diverge.

Contributory negligence has its roots in common law going back to England, and in its purist form is an extremely harsh doctrine in the world of negligence and personal injury issues. In its original form, the doctrine of contributory negligence stood for the principle that if the plaintiff contributed at all, regardless of how small an extent, to the accident, then recovery is barred. Taken literally, if the plaintiff was only 1% at fault in causing an accident, while the defendant was 99% at fault, the plaintiff would be barred from any recovery.

The unfairness of this interpretation is immediately clear and obvious. In any accident there is always the argument that the victim did, or failed to do something, albeit even trivial that contributed to, or could have prevented the accident. To allow culpable defendants to avoid liability because of relatively trivial contribution on the part of the plaintiff, contradicts the whole purpose and intent of negligence law. In practice, such a strict interpretation of contributory negligence was never applied to any substantial extent in the United States, with courts generally requiring some substantial negligent act or omission on the part of the plaintiff before barring recovery. The problem with this approach is that it was at the discretion of individual judges as to when a finding of contributory negligence would be made, and from the defendant there was always the potential of an appeal, since the law mandated a dismissal of the complaint upon a determination of ANY negligence on the part of the plaintiff.

The response to this potentially unfair quagmire was to formalize the determination of the extent of negligence on the part of the plaintiff and set a framework in which the issue could be objectively analyzed. Comparative negligence is the result of that effort. Comparative negligence unlike contributory negligence is usually a creature of statute, although there are jurisdictions where the concept of contributory negligence has been morphed into a comparative negligence approach by virtue of one or more appellate decisions. Comparative negligence basically determines degree of fault and assigns liability based on a mathematical approach centered on percentage of liability. In the typical comparative negligence jurisdiction there are two possible outcomes depending on the degree of fault of each party. First, if the plaintiff is found to be more than fifty percent at fault, they cannot recover. This is the same result as in a contributory negligence environment. This of course makes sense. If an accident occurred, and you were the major cause of it, on what logical basis should you be entitled to recover anything from the other person?

The second prong of comparative negligence is to ascertain damages in those cases where the plaintiff is less than fifty percent at fault. Typically the damages, that is the amount the plaintiff can recover, are determined in a two step process. First, total damages are determined. Then that amount is reduced by the percentage at which the plaintiff is determined to be at fault.

Thus, if a jury in such a case determines that the defendant is eighty percent at fault, while the plaintiff receives twenty percent of the fault, the total damages that the jury finds attributable to the accident are reduced by the plaintiff's twenty percent "fault".

Because the doctrine of contributory negligence originated in common law, and comparative negligence is an offshoot of contributory negligence, it is important that you carefully research these concepts in your jurisdiction. In some states there are specific statutes that specify that comparative negligence is the law and specify the way in which liability is ascertained and assigned. Those statutes effectively override any prior common law that may have held contributory negligence to be applicable. In other jurisdictions there will be one or more benchmark appellate court decisions that effectively determine, based on the decision of the supreme or highest court of that jurisdiction that henceforth contributory negligence is to be government by specific limitations and principles, effectively making comparative negligence the law by judicial interpretation.

Regardless of how a jurisdiction arrived at whatever standard it uses, it is important for you to have a thorough understanding. Failure to properly plead may result in a dismissal. An example can be found in some comparative negligence jurisdictions which require that the complaint contain some language to the effect of:

> the proximate cause of the accident was the negligence of the defendant, which exceeded and was greater than any negligence of the plaintiff.....

You have to set forth the proper allegations in your complaint in order to survive a motion to dismiss. To do that, you must understand these issues and the law that applies to them. There are no shortcuts here.

Assumption of Risk

In addition to contributory or comparative negligence, another defense to claims arising out of personal injuries is the legal theory of assumption of risk. It means exactly what the name implies. It means that the plaintiff or injured party was well aware of the risks associated with a specific activity, knew that there was the potential for injury, and proceeded anyway.

There are some important limitations to this defense, the most important being that the limitation of liability is restricted to the specific risk being assumed, and the plaintiff must have had knowledge of that same, specific risk.

Nor is it always an absolute bar. It is intended to address those situations where there is some dangerous activity, everyone knows of the dangers, and the plaintiff elects to accept the risk of injury. It will not help a defendant who is grossly negligent, or help a defendant outside of the specific risk being assumed. An example would be someone who elects to go scuba diving from a commercial dive operation. This is accepted as a potentially dangerous activity with risks associated with it. So if the plaintiff goes diving and gets stung by an underwater creature, or suffers some physiological issue resulting from diving, the operator will probably be able to successfully defend a claim by arguing that the plaintiff assumed that risk. On the other hand, if the plaintiff was injured because the dive boat struck him, or because equipment that he rented from the operator was not properly maintained, those would be outside of the risk assumed and the operator could not avail himself of the defense. Put another way, the diver accepted the risks associated with diving. He did not accept the risk of getting run over by the boat.

Suffice it to say at this point that in any personal injury claim that you bring, you will see it appear in the responsive pleadings. It is an affirmative defense, so if it is not raised it is waived. And because it is an affirmative defense, the defendant has the burden of proof to establish it.

Release from Liability

Akin to the assumption of risk concept is release of liability. Everyone is familiar with the releases from liability that surround us. Many dangerous activities that we engage in require us to sign ahead of time a release agreement. In these documents the signer acknowledges the risk surrounding the activity and agrees that the potential defendant is absolved of any liability. Think of it as a form of assumption of risk in writing. Some of these releases purport to require no signature. Sometimes tickets sold for events or activities have imprinted a form of release, stating that the purchaser, in purchasing the ticket and engaging in the activity has agreed to the terms of the "agreement". More common are limitations on liability. Probably the most common of these in terms of being exposed to them in daily life is an airline ticket. With electronic tickets now being the norm, these agreements are found on the airline website and you must always indicated agreement before being allowed to proceed and purchase a ticket. Before electronic tickets they appeared in fine print on the backs of tickets and boarding passes.

They limit the liability of the airline in the event of an accident.

For the purpose of representing yourself in a personal injury claim, the important thing for you to understand is that the law is complex surrounding these agreements, and if a release agreement becomes an issue, must be carefully researched. Under no circumstances should you blindly accept the existence of a release agreement as an absolute bar to recovery. Even if you have signed a release, or agreed to the terms of a release agreement, it is far from certain that it will be enforceable or apply to your situation. There is a significant body of law that deals with the validity and scope of these agreements, and more often than not there are numerous ways to avoid their effect.

Gross Negligence and Recklessness

Another subset if you will of negligence in its different forms is the concept of gross negligence and recklessness. There are times when the alleged conduct of the defendant is so egregious that it far surpassed simple negligence, rising to a far higher level of misconduct. Gross negligence is sometimes referred to as negligence that amounts to a voluntary disregard of the safety of others. Recklessness occurs when the actor takes no heed to the consequences of an act, or when one is indifferent to consequences.

Common sense tells us that the degree of culpability associated with gross negligence or recklessness should be far greater than simple negligence. And logic dictates that they be addressed differently. In the realm of personal injury law this degree of negligence typical affects two aspects of a case.

First, gross negligence and recklessness typically open the door to punitive damages. Punitive damages are those awarded by a court not to compensate the victim so much as to punish the defendant for improper behavior. They are separate and apart from actual damages which encompass such things as medical bills, lost wages, pain and suffering, etc., and will always be broken down as a separate award.

Second, if a defendant is found to have been grossly negligent or reckless, the comparative or contributory negligence offset or defense does not apply. So even if a plaintiff is found to have contributed to the accident by being negligent, that will not help the defendant that has been determined to have been grossly negligent or reckless.

Premises Liability

A distinct category of personal injury cases involves injuries that occur on someone else's property. Note that it is not different from the concept of negligence already discussed at all. It is simply a specialized kind. The

547

principles of negligence are still alive and well: a duty accompanied by a breach, that results in injury. The only distinction in these cases is that the duty arises from ownership or control of property or premises. What will also be clear is that the duty referred to is often related to a failure to do something as opposed to other forms of negligence where the transgression involves some sort of negligent act or conduct.

The law of premises liability concerns itself with the nature and extent of the duty that is owed to a landowner or person in control of premises to people who come onto, or enter the property. Where things become a little more complicated is the manner in which people come to be on the property or within the premises. Distinctions are made between people that have been invited versus trespassers, between those present socially or permissively, and those who are business patrons.

The laws pertaining to premises liability derive as does all negligence law, from the common law. In this area though, almost all jurisdictions have codified this law into statutes that specify the extent of liability. Finally, it is important that you understand that this area of the law more than most others requires careful and detailed research within your jurisdiction because the nature and extent of the liability imposed across the country is all over the board. It ranges from the more conservative jurisdictions where the cases hold that a property owner owes a person on his property no more than a duty not to create a dangerous condition, to other more liberal jurisdictions where a landowner, especially with respect to people as business patrons, becomes a virtual guarantor of against injury of any kind, and everything in between. To put it another way, because of cases that receive a lot of notoriety, many people believe that the mere fact that they are injured while on another's premises, especially in a commercial setting, entitled them to recovery. To varying degrees this is a misconception and whether there is entitlement to recovery depends on a lot of different factors.

Types of Guests

One of the biggest factors determining the nature and extent of the duty owed by a landowner or person in control of premises, and in turn whether there will be liability for an injury, is the question of what the injured person was doing there. For the purpose of this discussion the term "guest" will be used to discuss a person on the premises of another, not to be confused with guests at a hotel or event. It's just easier to use one term.

Guests, again, people that come upon or into the premises or land of another fall into several broad categories that in part define the duty owed to them. Both the law as well as common sense tells us that a landowner owes more protection, and needs to take more steps to protect someone whom he has invited onto the premises to do business, e.g. a store owner who has invited the public, than would be required to protect someone who wanders onto property in the face of "no trespassing" signs.

And indeed, the law across the country imposes different duties upon landowners depending on the category into which a visitor falls.

Trespassers

The least protected category of "guests" are trespassers. Common sense supports that premise. If someone is not even supposed to be on the premises at all, then the landowner will have less of a duty to protect them. That is not to day that there is no duty at all. There is. It is just not as great, and does not rise to as high a level, as with respect to other categories. Within the category of trespassers are two subcategories; discovered and undiscovered trespassers, and they are treated differently. With respect to the undiscovered trespasser the landowner generally owes no duty other than to not intentionally harm them. You can't shoot a trespasser just for kicks. The discovered trespasser is one who the landowner knows or has reason to believe is coming upon the property. An example would be people walking across the property of another by way of a shortcut. Here the landowner owes more of a duty and that is to warn of dangerous conditions. There is an important exception to the trespass category and that is with respect to children. Often called the attractive nuisance or dangerous instrumentality doctrine this theory places a higher duty on a landowner when there are conditions (such as a swimming pool) that would be attractive to children.

Licensees

This category includes people that are allowed onto the premises, but not necessarily there for the benefit of the landowner. It includes most social guests. When a licensee sustains an injury caused by a condition on the land the landowner is subject to liability only if, (a) the landowner knows or has reason to know of the condition and should realize that it involves an unreasonable risk of harm and should expect the licensee will not realize the danger, and (b) the landowner fails to use reasonable care to make the condition safe or warn the licensee of the condition, and (c) the licensee does not know or have reason to know of the risk involved. In other words, the landowner is responsible for things he is aware of but has no duty to inspect or to ensure that the premises are safe.

Invitees

Invitees are owed the highest degree of care. Invitees are those guests who presence is advantageous to the landowner, such as customers. They have been probably not only invited, but encouraged to come upon the premises. Invitees are owed all the duties of licensees and in addition, the landowner has a reasonable duty to inspect and make the premises reasonably safe. In many jurisdictions the property owner has almost an absolute duty to make sure that the premises are safe, even from hidden or unknown conditions.

Statutes and Regulations

Do not lose sight of the fact that the principles just discussed refer to common law, much of derived from very old common law. In almost all jurisdictions there are a variety of statutes and regulations that change the entire complexion of premises liability law.

Recall that in terms of basic negligence law, violation of a statute is often deemed negligence per se. That is once you have a violation of a statute or a regulation, it is very difficult to get beyond that and debate if it is reasonable or not. Moreover, if the violation is intentional, it often takes the conduct into the gross negligence/recklessness realm so that even of the plaintiff is also negligent, there will be no defense.

As a practical matter anyone exploring a potential claim for injury that occurred on the property of another must begin with the foregoing principles, but be careful not to stop there. Just because there are modern statutes does not mean that the common law is not relevant – it certainly is. It does mean though that your inquiry cannot stop with the common law. Regard it as a starting point. Once the common law has been checked, your research must go on to include statutes and relevant regulations in your jurisdiction. The point is that there can be duties imposed above and beyond the common law. You have to explore both. A perfect example would be in the case of the attractive nuisance discussed above in the context of a licensee. Where under the common law there may be no duty inspect the property and no liability for dangers that the owner is not aware of, if there is a statute requiring the property open to the public to be kept safe from all hazards and to be inspected, obviously the statute trumps common law and there is a new and different obligation imposed.

Vicarious Liability

While a separate principle, for the purpose of pursuing claims for personal injury, and to protect yourself if you're on the other side, it is important to understand the concept of vicarious liability. In a nutshell this is a legal principle that makes an employer liable for the acts of its employees acting in the course of their duties. For the personal injury plaintiff is it extremely important in terms of being able to secure a recovery. Going far back into the book, recall the discussion about identifying the proper parties to name in any lawsuit or claim. The point is that it is pointless to commence a lawsuit against a party from which you can never hope to collect. This is especially relevant in terms of personal injury claims. If you are a pedestrian, struck by a delivery truck, chances are pretty good that it will do little good to sue the minimum wage delivery driver. On the other hand, the company that he works for and that owns the delivery truck is a much better prospect.

This is where the principle of vicarious liability enters the picture. It provides that so long as the driver was performing duties arising out of and in the course of his employment, the employer will be liable for any negligence on his part. The principle arises from the old English common law master and servant doctrine. Under this principle, and it carries through to American common law today, the servant, acting under the direction and for the benefit of the master was in effect an instrumentality of the master and thus the master would be liable for anything done by the servant. In the United States that principle has been tempered somewhat in that it is fat from an absolute that an employer will be held liable for anything that an employee does.

To begin with the conduct must arise out of and in the course of the employment. That often becomes a point of major contention and dispute. As with so many things in the law, some situations are clear cut, others not so clear. If the deliveryman is on his way to make a delivery to a customer, during working hours, there will rarely be much doubt that his activities arose out of and in the course of his employment and that if he caused an accident, the employer would be liable. It is just as clear that where another employee, say a janitor, sees the delivery truck with the keys in it and decides to borrow it, making his way to a local tavern, then getting into an accident, it will be very difficult to establish that this person was performing duties for his employer and thereby imposing liability upon the employer. Unfortunately, there are just as many cases that are less clear. What about the plumbing service technician who is on call during the weekend so is allowed to take a company service truck home for the weekend? If he then uses the truck to go on a personal errand, such as to the grocery store, and gets into an accident, the question becomes much more complicated. You could argue on the one hand that the trip to the grocery store had nothing to do with being on call to answer a service request. On the other hand, it could be argued that by using the truck, he could by responding on his mobile phone respond to a service call more quickly by not having to return home first.

This issue presents questions that must be resolved on a case-by-case basis, but they are often critical to how a claim for personal injuries will be resolved.

Dram Shop Laws and Principles

Because so many motor vehicle accidents are alcohol related, another body of legal principles that should never be ignored are laws in various jurisdictions that apply to those who serve alcoholic beverages. If you are seeking recovery for injuries sustained in an accident, do not overlook these as a potential source of recovery.

Dram shop liability is almost always based on various statutes instead of common law. Indeed, cases where liability was sought to be imposed as a form of negligence consistently held that there was no liability in that there was no proximate cause between the serving of an alcoholic beverage and subsequent injury to a third person. The legal argument was that it was not the serving of the alcohol but the drinking of it that created the risk and danger. Every jurisdiction in the United States has some statutory basis for finding liability on the basis of the sale and serving of alcoholic beverages though they vary in terms of basis and orientation. Some are found in the statutes that addresses torts and liability. Others can be found in the statutes that govern the licensing and conduct of establishments that serve or sell alcohol. The result is the same either way. Violation of a statute is usually prima facia evidence of negligence.

all the so-called dram shop statutes basically impose a duty upon those selling or serving alcoholic beverages to refrain from selling serving a person, either beyond a reasonable quantity or to a patron that is obviously intoxicated. Efforts to limit the liability by arguing that the statute benefited only the person being served have been eliminated either by statute or case decisions which make it clear that a person injured due to the intoxication of another, can seek recovery against the establishment, or establishments that continued to serve. In some jurisdictions this liability is limited to commercial establishments. In a growing number of jurisdictions though, it has been expanded to impose liability upon those who serve guests alcohol socially.

The overriding point here is that if you have been involved in an accident where there is any indication that alcohol is a factor, be sure to explore the dram shop and social liability statutes in your jurisdiction.

Third Party Liability

Finally, in terms of exploring potential contributors to the effort of recovering for injuries sustained in an accident, do not overlook potential third parties. Remember that the law of negligence imposes duties on all of us for a variety if things, in a broad spectrum of circumstances. Use your imagination and explore in any given situation things that someone did that they should not have done, or failed to do, that they should have done, to see if additional defendants might be available, or, if you are the defendant, if there is not some basis for a cross or third party claim.

Here are some examples, from actual cases, to give you an idea of potential third party defendants to add to the party.

An auto accident occurs as a car pulls out of a gas station into the path of an oncoming car. Clearly there has been a failure to yield the right of way. But there was also found to be liability on the part of the gas station that had placed a marquee advertising prices so close to the edge of the roadway that the driver of the car that pulled out had no way to clearly see oncoming traffic.

You're driving down the road when a car pulls out in front of you forcing you to brake hard. The car behind you hits the back of your car. Of course you pursue a claim against the car that hit you, but what about the car that caused the whole thing to begin with?

The reason for exploring these options is that in many jurisdictions the liability insurance requirements are inadequate. They result from statutes passed years ago and never updated. There are still states for example where the liability insurance requirement is $15,000 per person for bodily injury and $5,000 in property damage. Most would agree that a trip to the emergency room with perhaps some surgery will quickly burn up the $15,000, and there are very few cars that you can buy today to replace a demolished automobile for $5,000. This consideration is in addition to the fact that many drivers, in spite of mandatory insurance requirements in all states, operate without such insurance. It may therefore be essential for you, if you've been injured in an automobile accident to involve multiple defendants in order to recover an adequate amount. Identifying additional potential liable parties might be the only way to secure a fair recovery.

Still another potential ground for third party liability is referred to as negligent entrustment. This theory basically stands for the proposition that if someone knows, or reasonably should know, that a person to whom they entrust a vehicle or allow to operate a vehicle is reckless and irresponsible, they can be liable to anyone subsequently injured as a result. This theory is often used to try to get at assets of a parent or other potential source of funds for an accident caused by someone with less than adequate insurance. Often because of cost considerations and dismal driving records, parents require their teen-age children to register vehicles in their own name and obtain their own insurance coverage, which if course is almost always the absolute minimum in terms of coverage amounts. When an accident is caused by such an individual and there is inadequate coverage, consider making a claim against the parents for allowing the teen to drive. There will be a good chance of success if it can be shown by driving history that the teen was reckless, had numerous violations, and had engaged in questionable activities, such that a reasonable person would not have allowed them to drive.

Insurance

While not directly related to legal issues surrounding personal injury, no discussion of this topic would be complete without considering insurance.

By far the vast majority of personal injury cases involve automobile accidents, and every state in the country has laws that require minimum liability coverage to operate a motor vehicle. In addition premises liability cases almost always involve insurance. If the place of injury is a commercial establishment, there will usually be a

559

commercial liability policy in place. If someone's residence is involved, a homeowner's policy will often come into play.

With insurance coverage or issues likely to be involved, it is helpful to have at least a basic understanding of the applicable principles.

One thing to unravel is the relationships and standing of the various parties in any personal injury claim involving insurance. An insurance policy is nothing more than a highly specialized kind of contract, but what is important is that it is a contract between the insurance company and the insured. In a typical liability policy, whether for an automobile or for premises the language of the policy is that the insurance company will provide a legal defense and will pay on behalf of the insured any amounts that the insured is legally obligated to pay as a result of a claim covered by the policy.

Take a moment to read that again because there is a lot there!

First is the term that limits the obligation of the insurance company to pay on behalf of the insured any amounts that the insured is legally obligated to pay. That means that if it is not established that the insured is obligated, translate that to being at fault in an auto accident, or having liability with respect to premises, then the insurance company has no obligation to pay anyone anything. Likewise, if the accident or event is not covered by the policy, the company has no obligation.

Keep one thing in mind at all times and that is insurance companies are in business to collect premiums, not to pay claims. When the time comes, if there is any option or way to avoid payment, an insurer will latch onto it. Along the same line of reasoning it is imperative that you read and understand your obligations with respect to the policy in terms of handling any claims. There are things that you can inadvertently do or fail to do that might give the company an excuse not to pay a claim.

Specifics vary from state to state, but all have some common elements.

You must report a potential claim immediately. Even if an actual claim is not being made. Many people make the mistake of thinking that because in an accident the people in the other car said they were ok, it is permissible to "handle it on your own" by paying what appears to be minor property damage out of your pocket, to avoid increased premiums.

Wrong answer.

First, in this day and age of TV lawyers and billboards entitled "Who Can I Sue?" a personal injury claim, even from a car full of people that denied any injuries, is highly probable. That accident that appeared to be nothing and could be resolved for $500 worth of light body work has suddenly turned into a much, much larger claim and guess what? Because you didn't report it the insurance company may tell you that you're on your own, good luck.

If you are injured, even though it is not your insurance policy or company that is at issue, one of the first things that you should do is determine the name of the other driver's insurance company and notify them that you are making a claim.

Remember that insurance is a contract between the insurance company and the insured (the other driver). The insurance company will pay you only because their insured becomes legally obligated to pay you. But at the same time, you have a very strong interest to make sure that the insurance company does not have any excuse to deny the claim on a technicality.

This gets back to the bizarre relationship of the parties. Even though they insure the other driver, it is you that will get paid, so you need to do everything you can to make sure that you do in fact get paid. So by notifying them, even though you are under no technical legal obligation to do so, you head off any argument by the company later that they did not receive notification.

All liability policies provide that in exchange for defending and paying any claims, the insurance company effectively gets to control the case, make all decisions regarding the case, and decide whether to settle or litigate. This gets a little more complicated in a situation where there is insurance to cover an accident, but it is not enough. In these cases the insurance company has liability up to the limits of its policy, but the insured is liable for anything in excess. Finally, things get even more tortured and confused where you are involved in an accident with someone that either is not insured, or whose policy limits are inadequate, and your policy includes coverage for uninsured or underinsured motorists. Now your own insurance company steps in as though it was the insurance company for the other driver, and your dealings with them will be virtually the same as if they were the other driver's insurance company.

With the sometimes bizarre relationships created by the people involved in a case and the various policies of insurance, it is important to refrain from taking certain kinds of action without carefully analyzing the situation. This is because in addition to the obligation to defend and pay amounts which the insured may be or become obligated to pay, there are other issues such as subrogation.

Subrogation is the right of the insurance company to make a claim against a third party, in your name, for amounts that it has been obligated to pay.

Often an example is helpful. Recall the dram shop cases. Let's put a little different twist on things. Let's assume that you were in an accident caused by a driver that had been drinking at a local tavern, who was uninsured. Let's assume that you had uninsured motorist coverage on your own policy and that your insurance company stepped in, as it was obligated to do, and paid your claim. Under the principle of subrogation your insurance company now has the right to bring a lawsuit, in your name, against the at fault driver, and any other parties that might have liability, including possibly the tavern that served him.

The critical point here is that the case is brought in your name. It is one of those legal fictions and that results in a lot of potential confusion and misunderstanding. Here's the rub. If you sign the wrong document, as for example if the other driver offers to pay for your car if you sign a release, you could inadvertently destroy the ability of your insurance company to recover.

All of this becomes extremely complicated and the key thing to remember is to carefully analyze and examine things before you agree to anything, make any statements, or sign anything.

Attorneys

While the whole point of this book is to show you how to represent yourself, there are times when you should retain an attorney. There are times when you have to, such as when you have a corporation or a limited liability company.

But just because through necessity or good judgment you decide to hire an attorney, it does not necessarily follow that you should ignore the things you've learned about being your own lawyer. The legal profession has taught us that the technical aspects of a case demand the professional skill and judgment that only a lawyer could possibly possess. The corollary to that is to leave everything to the attorney and stay out of the way.

What nonsense!

If after reading this book you come away with nothing else, you should appreciate that there is no deep dark mystery about the law or the judicial system. Even if you have to hire an attorney, there is no reason you cannot actively participate in the case, especially the decision making process.

Will you run into attorneys that refuse to allow you to participate? Of course. Dump them! With a little looking you will find one that understands that you do not want to be a doormat and would like to take an active role.

The purpose of this section is help you know how to find an attorney to work with you and to understand how to deal with them, including how they should be paid.

Finding A Lawyer

There is no shortage of lawyers America. We have more lawyers per capita by a huge margin than any other country in the world. Lawyers are everywhere!

And that's the problem. Lawyers are everywhere! They smile at us from our television screens, assuring us that they are there to fight for us. Looking dapper and somber, surrounded by volumes of impressive looking law books, they confide that insurance companies fear them. On the internet should you have the courage to search for "lawyer" or "attorney", dozens of sites will pop up assuring you that the lawyers that have paid to be on their pages are the best there is, and on and on, ad infinitum. If you visit a site offering "free" legal advice, when you "ask the lawyer" what you'll get is some guy trying to get you to hire him.

Attorneys come in all sorts of styles and flavors. From the sole practitioner trying to do it all by themselves, to the huge mega law firms with literally hundreds of attorneys in different locations and specialties.

How to sort it out and how to find the lawyer that can do the best job for you at a reasonable price is a challenge, but not an insurmountable one.

First, let's narrow the field a lot before going any further and kick out of the prospect list what we want to avoid.

Assuming that you, your resources and your legal issues are not on the levels of Microsoft or General Motors, forget the huge firms. People often believe that big is better and that these large firms, with their impressive letterheads have more clout, or at least will intimidate or bully the other side into submission. That is simply not true. All that these firms do is rack up literally thousands and thousands of dollars in legal fees and in the end accomplish no more than any reasonably competent, reasonably conscientious, solo or small firm attorney could do. When you go into these firms, look around. The furnishings are awesome. Nice paintings on the wall. Persian rugs on the floor. The offices are always downtown in impressive buildings. When you've seen all that, once you've gotten over being duly impressed and awed (worked didn't it?) stop and realize who is paying for all that. Then consider further that the senior partners in these firms are soaking down mid to high six figure salaries, and think about who is paying those. Yep, you will be if you make the mistake of retaining a firm like this. These firms subscribe to the religion of billable hours. A young attorney working for one of these firms that does not bill sufficient hours is soon jobless. Unless you have a very, very deep pocket, shun these firms.

The next group to strike off your list of potential attorneys are the TV Lawyers.

You know who we're talking about. The fool that appear to step out of your television set. The ones who tell you how great and wonderful they are, and how insurance companies fear them. The ones who tell you that they hold the key to solving all your debt or financial problems. The ones that tell how they are there to look out for you. These attorneys are to be avoided like the plague. They are the ambulance chasers of the past. Under no circumstances should you even waste your time talking to these people. There is nothing that these TV lawyers can do for you that any competent solo practitioner or small firm can't do just as well and in the long run, probably for less money. Here is why any lawyer that advertises extensively should be avoided at all costs.

These attorneys deal on pure volume. They focus on cases where they can collect a contingent fee, generally personal injury cases, or cases like bankruptcy, where they can run an assembly line process. The cost of advertising is a major expense as is the overhead needed to deal with the sheer number of contacts that the advertising generates.

These people might be great marketers and business people but they are not by any interpretation of the term, competent attorneys. Their business model requires that large numbers of cases be processed quickly. They do not have time to go to court or to devote any meaningful degree of attention to your case. The need to settle cases quickly results in inadequate settlements. They would rather take less money for a case so that they can move on to the next one than hold out for a case's true value. The need to handle large numbers of cases with minimal attorney involvement results in an assembly line manned by non-lawyers often with inadequate supervision. Why should these lawyers be avoided? Again, the reason for advertising is to increase business volume. For an attorney, with only a limited amount of time each day, the larger the volume, the more clients the time must be spread among, and the less time available to focus on you and your case. Also, attorneys that have a good reputation, have done good work for their clients, and focus on quality versus quantity, generally do not need to do a lot of advertising.

So that now we've told you what to avoid, how do you find the right attorney?

First, define what you are looking for. Is this a criminal case? If so, what kind? If you are being accused of some business related crime, you want to find an attorney that is knowledgeable about white collar crime. The criminal lawyer that represents drug dealers or robbery suspects is not going to have the expertise to focus on business oriented charges. Has your son or daughter been arrested? You need an attorney that specializes in juvenile family law matters. Is your business being sued? You need to find a lawyer experienced in business litigation.

Now that you know what kind of attorney s to avoid, and what kind of attorney to look for, how do you find them? Well, you could go the easy route and just get on the internet and google whatever kind of attorney you're looking for. Problem is, you'll get a lot of paid advertisers, and often the search results won't be specific. A lot of attorneys, especially inexperienced ones trying to establish a practice will check off just about every area of the law when they complete the online registration for some of the legal directories. Come on, do you really want some kid right out of law school representing you just because he says he handles bankruptcy, divorce, estate planning, construction law, real estate, personal injury, workers compensation,, criminal law, business law and half a dozen other selections? Of course not. The internet is wonderful, but it has its limitations.

Finding a good lawyer will take a bit of research and legwork. Here are some suggestions:

Go ahead and search the internet, but be aware of how the entries make it onto a specific site. There are numerous sites that are advertising driven and do not charge for the posting of an entry. These are far more reliable than those that present attorneys based on the amount spent to be listed on the site.

If you are looking for an attorney specialized in a specific area, consult the bar website for your state to see the attorneys specialized in that area as a good starting point. Most states now have some form of specialization certification. A state bar certification means that the attorney has complied with experience, education and other requirements for that area of specialization. It is a far better indicator of qualifications than some web advertisement. While on the state bar website, also check to see if the attorneys you are looking at have any disciplinary issues. In days past attorney disciplinary matters were confidential and private. You could be being represented by an attorney who had been suspended for negligently handling legal matters and never know it. Things have changed and most states have provision for disclosing these matters to the public.

If you have used an attorney for some other matter in the past, ask them for referrals. Attorneys mix and socialize with attorneys. They often have a good idea from a myriad of clues and sources, of who is competent and reliable in a given area. Be sure though to take such a referral only as another source of information and not as gospel. It is just as possible that your former attorney may be clueless. Attorneys that do nothing but bankruptcy day in and day out are just not going to have a great awareness and insight into what's going on, and who the shakers and movers are over in family court.

You can also consult the more reputable and established legal directories such as Martindale Hubbell. Take these with a grain of salt though. They will give the most deference to and have the nicer things to say about the large firms that spend a lot of money with them. Also, the way in which they rate attorneys operates in favor of larger, established firms, to the detriment of smaller forms that may be competent but have not been around as long.

Depending on how sophisticated the court online docket access is in your jurisdiction, you can learn a lot from looking at these records. Many online systems will let you search or browse by attorney.

While this may not be much help if you are looking for a good estate planning attorney, if you are searching for a litigation attorney, it is an important resource to explore. After all, do you really want to hire an attorney to handle a court case for you whose name appears once or twice on the entire court roster? If you are looking for a litigation attorney, and if the online docket system is stout enough, you can learn a wealth of information. Going through the lists of cases, and the docket reports for specific cases, you can learn:

- how many cases does the attorney handle?
- what kinds of cases?
- do the cases he files have merit, or are most of them dismissed?
- does he win or lose the majority of his case?
- does he file a lot of motions?
- does he follow through to hearings on the motions filed?
- do the motions have merit or are there a lot of frivolous motions there?
- how do the judges rule on his motions?
- where motions are accompanied by legal briefs, are they thorough?
- is he diligent? Do things get done when they should?
- does he farm work out or does he do it?

Yes, you really can find out all that information from court filings. In federal courts, the Pacer system will give you the ability to research all of those points. There are some state systems in the larger metropolitan areas that are comparable. In other jurisdictions you may be limited to a docket report and have to go to the courthouse to actually see the documents. That's ok. It's all public record.

Once you've narrowed it down, then how to proceed depends on you. You should meet with a prospective attorney and discuss the matter you want them to handle. If the attorney is well qualified, expect to pay for this time. There are no free lunches in this world and the "free" consultations you see advertised are nothing more than an attempt to get as many clients in the door as possible to increase volume. Remember, an attorney's stock in trade is his time. Be wary of one that is giving it away.

Since you are paying for the time, you should not hesitate to ask questions. This is a two way street. The attorney is going to determine whether they are willing to handle your case. You are going to determine whether you want the attorney to handle your case. You should feel free to ask them if this is a matter they feel comfortable handling. Don't be afraid to ask them about track record. They should not be bothered by being asked how many cases similar to yours they have handled and so forth. You will want to know how they will charge. If they charge by the hour, their hourly rate as well as the rate that they will bill you for any assistants or paralegal time are legitimate questions. Ask the attorney their opinion as to the outcome of the matter you are discussing with them. If the attorney brashly tells you that this is a "slam dunk winner" and you have nothing to worry about, it is a sign that you might want to look elsewhere. A competent attorney, experienced in the field will first acknowledge that there are no "slam dunk winners". They will discuss the flaws and weaknesses as well as the merits of your case, and they will caution you regarding possible unfavorable outcomes along the way.

Working with an Attorney

Once you selected an attorney, it is important that you reach an understanding as to several issues upfront. Most attorneys will have a "standard" engagement letter. The purpose of that letter is to define what work the attorney will be performing, any limitations on the scope of representation and how they will be paid.

That's fine, as long as you understand that this engagement letter is not etched in stone, that virtually nothing in it is for your benefit, and there are some other things that need to be discussed and agreed upon.

The issue of outcome and probability of that outcome should be revisited once you have selected an attorney. Of course no attorney that you would want to consider working with can tell you with certainty, the ultimate outcome of your case or matter. They should however be able to give a realistic assessment of the likely outcome. You should be able discuss a general range of expectations, based on various assumptions, with the understanding of course that if the assumptions prove wrong, so too, likely will the outcome. You should be able to get a general assessment of how long, within a reasonable time frame the matter should last, and again, within reasonable parameters, how much time, and therefore cost will be involved.

Attorney's Fees.

One of the major issues in dealing with an attorney of course is that of fees. You need to know what the case is going to cost, at least in general terms and how the attorney will charge. There are three general types of fee arrangements; hourly, contingent and flat fee. The most common in general litigation is the hourly rate. Here the attorney has established an hourly rate and charges you a fee based on time spent working on your case. In some cases, notably personal injury cases, a contingent fee may be used. This is an arrangement where the attorney charges no fee as the case goes along, but will accept by way of compensation a portion of any recovery. Typically such fees will be in the range of 30-50% of whatever the attorney is able to obtain for you. The justification for such a hefty portion of your money to be paid upon recovery is that first, you are not required to pay anything upfront, and second, you pay a fee only if there is a recovery. A flat fee arrangement is just what it implies. A fee is quoted based on the nature of the case and the amount of time expected to be required. The fee remains unchanged even if those underlying assumptions prove to be false. These arrangements are most often see in criminal defense cases.

Here is where you need to discuss how the fee will be based, if hourly, the hourly rate, at what rate you will be charged for different activities and so forth. There should also be some estimate, at least in general terms of the total amount of time expected to be involved. Should you expect an attorney retained on an hourly basis to tell you that the case will involve no more than a specific amount of time? Of course not! There are too many uncertainties and too many things the attorney cannot control. He has no way of knowing for example how many depositions the other side will schedule, whether documents will be produced on request, or whether a hearing will be required.

Nonetheless, an experienced attorney should be able to give a workable estimated range based on the complexity of the case, the issues involved and the amount in controversy, of both how long a case will take to resolve and again, within a reasonable range, how much time will be involved.

On the topic of fees, many attorneys will want a retainer paid in advance. The retainer assures the attorney that if work is begun on a case, there is a source for payment for the time involved and the costs incurred. An attorney requesting a retainer is acceptable as long as the amount is reasonable and the unused portion is refundable if services are terminated. There are some attorneys that demand a non-refundable retainer. There is no reason for a reputable attorney to expect to be paid a substantial fee in advance, for work that has not yet been done, and expect to be entitled to keep it if his services are terminated. In many states there are rules flat out prohibiting non-refundable retainer fees. If an attorney even mentions non-refundable retainer, he has done you a favor by displaying ahead of time his lack of ethics and integrity. Thank him for his time and leave.

Now in fairness, do not confuse a non-refundable retainer with a flat fee. Attorneys will sometimes quote a flat fee for handling a matter. It is of course up to you whether to agree to such a fee arrangement, but if you do, it is perfectly reasonable for the fee to be paid with the understanding that it is not refundable. A flat fee and a non-refundable retainer are two different things.

What constitutes a reasonable retainer depends on how complex the case is, how much work may be involved initially, if and when the attorney may be entitled to additional payment, and how difficult it is for an attorney to remove themselves from the case.

If the attorney bills monthly, it is not unreasonable for them to request that a realistic estimate of the value of the work to be done during the first month be paid in advance. There are other instances where a larger retainer may be appropriate. In business bankruptcy cases, after the initial payment, the Court determines when additional payments can be made. These additional payments are often not authorized for several months into the case. In such a situation it is not unreasonable for an attorney to request enough of an advance retainer to insure payment of fees until future court approval is anticipated. Finally, attorneys cannot just quit if they're not being paid. In almost all jurisdictions once an attorney makes an appearance in a case, approval of the court is required in order for them to withdraw. There are some jurisdictions where this is far from automatic, especially in criminal cases. A lot of judges will be very reluctant to allow an attorney to withdraw from a case in advanced stages because they have not been paid.

So all of these factors weigh into the equation of what is a reasonable retainer. Regardless of the size of the retainer, it should be understood that it will be deposited into the attorney's escrow account and withdrawn only as fees are earned or costs incurred and that any unused portion will be refunded upon termination of the representation.

Other points to address.

You should reach an understanding immediately as to who controls the case. Different attorneys have different attitudes regarding this issue. You should make it clear to the attorney that you intend to take an active role in the case and to please let you know up front if that will be problematic.

A major consideration is that in virtually all jurisdictions, a client is bound by agreements, representations and stipulations made by his attorney. That means if your attorney states to the judge for example that you agree to arbitrate, or agree to a trial without a jury, etc., you are bound by that. The fact that you may not have agreed to it with your attorney, or even known about it ahead of time is completely irrelevant. You are bound by your attorney's actions. Because of this you must make it clear to the attorney that you expect to be consulted on ALL significant issues and demand input into all aspects of the case. Significant issues include:

- depositions - if you're paying, you decide who to depose or not

- you expect to be notified of all depositions so you can decide whether you will attend. The emphasis is if you, not the attorney, decides.

- any agreements with the attorney on the other side require you to at least be notified. Things like granting extensions of time to respond, postponing a hearing, etc, you need to at least be notified of and have input.

- no significant agreements, such as a substantial continuance, adding parties, trial without a jury, or a smaller jury, are to be entered into without your knowledge and consent.

-        any form of alternative dispute resolution must be approved by you. Most jurisdictions now require the parties to participate in some form of arbitration or mediation, but often leave it to the parties to elect among options.

Make it clear to your attorney that he is specifically NOT authorized to enter into any agreements unless and until you have been notified and consented. You may get some resistance on this. If you do, find another attorney. There is a too common attitude among professionals that clients are not able to make important decisions and that the professional, being far wiser and more experienced, is better able to make those decisions. It is not limited to the legal profession. Doctors have long been guilty of the attitude that the "patients really don't have the knowledge to make decisions, so we'll just make decisions for them". Unfortunately, many attorneys have the same attitude. If you encounter one of these, you might be better served elsewhere. You certainly don't need to tolerate this paternalistic attitude from your attorney. A reputable, competent attorney will never be offended at you wanting to participate and to be kept informed.

Make clear to the attorney that you expect copies of everything in the case. To save expense and trouble make it clear that an email copy will suffice. In this day and age it is hard to find an attorney that does not scan documents and maintain them in electronic format. It takes only a couple of mouse clicks to shoot you a copy. Most correspondence between lawyers and between lawyers and the court is via email now. Make it clear that you are to be copied on EVERYTHING (email being free, this will not rank as a major expense) and that a copy of anything incoming is to be forwarded to you.

You should reach an agreement with the attorney as to how other communication will be handled, in particular, telephone calls. Telephone calls are a sore spot in attorney client relationships to the point that surveys of bar complaints against attorneys have shown that one of the largest single reasons for a complaint by a client is the failure of attorneys to accept or return telephone calls.

It is not exclusively the fault of attorneys though. Incessant telephone calls from clients are distracting and inject friction and resentment into the attorney client relationship.

There is nothing more infuriating or distracting for an attorney than to be in the middle of working on something and be interrupted by a telephone call from a client asking when something will take place, has anything been heard regarding an offer, a decision be a judge, etc., or just in general, how the case is going.

What happens? The attorney succumbs to human nature and viewing the client as an inconsiderate pest, stops taking his calls. The client is anxious about his case and resents the fact that he is paying the attorney but can't talk to him. The relationship deteriorates when there is in fact no need for this to happen.

To avoid these problems different techniques and arrangements can help. The biggest thing is to keep the client in the loop. That is why we suggest requesting copies of everything. If you know what's going on there will be less need to call the attorney to find out.

Second, reach an agreement that there will be scheduled telephone calls periodically to discuss the case. You will know that the attorney will call or accept a call at a specific time. The attorney will be expecting to discuss your case and will be prepared. And in fairness, both attorney and client should prepare for these periodic conversations. This is when the client should present any questions – when both client and attorney are focusing on the client's case and when the attorney should bring the client up to speed on what is happening in the case.

A lot the problems with telephone calls can be eliminated by using email instead. Email gives the attorney the opportunity to respond when he can address the question and is not distracted. An attorney may be much better able respond to a question if there is an opportunity to review the file. Of course if you use emails, use them judiciously and ask specific questions. An email that just says "Hi, what's going on with my case?" is just stupid, wastes everyone's time and probably will not get a meaningful response.

Monitoring the Case

In the context of court cases, there are two kinds of clients. One group takes the position that they've hired an attorney and the attorney will handle everything. These people want only general progress reports and to be told at the end how the case came out. The other group wants to actively participate in the case, wants to be informed and kept up to speed so that they can make prudent decisions when the time comes. This book completely disregards the first group, because it is highly unlikely that they will read a book such as this at all. On the other hand, this book is aimed directly at the second group. Just because you have retained an attorney does not mean you should disregard everything you've learned in this book and blithely ignore what's going on in your case to await the outcome. Hopefully you will have learned enough when you finish this book to know how to monitor what is going on and understand the significance.

You should already have directed your attorney to copy you on everything in and out of his office that pertains to your case. In addition, if the court you are in has electronic filing, monitor it frequently to see what is going on. This allows you to confirm that your attorney is sending you materials as agreed, and in addition, to be aware of things being filed in the case that may not have been sent to your attorney for one reason or another. Finally, monitoring the court file allows you to know where the case is in terms of working its way up the roster for trial, and what things are upcoming. With the court file being accessible in many jurisdictions with the click of your mouse, there is simply no excuse not to know what is happening in your case.

This is also a good way to keep track of the things your attorney is charging you for and whether they are a prudent use of your money. For example, is your attorney filing silly motions (like a motion to dismiss when all the other side needs to do is amend their complaint), or are they doing things that matter and will affect the outcome of your case.

Do not be afraid to question what is going on. Many clients wrongfully assume that the attorney knows best and all decisions should be left to the attorney. If your attorney has filed a motion to dismiss and there is no apparent benefit to the outcome of the case, ask them why the motion was filed and what the objective was. Make it clear when you speak with them that you understand the significance and mechanics of these motions and do not expect to see a lot motions that accomplish little in the long run.

Contrary to the expectations of many people, most attorneys will be neither upset nor annoyed at these questions. They will though, understand that you are on top of the case and have made it your business to know what is going on. Moreover, only by having a current perspective of the progress of the case can you make viable decisions with your attorney.

In a nutshell, there are three tricks to being happy with an attorney.

First, pick the right one. Eliminate the people that you don't want to deal with. Pick an attorney that is first, right for your case. You don't need Clarence Darrow to handle an uncontested divorce. Pick an attorney that is experienced in the area of your case or matter. Pick an attorney that you're comfortable with.

The second trick is to communicate openly and candidly and have an understanding on how the matter will be handled.

Third, actively keep track of and monitor everything that is happening in your case.